E WEEK LOAN

Hedge Funds

Hedge Funds

Courtesans of Capitalism

Peter Temple

JOHN WILEY & SONS, LTD

Chichester · New York · Weinheim · Brisbane · Singapore · Toronto

Other Wiley Editorial Offices

John Wiley & Sons, Inc., 605 Third Avenue,
New York, NY 10158-0012, USA

Wiley-VCH Verlag GmbH, Pappelallee 3,
D-69469 Weinheim, Germany

John Wiley & Sons Australia, Ltd, 33 Park Road, Milton,
Queensland 4064, Australia

John Wiley & Sons (Asia) Pte Ltd, 2 Clementi Loop #02-01,
Jin Xing Distripark, Singapore 129809

John Wiley & Sons (Canada) Ltd, 22 Worcester Road,
Rexdale, Ontario M9W 1L1, Canada

Library of Congress Cataloging-in-Publication Data

Temple, Peter.
　　Hedge funds : the courtesans of capitalism / Peter Temple.
　　　　p. cm.
　　Includes bibliographical references and index.
　　ISBN 0-471-89973-9
　　1. Hedge funds. 2. Hedge funds—United States. 3. Capitalism. I. Title.

　　HG4530 .T45 2001
　　332.64'5—dc21

　　　　　　　　　　　　　　　　　　　　　　　　　2001017601

British Library Cataloguing in Publication Data

A catalogue record for this book is available from the British Library

ISBN 0-471-89973-9

Typeset in 11/15pt Goudy by Dorwyn Ltd, Rowlands Castle, Hants.
Printed and bound in Great Britain by Biddles Ltd, Guildford and King's Lynn
This book is printed on acid-free paper responsibly manufactured from sustainable forestry, in
which at least two trees are planted for each one used for paper production.

Contents

Acknowledgements   vii

1   Courtesans of capitalism   1

2   Masters of the Universe   21

3   Speculators and hedgers   45

4   Rogues, philosophers and philanthropists   69

5   The Archimedes of Greenwich   89

6   Toxic waste and vultures   113

7   Highwaymen of the global economy   133

8   The hedge fund in your bank   153

9   Finance's four-letter word   171

10   Dance of the seven veils   189

11   Attaining respectability   211

12   Taming Archimedes   229

Bibliography   245

Index   263

Acknowledgements

Writing a book about hedge funds has its pleasure and pain. One great joy has been the amount of information available on the web about hedge fund managers and various issues related to the hedge fund industry, its methods, and the regulatory environment.

As a group, however, hedge fund managers are a taciturn and reclusive bunch. A questionnaire I sent to around fifty leading hedge fund managers elicited little response, although as the book progressed I began receiving some interested approaches from sources I had not previously contacted. I am grateful to them for taking the trouble to seek me out and offer help. Nicola Meaden of TASS and Johan Wong and Greg Barrett of Hedgeworld deserve special mention for the information and contacts they have provided to me, including unfettered access to the Hedgeworld.com site.

Several members of the hedge fund community have helped with information and interviews. The hardier among them were also kind enough to read and comment on the manuscript in draft form and made a number of valuable suggestions that have resulted in a much better book. In particular, Adam Sorab at Deutsche Bank (then at CSFB), Kevin Gundle at Aurum, Colin McLean at Scottish Value Management, Nils Taube at Taube Hodson Stonex, Les Allen at Lehman Brothers, Martin Harrison at GAM, Joe Toms at Hilspen Capital Management, Michael Lewitt at Harch Capital, Michel Serieyssol at Bear Stearns, and Jeff Summers at Klesch & Company all have my thanks, as do John Trammel at Argonaut and Patrick Hess at USCG. They bear no responsibility for any errors or imperfections that remain. Nor are my views on hedge funds necessarily theirs too.

As usual my wife and business partner, Lynn Temple, helped in many ways. The research for Chapters 4 and 10, as well as the bibliography and index are largely down to her painstaking attention to detail. She has my grateful thanks, as ever.

Peter Temple
January 2001

1

Courtesans of capitalism

Courtesan. N. It. Cortigiana (f. of cortigiano – courtier) A prostitute,
especially one whose clients are wealthy or upper class
Oxford English Dictionary

This is a book about hedge funds and their influence on the financial markets, and on you and me. It is not about upmarket prostitutes or the seamier side of life. Yet when I began writing this book, the parallel struck me forcibly between the courtesans of a bygone age – their trade since undermined by a less rigid moral code – and the grip that hedge fund managers exert on their clients.

So the courtesan comparison is an entertaining one on several levels. The French, not surprisingly, have a word for them. In fact, they have not just one word, but several phrases: *poules de luxe* 'luxury chicks' and *grandes horizontales* 'the great horizontal ones' are only two of the more entertaining.

Putting aside the euphemisms, they are upmarket tarts. Not quite the way hedge fund managers would like to view themselves. But whether by accident or some form of inspired marketing, the courtesan word seems to convey more than this, just as hedge fund managers succeed in seeming more than mere speculators.

Whether supporting military and political leaders, comforting kings and princes, spying by passing secrets acquired during pillow talk, or bringing scandal in their wake and toppling governments, courtesans have often played a pivotal role in history. Hedge funds have broken currencies, bankrupted economies, and threatened to destabilise the financial system.

They have been the stuff of news stories. Hotels have been built to honour their memory. The distinctive cupolas of the Carlton Hotel in Cannes – one of the premier hotels on the Côte d'Azur – were reportedly modelled on the statuesque Bella Otero, a leading *horizontale* at the time it was built. Hedge fund managers seek more subtle memorials.

Courtesans have been immortalised in books and opera. Alexandre Dumas created *La Dame aux Camelias*. This was the story of Violetta Valery, a Parisian courtesan who succumbed to consumption. In turn the story became the subject of the opera *La Traviata* by Verdi. Operas have not been written about hedge fund managers, and what books there are have been a dry read. Then again there is Mata Hari, born Gertrude Margaret Zelle in Holland in 1876, who used her charms to spy for the Germans in World War I and was executed by the French for her pains in 1917. Hedge fund managers rarely fade away quietly either.

Or take the case of Veronica Franco, a Venetian courtesan who lived in the second half of the sixteenth century. Among her paramours was King Henry III of France. She had rich and powerful patrons, but she fell foul of those whose positions of patronage she threatened. Tried as a witch by the Inquisition, she was saved only because her many clients were shamed into pleading her case. There are parallels with hedge fund managers, not least with Long Term Capital Management (LTCM) and John Meriwether.

*   *   *

So they are the upper echelon of the world's oldest profession. What distinguishes them from their humbler sisters is that their clients are invariably drawn from the upper stratum of society, and wealthy to boot. Why make the comparison between courtesans and hedge fund managers?

They have plenty of apologists, many of which believe that the services they perform are a healthy outlet for basic instincts. Yet sometimes their clients get more excitement than they bargained for. They have, or claim to have, superior skills to their less well-known counterparts, for which they are paid very handsomely. They have achieved a certain level of notoriety. They are used by the wealthy and have a small and exclusive clientele.

For some at least, they provide an exciting alternative to more conventional relationships – with an air of risk and danger. Plenty of otherwise respectable institutions are happy to provide them with the support and services they need to practise their profession. Their actions have had adverse effects on the vulnerable. Those responsible for policing them sometimes turn a blind eye to their activities. They seek respectability, yet are never quite accepted as members of polite society, even by those who employ them. Sometimes they meet an unpleasant end.

We could have been writing here about the famous courtesans of history. Or writing about hedge fund managers. The parallels are strong.

*   *   *

Hedge funds and their managers have no shortage of apologists. Those who criticise what they do are often accused of not understanding the benefits they bring to the body of the financial system, of being overly conservative or prejudiced. Or else the charge is one of being envious or embittered, or threatened by their success.

But the benefits they confer are hard to measure. Hedge fund managers enrich themselves through incentive fees and management charges, but whether or not they provide long-term benefits for their investors is another matter. Occasionally they go spectacularly wrong.

While many hedge funds have been successful, it is the less fortunate ones that attract attention. Often this attention, though uncomfortable, is wholly merited. The case of LTCM and John Meriwether is only the most highly publicised in a string of failures, which include Victor Niederhoffer's Niederhoffer Investments and David Askin's Askin Capital Management. More recently, other hedge funds have been laid low by fraud and deception, usually centring on the falsification of performance figures.

Not only this, and perhaps to the consternation of their customers, but the hedge fund style of trading is practised by large banks around the world, and has been responsible for some high-profile collapses or enforced takeovers. Quite apart from the obvious example of Barings, consider SBC's takeover of UBS. It was later found this had been completed after UBS discovered a large loss on its trading book. Bankers Trust was taken over by Deutsche Bank in similar circumstances. Most of Britain's big high-street banks have been through periods when they have made heavy losses on trading, and one way or another their customers end up paying.

Many courtesans became fabulously wealthy. Hedge fund managers and bank traders share one thing in common: a remuneration structure that rewards them when things go well, but may not penalise them unduly if things go badly. That is to say, incentive fees and bonuses do not have to be paid back if performance later turns sour, even if it proves to be the result of excessive or ill-judged risk taking.

The worst that can happen to a trader is the sack, probably followed by a highly paid job somewhere else; trader's mistakes are usually written off as bad luck. Hedge fund managers may have to make up losses before their performance fees resume. Mostly, but not always, they have some of their own money at stake. Only rarely, if at all, do all the performance fees earned go back into the fund. It is a one-way bet that in recent years has appropriately earned the name 'moral hazard': Heads you and I win; tails you lose but I don't.

Courtesans draw their clients from the rich and famous. Hedge fund investors have historically been a select bunch, characterised by their wealth and their appetite for risk. Because they are structured as offshore limited partnerships and may not, according to US laws, have more than 99 investors, hedge funds have mystique, notoriety and exclusivity. With the funds almost all administered from offshore tax havens, their investors have anonymity if they wish it – which some do. One may draw one's own conclusions.

Jut as the average courtesan needs accommodation sufficient to project an air of successful opulence to potential clients, so too do hedge fund managers need office space, clearing services, bank loans and a variety of more technical facilities to ply their trade. They usually have no shortage of suppliers. These range from banks, which supply the loans to allow them to 'leverage' their portfolios, to so-called prime brokers, who supply a package of services. An article in the business magazine *Forbes* about prime brokers said, 'They are the bordello keepers, and the hedge funds are the girls, and it's easy to guess who is likely to make the most money in the long term.'

Men make fools of themselves with courtesans, and in the process innocent bystanders get hurt. Harming the vulnerable is a hard charge to prove. But certain types of hedge fund have a raison d'être based around targeting what are regarded as unsustainably overvalued or undervalued currencies and stock markets and forcing a correction of the supposed anomaly.

This can be viewed as simply making sure the free market functions as it should. But one might sometimes question whether or not the over- or undervaluation is real. Or does it simply exist in the mind of the hedge fund manager? Because of the market power hedge funds exert and the degree to which other traders follow them, their actions can produce a classic self-fulfilling prophecy.

Britons may have cause to thank George Soros for driving sterling out of the European exchange rate mechanism (ERM) in September 1992, but the value of the pound is currently higher now than it was then. And should the Malaysians be so grateful to the Soros camp? The Malaysians endured capital controls for more than a year, instituted (and seemingly successfully) to protect them from similar depredations. More recently these capital controls were quietly and successfully removed, but Malaysian Prime Minister Mahathir Mohamed continues to press for concerted international action against hedge funds.

Courtesans are discreet, well connected and so able to avoid the attention from law enforcement that their lower-paid sisters attract. Hedge funds fall between the gaps in regulation. Because legally they are offshore entities, they are difficult to police. One suspects, however, that were some of them other than generally very discreet about pursuing their profession, they would attract the attention of the authorities. As it is, it is those who provide them with money (large clearing banks and investment banks), in the form of loans (or other forms of leverage), that have attracted the attention of regulators.

Nonetheless, they do present the authorities with a more complex problem. When large hedge funds use leverage, they become very big indeed, but not perhaps as big as some of the internal funds run by large banks along hedge fund principles. When LTCM collapsed, irrespective of the official reasons advanced to justify the bailout, people asked, Was the fund was too big to fail? It never got a satisfactory answer.

LTCM could have been allowed to disappear without intervention. But had there been no intervention, the consequences for the markets in which it had invested might have triggered losses at other, more pivotal institutions in the financial system. Add to this the fact that key executives at some of these institutions were themselves personal investors in LTCM, and we have a very complex situation for regulators to police.

LTCM's investors may have been too big and too well connected for too much fuss to be made. A discreet and unpublicised clipping of the wings may be the only punishment meted out. But they suffered in more subtle ways. According to one fund manager well placed to know, 'It was one of the industry's dirty little secrets. All of the banks connected to LTCM mimicked the trades they knew about and were asked to facilitate. There was an audible sigh of relief as they were each unwound.'

Courtesans in history have craved legitimacy and respectability, but rarely achieved it completely. Similarly, many hedge fund managers' attempts at acquiring respectability have an almost surreal quality. George Soros has attempted, probably unsuccessfully, to stake his claim to be a major contemporary philosopher. More likely he will be remembered as a philanthropist. Other hedge fund managers personally donate large sums to causes that range from the worthwhile to the bizarre.

Courtesans sometimes died spectacularly dramatic deaths. Whether, like Mata Hari in front of the firing squad, or like those of the court of Louis XVI, beheaded by the guillotine. Or like Violetta, from tuberculosis. It is too early in the day to know what fate befalls hedge fund managers who fail spectacularly.

The hapless Nick Leeson, the internal hedge fund trader who brought down Barings, may not qualify, nor may Mike Milken, the junk bond king of Drexel Burnham. Nor may Ivan Boesky, although minus the inside information he used for his trading edge, his method, essentially merger arbitrage, worked much as some hedge funds work today. All three served some time in prison. Milken and Leeson contracted life-threatening diseases but have seemingly overcome them.

Some unsuccessful hedge fund managers, such as Victor Niederhoffer or David Askin, simply fade from view, selling off a few antiques, doing a little trading here and there. Or like LTCM's John Meriwether, they may re-emerge chastened in another vehicle, exercising their persuasive powers on investors. In spite of Meriwether's undoubted persuasive powers and a recent public expression of remorse, his recent attempt to raise money for his comeback has met with a mixed response, the initiative raising only some $400m out of the $1000m sought. It is all a far cry from the origin of hedge funds as essentially conservative investments.

* * *

When you begin researching a book on hedge funds, the name of Alfred Winslow Jones pretty soon begins to come up. Jones is rightly regarded as the originator of hedge fund investing, although we can perhaps speculate that he might be appalled to see some of the ways in which his original, simple investment concept has been corrupted.

Jones was born in Australia in 1900 but came to America with his family when he was four years old, doubtless passing through Ellis Island, as virtually all immigrants did around that time. He survived the experience. Graduating from Harvard in 1923 he set out to travel the world, working as a purser on a passenger liner for the best part of ten years. In the early 1930s he surfaced in Berlin as a vice consul at the American embassy. He was a reporter during the Spanish Civil

War and returned to the United States to study for a doctorate in sociology at Columbia University.

His thesis had the worthy if less than snappy title 'Life, liberty and property: a study of conflict and a measurement of conflicting rights'. It explored attitudes towards corporate property in Akron, Ohio. But it did become a standard sociology text and still features on library catalogues at universities throughout the United States. This study, and probably his experiences in Europe in the 1930s, left Jones with what one writer describes as an active concern for those less fortunate and an interest in schemes for the relief of poverty, many of which had a distinct left-wing tinge.

Academia didn't exert much pull on Jones. And, social conscience or no, the one-time diplomat and steamboat purser turned seriously to studying capitalism in the early 1940s, working as an associate editor at *Fortune* magazine and writing for *Time* and other business publications.

A few years later, towards the end of 1948, Jones was researching material for an article on forecasting trends in the market. In the course of this work he interviewed many of the most prominent analysts, forecasters, technical analysts and other assorted experts on Wall Street. Every expert he interviewed said that it was impossible to forecast the direction of the stock market with any degree of consistency. The article was published in *Fortune* in March 1949, but by then Jones had had the germ of an idea and had already formed an investment partnership to see if it could be exploited.

Jones's idea was to generate profits while attempting to eliminate market risk, and hence shift the onus of the fund away from predicting the direction of the overall market, something his interviews with forecasters had told him would be impossible with any consistency. The method to be used was to pick both undervalued stocks, which he would buy, and overvalued stocks, which he would sell short.

Short selling is a peculiar investment technique – selling securities one doesn't own, but has simply borrowed, in the hope of buying them back at a lower price to return to the lender, while pocketing the profit. The basket of stocks that had been sold short was the insurance, or 'hedge', against a drop in the market. Jones also used borrowing to enhance returns, but did not take big overall bets on the market's movement up or down. Hence the term 'hedge fund'.

Imagine, for instance, that Jones had $10 000 to invest. He would borrow 50% of this figure, then buy perhaps $10 000 of stocks and sell short $5000. Capital had to be put up to enable the short sales to take place, or held in reserve for topping-up 'margin calls' if they didn't perform as expected. So while the total involvement in the market represented $15 000 (or 150% of his capital), his net exposure as a percentage of his capital was only 50% (the $10 000 of stocks he had bought less the $5000 he had sold short). If the stocks he had bought (or was 'long' of) went up and the 'shorts' he had sold went down, returns would be magnified accordingly.

Another way of looking at this is that a fund constructed along these lines has a hedged portion and an unhedged portion. In the gross exposure of $15 000, $10 000 is hedged, with the stocks purchased matched by short sales of different stocks. The overall returns from this portion are in theory much less likely to be affected either way by a movement in the market in either direction.

The remaining $5000 was, in this example, invested in specially selected 'longs'. This overall position was probably a natural one for Jones, who may well have believed, correctly for the most part, that over time the market would tend to rise. Either way, the basis for the expected returns is successful stock picking, but stock picking with a difference. That difference is that overvalued stocks, which are expected to fall in price, are also selected and sold short, in addition to the more normal practice of so-called long-only analysts and fund managers – researching and buying undervalued stocks but leaving alone those they consider overvalued.

The idea was spectacularly successful. In April 1966 *Fortune* magazine, for whom Jones had previously worked, published an article by Carol Loomis with the title 'The Jones nobody keeps up with'. A short piece, the article had explosive significance. It outlined his methods and highlighted that Jones's fund had outperformed the next best performing mutual fund by a margin of 44% over five years and by an

87% margin over ten years, even after deducting a 20% incentive fee calculated on realised profits. The article was influential because Jones had managed to keep his fund, and his investment methods, largely secret up to that point.

Before long, his investment style was being widely imitated. One estimate puts at several hundred the number of hedge funds that were set up over the three years following Loomis's article. Many of Jones's would-be imitators were to be culled by the savage early 1970s bear market since, in the gung-ho atmosphere of the times, they had not followed Jones's relatively conservative principles and kept a significant proportion of their fund hedged.

Prominent survivors of that period, such as George Soros and Michael Steinhardt, went on to greater things. Jones's own partnership also acted as an incubator for at least two other employees, Carl Jones and Dick Radcliffe, who absorbed the Jones method and left to set up their own respective operations.

Jones died rich in 1989. He was a shy, quietly spoken and modest man, in sharp contrast to some of today's self-styled hedge fund superstars. By the time he died, the partnership he had started had been converted into one that, rather than manage its own portfolio directly, was more akin to a fund of funds. This is a fund that invests in other hedge funds, spreading money among different managers and styles of hedge fund to reduce risk.

There are many significant lessons from the ideas that Jones pursued so successfully. First is that his spectacular returns were achieved by reducing market risk and by astute picking of undervalued and overvalued stocks, not by making large bets on the direction of major markets. Second, the borrowing in his funds was relatively modest, and the performance he generated appears to have been achieved without resorting to complex mathematical techniques. Third, although Jones's fund worked on the basis of an incentive fee, the fee was based on *realised* rather than paper profits. And no management fee was charged. All the fund's expenses were paid out of the annual incentive payment. In addition, all of Jones's own capital was invested in the fund.

Remember too that Jones started his fund well before the application of computers to finance, and before the widespread use of sophisticated financial derivatives, futures, mortgage-backed securities, collateralised mortgage obligations and all the other paraphernalia supposedly necessary to generate superior performance by some of today's hedge funds. Related to this point is that, largely through his own common sense, Jones hit upon a truth which took academic financial economists several more years to identify and explain. Jones realised that the risk of investing in a market was distinct and separate from the risk inherent in investing in a stock, and it could be identified, reduced and even more or less eliminated by appropriate hedging.

There is also delicious irony in the fact that Jones, a journalist, devised a successful investment method through intuition and common sense and practised it successfully for forty years. This contrasts sharply with the fact that two of the prominent participants in the LTCM debacle, which happened nearly ten years after Jones's death, were Nobel laureate financial economists. One of them was Myron Scholes, half of the Black–Scholes partnership that derived the formula for accurate pricing (and therefore tradability) of financial derivatives.

*   *   *

Investment genius, it is sometimes said, is a short memory in a rising market. In the wake of Loomis's article there was no shortage of hopefuls out to prove they had what it took to make money. Only a select few were heard of again.

Most statistics relating to the spectacular growth of hedge funds date from 1990, perhaps because figures that take in the 1987 stock market crash do not make such pretty reading. Yet the so-called Reagan bull market began in 1982 and was probably a propitious time for some hedge fund operators. And we know that many hedge funds were active and successful even prior to that period. In *The Alchemy of Finance*, for example, George Soros writes at length if not particularly entertainingly about his trading experiences in the mid 1980s.

Even in 1981 *Institutional Investor* magazine was writing about Soros's performance record, commenting how he had multiplied a fund worth only $15m in 1974 to one worth $381m by the end of 1980. Julian Robertson, another big player who boasted Margaret Thatcher as a director of one of his funds, reputedly turned $8m in 1980 into over $7bn in 1996, and more than three times this number a couple of years later (although his star had waned somewhat by mid 1999 and he effectively wound up most of his funds in early 2000).

But performance figures such as these are sometimes not all they seem. Even figures as straightforward as the estimates (and that is all they are) of funds under management in the hedge fund industry are partly a reflection of the performance of the funds in question, partly a reflection of the increased money flowing into the industry, and partly due to the increased numbers of funds themselves.

Take the commonly stated figure that hedge fund assets under management have risen from $20bn in 1990 to about $400bn now. This twentyfold growth seems impressive, but it has to be seen in the context of an increase in the number of funds from 200 to over 3000 during the same period. If you assume that each of a fund's 99 investors, the maximum allowed, contributed $1m, making each fund worth $99m, this alone would explain $300bn of the $380bn increase in value between those dates. In reality some funds are smaller than this and the increase as a result of performance somewhat greater.

According to figures from TASS, an industry database which takes in figures from most but not all hedge funds, the flow of new money into hedge funds has been of the order of $60bn since 1994 and performance has contributed $100bn to assets over the same period. The movement does, however, conceal big shifts in the manner in which the funds are invested.

One of the themes that we will return to later in this book is the secrecy under which hedge funds operate. In a way the penchant for secrecy is understandable. The less information the market has about their activities, the easier it is for them to steal a march on it. To use jargon, the greater the secrecy, the less the 'market impact' of them dealing in a particular security, currency or other financial instrument.

But secrecy is a double-edged sword. It opens up hedge funds to the accusation, justified or otherwise, that a minority of their investors may be less than wholesome. The size of this minority one just cannot know – it's a secret! Almost all hedge funds conduct extensive vetting to prevent situations like this occurring, but inevitably they rely to some degree on the integrity of those who introduce investors to them.

Secrecy can also be turned on and off like a tap, and some observers are not impressed. In a detailed critique of hedge funds, the Wall Street investment consultants Chapman, Spira and Carson say, 'Unregistered hedge funds with less than 100 investors are exempt from a public reporting requirement. When superior results are attained, the fund management will arrange press conferences to bombard the public with their results. Underperformance is accompanied by evasion and silence.'

'One manager,' says Chapman Spira, 'broadcast substantial trading profits during a period when he had actually wiped out the majority of the fund's investors. The "Alice in Wonderland" performance, though unverifiable, continued to attract gullible participants.' Having said that, there are perfectly reputable statistical services which take statistics covering the whole gamut of hedge funds and put them in the public domain, and one has no good reason to suspect that their figures are anything other than reasonably accurate. A little more transparency, though not complete clarity, may be on the way.

You might think, however, that the measurement of hedge fund performance would be a statistically rigorous process based around complex formulae containing lots of Greek letters with subscripts and superscripts. This is the case to some extent. But measuring hedge fund performance is nonetheless comparatively easy to understand as a broad concept. A fund generates a return month by month, which can be averaged or converted to an annual figure. The return may come from capital appreciation or investment income – the two components are added together to produce a so-called total return figure.

But this isn't the whole story. If the manager is being true to the principles of hedge funding devised by Jones, and not all of them are, then those returns should be consistent. In other words, because of the way the fund's investments are structured, with investment both on the long side and the short side, a classic hedge fund's returns should be less volatile than those of the market as a whole.

While this is the theory, it certainly doesn't fit with the popular image of hedge funds as institutions that sashay around the capital markets, making and breaking currencies, forcing governments to institute capital controls, breaking the careers of politicians, and even threatening the very well-being of the global financial system. The acid test for an investor is whether or not a fund can generate its return without undue volatility in those returns. Clearly one has to be balanced against the other. It is an axiom of investment, often forgotten in the heat of the moment, that risk and return are indivisibly entwined.

So the higher the return generated by a fund today, the greater have been the risks to generate that return and the greater the risk that this return will not be available in the future.

*   *   *

In financial markets, the usual assumption is that risk equates to volatility. The more the price of an investment swings around its normal trend, the greater the risk of losing money if you have to sell. It can be measured statistically; in the jargon it is called the standard deviation of the investment's price change, or return, from the average. Imagine a straight line drawn through a chart of monthly returns over time, with the line representing the average return, then the standard deviation is a percentage measure of how violent the zigzags around that line are likely to be.

There are easier ways of thinking about this without getting ensnared in statistical buzzwords. For example, as an investor, would you rather have a return of 8% but a 90% chance that the return could vary between a loss of 8% or a gain of 24% in any one time period, or a return of 5% that is 90% likely to vary between 3% and 7%? The answer depends to some extent on your appetite for risk, but the conundrum can be solved logically by using something called the Sharpe ratio.

MBA students specialising in finance are taught, almost by rote, the theories of a select group of financial economists and mathematicians, including Franco Modigliani, Merton Miller, Eugene Fama, Myron Scholes and Fischer Black, and Harry Markowitz. In 1952, more than a decade after Jones had devised his hedge fund model, Markowitz formulated the theory which demonstrated how it was possible to combine a group of relatively volatile and risky investments and for that portfolio to have a lower volatility than its separate constituents, provided their businesses were not correlated.

Students of modern portfolio theory, as Markowitz's ideas have come to be known, develop a quick affinity with the initial letters of the Greek alphabet. The Markowitz theory, and I am adapting pretty freely here for the sake of clarity, suggests that any investment, be it an individual share or a fund, has two salient characteristics, known respectively as alpha and beta. Alpha describes the return that might be expected from the investment if the market were unchanged. Beta is a multiplier that describes the effect of the market on the performance of an investment.

Or if you prefer the official statistical explanation according to one tome on the subject: 'Alpha and beta are descriptive statistics of a linear regression of a manager's monthly or quarterly results plotted against the market. Alpha is a number that shows the expected statistical return if the market was unchanged. Beta is a multiplier which reflects the effect of the market on the manager's results.' Substitute the word 'investment' for 'manager' if you prefer; the theory is the same.

If a fund (or a share) has an alpha of 3% and a beta of 1, in a market up 10% it should in theory rise by 13%. The beta of 1 means that this component of the return would be identical to the market's return of 10%. To this is added the individual return (or alpha) of 3%. If the market were to fall by 10%, the performance of the same investment should in theory be a drop of 7%. The market return component would be a fall of 10%, offset in part by the positive return attributable to the investment of 3%.

Without all the Greek paraphernalia, Alfred Jones arrived at essentially the same conclusion. In the Jones fund, the effect of beta was neutralised by the hedged portion of the portfolio, and the alpha magnified by leverage of the remaining 'long' portion of it.

Where does this get us in terms of looking at hedge funds? The answer is relatively simple. What interests the hedge fund manager is positive absolute performance; that is to say, a high alpha. A high enough alpha may be sufficient to offset a declining market. The reason – the hedge fund manager's pay depends on absolute performance rather than relative performance.

For many investors, however, what matters more than this is whether or not the return being generated is being produced for an acceptable level of risk. Which is where Sharpe comes in. William Sharpe was a student of Markowitz and developed his teacher's theories in a number of directions. One of these led to the devising of the Sharpe ratio, which has found its most productive use in the measurement of hedge fund performance.

The Sharpe ratio deals with the relationship between risk, return and the risk-free rate of return. The idea is to separate out the extra (or 'excess' in the jargon) return that derives from the risk of an investment, and then measure it against the risk involved. The risk is defined as the volatility (or the standard deviation) of the return. In simple terms, the Sharpe ratio is the annual return on a fund, say, minus the risk-free rate of return (usually expressed in terms of the yield on three-month US Treasury bills), divided by the percentage volatility of the returns.

Let's say for the sake of argument that we have two funds: one with an annual return of 24% and a volatility of 20%, and one with a return of 16% and a volatility of 10%. The rate of return on three-month Treasury bills is 4%. The Sharpe ratio for the first fund is

$$\frac{24 - 4}{20} = \frac{20}{20} = 1.0$$

The Sharpe ratio for the second fund is

$$\frac{16-4}{10} = \frac{12}{10} = 1.2$$

What this tells us is that although the second fund appears to perform less well, in fact it offers a greater amount of return per unit of risk. The higher the Sharpe ratio, in theory the better the investor is doing in generating return while minimising risk.

Before leaving the subject of jargon, financial economists would not be the wonderful people they are if they hadn't managed to complicate this elegant concept. One result is the Sortino ratio, a variant of the Sharpe ratio. The idea behind this is that what worries investors is not deviation in both directions around the mean return – as measured by standard deviation (or its synonym of volatility) – but only deviation *below* the mean. Hence the Sortino ratio is calculated in the same way as the Sharpe ratio. The numerator is still the return minus the risk-free rate, but the denominator is the deviation below a specific mean or target return.

Another piece of jargon is the word 'drawdown', which in effect is a euphemism for losing money. Hedge fund statistics often include a statistic that gives the maximum drawdown. This is the biggest fall from peak to trough over any period in the fund's history. Jargon like this is all very well, but what it all comes down to is that as a hedge fund investor, or indeed a hedge fund manager, the degree to which you are attracted to absolute return irrespective of the risk involved, or whether you want a more controlled approach, depends on how comfortable you are with risk.

Risk aversion varies from individual to individual, and it may decrease with increased affluence (although some rich people I know are also the most risk-averse, or more accurately the meanest, people I have ever met). My own experience suggests that risk aversion increases with age, but perhaps that's just me.

*   *   *

There is little doubt that the model postulated by Jones was essentially a risk-averse model, and to that extent it is fair to say that many of today's hedge fund managers, by worshipping at the altar of leverage (borrowing heavily to enhance returns), have corrupted Jones's ideas. Jones's model defined the characteristics of a hedge fund: a fund having both long and short positions, some leverage and an incentive-based fee structure for the managers. But more modern definitions of hedge funds you might come across these days suggest that a fund can be called a hedge fund if it possesses two of these three Jones characteristics.

Since managers are unlikely to give up their fees, what this essentially means is that the definition holds if the fund is one that goes short as well as long, or if it is leveraged, but not necessarily both. As we will see later on, many of the problems experienced by some hedge funds have essentially related to excessive leverage and a propensity to ignore either the short side of the equation or the issue of market liquidity.

It is evident to even the most untutored eye that leverage and a lack of hedging amounts to speculation on a grand scale, driven along by the desire (or the greed) of the manager for performance, and the fame and fortune that goes with it. It is often said that stock markets are driven by fear and greed. Nowhere is this more true than in hedge funds.

You will see from these comments that I approach the issues surrounding hedge fund investing with a somewhat baleful eye, certainly a much more sceptical one than you might find in many other books on this subject. I do believe, however, that there are a large number of hedge fund managers who have remained true to the ideals of Alfred Winslow Jones and whose efforts are somewhat devalued by the activities of the higher-profile practitioners in the field – the courtesans of capitalism – not least those whose investment strategies lead to harm for themselves, their investors and innocent bystanders.

The growing institutionalisation of the hedge fund industry (as shown by, for instance, large pension funds looking to make controlled investments in them), and moves to regulate it, may lead to easier identification of these 'true' hedge funds and their greater accessibility to the broader mass of investors. I think this is a development whole-heartedly to be welcomed, and it is one which I explore in some detail later in this book.

But bear in mind that it won't in the meantime prevent some of the existing large pools of capital from occasionally playing havoc with the financial system. To know what hedge funds can do, we need to look at the character of hedge fund managers, examine how hedge funds work, and consider the different forms they take. These are the subjects of the next two chapters.

2

Masters of the Universe

Victorious warriors after the fray . . . Masters of the Universe
Tom Wolfe

The courtesans of history were famous not simply for their talents in the bedroom, but as individuals in their own right: for writing books, for throwing parties, for spying and making enemies. To gain an understanding of the way hedge funds function and what is both wrong and right about them, it's essential to get to grips with the complex, multidimensional individuals who manage them.

As well as the courtesan analogy, the idea that hedge fund managers are also akin to 'Masters of the Universe', a term from Tom Wolfe's novel *The Bonfire of the Vanities*, is also apt. Walking into his office at investment bankers Pierce & Pierce, Wolfe's character Sherman McCoy thinks pretty highly of himself too. Wolfe describes him thus: 'He considered himself as part of the new era and the new breed, a Wall Street egalitarian, a Master of the Universe who was a respecter only of performance.' It sums up how some hedge fund managers view themselves.

There are thousands of hedge fund managers, of course, most of whom labour away unnoticed. The heavy hitters in the industry do get noticed, however, and sometimes do not welcome the attention they get. Not that all hedge fund managers are especially publicity shy, especially when things are going well. But they tend to be cagey in the way they approach the press. That they are written about is testimony to the fascination that financial notoriety holds for newspaper and magazine readers. Here's how Richard Thomson puts it in his book *Apocalypse Roulette* :

The world of hedge funds is undeniably strange. Hedge fund managers are by nature solitary and often difficult people, the hermits of the financial markets. . . . Many of the most successful hedge fund managers have not been to business school or even worked for a major Wall Street or City firm.

Hedge fund managers are not, in general, modest people, which is one reason why they tend not to operate easily in large organisations. They have a tendency to think they are right while everyone else is wrong which, to more corporate-minded folk, can be intensely irritating – particularly when it turns out to be true.

One hedge fund manager puts it slightly differently:

The key thing to understand about hedge fund managers is that they tend to be non-institutional types who want to work for themselves, not a big organisation. They do not want to deal with the politics and the other nonsense you get in a big company.

Here is the view of an investment banker who spends much of his time dealing with hedge fund managers:

They are confident without being arrogant. They are all highly trained, they come from all types of background, but they all have some special magic.

A UK fund manager who also operates a hedge fund observes:

They are often contrarians, but what is more important is a flexibility in thinking, a willingness constantly to explore alternative scenarios, and to look for asymmetry and illogicality in the market.

This diversity of views makes researching the people behind the headlines more difficult than normal. But it is not impossible. The profiles that follow have been drawn from a wide variety of printed sources, including press articles, books and published interviews, as well as my own interviews with various sources, most of whom prefer to remain anonymous.

* * *

Most profiles of hedge fund managers start with George Soros, the best known to European readers because of his role in the forcible ejection of sterling from the European exchange rate mechanism (ERM) in September 1992. Seminal though it was, this event was by no means Soros's first success, or the only controversy in which he has been involved.

Soros was born in Budapest in 1930 with the Hungarian name Dzjchdzhe Shorash. His father was a lawyer, but had spent some years in Russia in the immediate aftermath of the revolution, and was by all accounts a survivor, unconventional and wily. The family spent the period after the Nazi invasion of Hungary in hiding under false papers and Soros later left the country for Switzerland in 1947, shortly thereafter moving to London, surviving by doing odd jobs, later studying at the London School of Economics. Subsequent jobs included selling ladies' handbags in Blackpool – a seedy resort town on England's north-west coast.

Soros eventually gravitated to the City with a job at merchant bank Singer & Friedlander, becoming a trader specialising in arbitraging gold stocks. Arbitrage means trading so as to profit from small price anomalies between similar stocks in different markets.

Finding London merchant banking too stuffy, he moved to New York in 1957 and continued working as an arbitrageur for the firm of F.H. Mayer, later moving to Wertheim. There he continued his arbitrage activities, ferreting out discrepancies in value in both US and international stocks. In 1963 Soros moved to A. & S. Bleichroeder, a leading US firm with a bias towards international markets.

According to an unauthorised biography of Soros by Robert Slater, Edgar Astaire – a business partner of Soros at times – describes him as 'a good psychologist . . . quite perceptive'. But he continues, '[Soros] made sure that others didn't get to know what his personality was like. He often says contradictory things for effect. He pontificates a lot of nonsense. He sometimes just says things for himself. He's not loveable.'

Soros's contrarianism, his global outlook, his background in arbitrage, all suggest a macro trader in the making. Macro traders bet on changes in the 'big picture'. Soros's father is also reputed to have instilled huge self-confidence in his children, so much so that, according to Slater, as a child George thought of himself (privately of course) as having godlike qualities of infallibility and genius, harbouring ambitions to be the new Einstein.

More crucially perhaps, Soros senior also taught his son that it was acceptable to take risks, as long as one did not risk all one's capital doing it. And he taught that perceptions were often more important than reality. Others suggest that Soros's background may have given him a nose for political instability that he has been able to profit from handsomely in his trading activities.

Soros started the Quantum Fund in 1969. It proved outstandingly successful for those investors who stuck with it long-term, achieving compound annual returns of over 30% per annum for much of the period since inception. Only in the last few years, and particularly in 2000, has its performance been less notable.

One of the strengths claimed for Soros's past approach is that it was flexible, adapting its style to changing circumstances and different market conditions and employing a mixture of assets within the fund, which ranged from straightforward long and short equity and bond positions, through to index futures, currencies and property. Soros is also held by many observers to have a superb intuitive understanding of leverage and the role it should play in investing, arguing that gearing up some types of asset is inherently 'safer' than doing it with others.

One of Soros's pet theories is that, put simply, financial markets do not tend towards equilibrium, as conventional theory would argue, but feed on their own misconceptions about events to produce exaggerated movements, which produce new misperceptions. This two-way feedback between perception and reality Soros describes as his theory of 'reflexivity'. It is, he claims, something that the shrewd investor can exploit by following the trend till it reaches the peak, and then, having identified what Soros calls the 'inflexion point', switching to the opposite tack.

Soros's theories are interesting, although some might argue they are nothing more than a stating of the obvious dressed up in the sort of psychobabble beloved of some Americans. Soros's almost comical attempts to present himself as one of the twentieth century's greatest philosophers, in addition to being one of its greatest investors (the latter claim clearly has substance), are not entirely convincing. Not only do we have the comment of his colleague Edgar Astaire as evidence of Soros's predilection for pomposity, but also a coruscating review of his book *The Crisis of Global Capitalism*, published in the December 1998 issue of the *Economist*. This extract gives a flavour of what it says:

> Because of who he is there will always be buyers for his books, publishers for his books, and cash-strapped academics to say flattering things about his books. None of this alters the fact that his books are no good. . . . A remarkable thing happens to money when it passes through Mr Soros: it emerges multiplied, but otherwise unchanged. With other inputs the results are more disappointing – to be blunt, more in line with biology. Mr Soros gorged on chopped philosophy, mashed economics and facts and figures swimming in grease. It was too much. Before he knew what was happening, out rushed this book.

Though arguably no great shakes at either authorship or philosophy, there is little doubt that Soros has a feel for market opportunities. Among Soros's coups were substantial gains made in the UK gilt-edge market in the late 1970s, his Black Wednesday demolition of sterling in 1992, and raids on emerging market currencies in 1998.

One of Soros's first major coups was in the UK gilt market in the late 1970s. It entailed pumping several millions, at that time a sizeable portion of the fund, into new stocks that were being issued in partly paid form. In one issue reckoned to be especially popular with investors, Soros needed to ensure that he was allocated a generous slice of the issue. His broker made hundreds of applications in small lots that would be more likely to be allotted in full. The result: the Soros fund got a massive allocation, and the stock itself went to a 10% premium in a matter of a few hours. The broking firm concerned is long since defunct.

On the negative side, Soros's calling of major currency moves has not always been infallible; witness losses made betting against a strong yen in 1994 and 1996 and a failure to anticipate the major inflexion point, to use his own terminology, represented by the 1987 stock market crash.

Soros's sterling coup in 1992 disproves the claim Soros made before the US Congress in 1994. He was asked if it was possible for an investor like him to amass enough capital to manipulate the value of a currency. Soros's reply was: 'I do not believe that any market participant can, *other than for a very short time*, successfully influence currency markets for major currencies contrary to market fundamentals. . . . Hedge funds are relatively small players given the size of global currency markets' (my italics).

Deliberately or otherwise, this misses the point. Influencing markets for a short time, given the leverage at their command, is all that hedge funds need to do to make profits. Second, the essence of the power wielded by high-profile investors like Soros is that other investors follow them, adding to their influence and producing the desired effect.

But other less successful forays seem to bear out the theory that, if manipulation like this does occur, it is less cause and effect than a happy conjunction of circumstances. Other bets made by Soros's funds look all too fallible. Returns from Soros's funds have been less than inspiring in recent years. Since 1995, when returns of 40% were seen, they have struggled to reach the 20% mark and in some periods have been negative. In fact, the Soros group's record in more esoteric areas of the market has been flawed. Its funds lost heavily from the poor performance of the euro and in the sharp downward move in technology stocks in March/April 2000. But apportioning all the blame to George Soros himself is perhaps unfair, not least because, even after these losses, the Soros funds were collectively worth some $14bn prior to their restructuring.

Soros's acolytes supposedly masterminded the move into technology, although Stanley Druckenmiller (see below) has confessed to a dislike of the technology sector. Ironically, it may have been largely responsible for the problems the Soros funds encountered. It gave the funds good performance in the second half of 1999 but a disastrous performance in the first half of 2000, prompting fund manager departures and a shift to a more conservative style of hedge fund investing involving a new clutch of external managers, some of whom were previously partners in Soros Fund Management. Robert Soros, George Soros's son, is also said to be assuming a more prominent role in the running of the firm. Soros has said that he sees his funds' future role as being mainly to provide cash for his philanthropic activities. In the meantime he has more pressing problems. Recent press reports suggest that, after a twelve-year investigation, Soros is one of several people who may face trial in France over alleged insider dealing in Société Générale in 1988.

*   *   *

Though they hardly fit the description of minions, in the course of his career Soros has sought to employ others to do much of the day-to-day work of managing his funds; the two most prominent managers were Stanley Druckenmiller and Nick Roditi.

For an extended period of time, George Soros stepped back from active management of the Quantum Fund and handed over much of his role to Stanley Druckenmiller. Originally from Palm Beach, Florida, the 47-year-old Druckenmiller is married with three children. He began his career as a securities analyst with Pittsburgh National Bank, achieving promotion at startling speed, and started Duquesne Capital Management in 1980. In 1986 he was recruited by the fund management group Dreyfus but allowed to continue managing his own fund at the same time. He left two years later to join Soros.

The family man image ends there. Druckenmiller's style arouses strong passions. One leading British fund manager, approached by Druckenmiller with an offer of a job at the Quantum Fund, describes him in very unflattering terms. Another instance of Druckenmiller's brusqueness is his habit of giving outside fund managers a matter of minutes to explain their complex investment techniques.

Newspaper reports also describe Druckenmiller as an outspoken right-winger, sharply contrasting with the more liberal views of George Soros. In the middle of the dispute between President Clinton and the US Congress over the federal budget in 1995/96, Druckenmiller suggested that the US Treasury be allowed to default on its debt and took a full-page advertisement in the *Washington Post* to argue the case, saying that Republicans should not allow fears of temporary market instability to deter them from forcing spending cuts on the president.

As a fund manager, however, such outspokenness may be less becoming. Druckenmiller has had his ups and downs in the markets, as has Soros. His biggest coup was correctly predicting the strength of the Deutschmark in the wake of German reunification and the reining in, through high interest rates, of the subsequent inflationary tendencies it produced. Druckenmiller took a huge $2bn position in the German currency, one so large that, according to one source, it was hard to exit when the time came. The results of this and other similar positions were returns that averaged 50–60% for several years.

Much less successful were highly geared bets in mid 1999 that the euro would rise against a dollar weakened by a record US trade deficit, followed by another pasting as the fund took a long position in the yen, only to see things go awry as the Japanese government decided unexpectedly to accept a weaker currency, although Druckenmiller was not alone by any means in reading the market wrongly in this instance.

In 1999 Druckenmiller took a big long position in technology stocks, which produced excellent returns that year, but a sharp drop in value in early 2000 following a big correction. At this point, Druckenmiller and Soros parted company, and the Soros funds are now expected to pursue more conservative strategies. Druckenmiller meanwhile is to return to managing his own Duquesne fund and says that his departure from the Soros group had been planned for some time. He was joined in August 2000 by Stanley Shopkorn. Shopkorn is a former head of equities at Moore Capital, another large hedge fund.

For many years, Nick Roditi played counterpoint to Druckenmiller's reputed aggressiveness in the Soros stable of managers. A quietly spoken 54-year-old who craves anonymity, Roditi, who was never directly employed by the Soros group and who has other fund management clients, ran the Soros Quota Fund which posted stellar returns over a five-year period to mid 1999, increasing in value by more than 400%. Indeed, Roditi's returns in 1996, his first full year working for the Soros interests, bailed out the group from one of its periodic disastrous bets on the yen, mentioned earlier.

Born in Zimbabwe, Roditi divides his time between Europe and Africa, especially South Africa, where he owns a fruit farm and a vineyard. After Peterhouse College in Zimbabwe, where he was a contemporary of Rupert Pennant Rea, former deputy governor of the Bank of England and ex-editor of the Economist, he first came to London as a student in 1969 and attended City University.

When in London, he works quietly from a small office near his multimillion pound home in Hampstead, an upmarket enclave in North London where he lives with his wife and son. He is reputed to collect small items of art. Roditi gained degrees in law and commerce at the University of Cape Town and was a director of the merchant bank Schroders between 1970 and 1982, after which time he was managing director of Schroder Securities. In 1985 he joined Jacob Rothschild's investment business as an employee; he worked there until 1992 before leaving to run his own fund management activities.

Observers say that Roditi's special talent is predicting interest rate movements, and placing associated geared-up bets on resulting currency movements to take advantage of them.

Roditi appears to have been dogged by ill health. Newspaper reports have him variously suffering tuberculosis as a child and asthma as an adult, but he has never commented publicly on this. Some reports suggest that his reason for starting his own fund management business were partly health-related. In late 1998, in the wake of the LTCM crisis, Roditi took leave of absence for three months on health grounds, returning to manage the Quota Fund in January 1999. Like Druckenmiller he made big bets in technology stocks that year and has since also ceased to manage Soros funds.

Estimates of Roditi's earnings have been scattered over the press, some reports suggesting that in 1996, one of his best years, he earned some $125m, putting him ninth in a list of Wall Street highest earners.

Something of a recluse, Roditi has always declined to comment on estimates of his personal wealth.

*   *   *

While George Soros, rightly or wrongly, is regarded as the doyen of hedge fund managers, there are at least a couple of others with a legitimate claim to the title, both now seemingly in retirement.

Julian Robertson has long been regarded as one of the giants of the hedge fund business. A 67-year-old native of Salisbury, North Carolina, he is big and burly with a booming Southern drawl and reputed to have a short fuse. Robertson's Tiger Management has been in business since 1980, when it had $8m under management. Its assets reached a peak of $20 *billion* in the summer of 1998, but fell back to around $8bn at the time it was wound down in early 2000. Observers describe the recent moves as a regrouping rather than outright retirement.

Robertson styles himself as a typical small-town boy, but his family circumstances appear to have been comfortable. Despite a demanding father, a senior executive in a textile business, Robertson was not a conspicuous achiever either at school or university and is happy to have himself described as having been a late developer even in mathematics, which most would now regard as his forte.

After service in the navy, he moved to New York to join Kidder Peabody – the firm later brought to its knees by the activities of alleged rogue trader Joe Jett – and stayed there for twenty years. Robertson then discovered fund management and left with another former Kidder employee to form Tiger. The partner, Thorpe Mackenzie, soon went off on his own, perhaps recognising that Robertson would emerge as the dominant of the two.

Robertson built his funds and his personal fortune on stock picking and was an advocate of detailed investigative analysis to identify undervalued situations. Tiger has consistently had the largest team of industry analysts among major hedge fund groups, and this pattern continued to the end.

Despite substantial personal rewards, one common inference was that Tiger's employees found Robertson's predilection to 'lose his cool' (as he himself puts it, with what others would regard as some understatement) more than a little off-putting. Another 'problem' faced by the Tiger funds was reputedly Robertson's apparent insistence on retaining control of all fund management decision making, which outside commentators say has become something of a handicap for the funds in recent years.

Much of Robertson's performance record was built when Tiger was relatively small and able to hunt out small stocks to take positions in. As the funds grew in size, achieving this stock-based performance without also taking big macro bets – something which Robertson may be less good at than stock picking – became more difficult.

In the latter stages of Tiger's life, Robertson was forced to confine his stock selections to the world's largest 200 companies. The performance of the fund was also not helped by the fact that Robertson, who made his name as a so-called value investor, had an investment philosophy which for a period in the late 1990s was distinctly out of favour. Prior to the wind-up there were signs, however, that Robertson was mellowing, even going so far as to allow selected staff to manage part of the firm's capital.

While Tiger made astute bets in the early 1990s, 1994 was a bad year and key employees left the firm, further inhibiting its ability and management depth in this area. Bad bond market calls in 1994 and an underweight position in stocks in 1995 compounded the problem, although after that the firm's performance took a turn for the better.

After a highly critical article on him appeared in *Business Week* (ironically on April 1, 1996), Robertson issued a writ for libel against the magazine and eventually, at the end of 1997, settled for an apology from the magazine, establishing the fact that his performance in 1996 and 1997 had demonstrated that he was not, as the magazine had said, losing his touch and that contrary to suggestions in the article, he was continuing actively to meet company managements.

No money changed hands, however, leading to the suspicion that some of the other assertions in the article, notably over the firm's muscular hire and fire techniques, contained more than a grain of truth.

Robertson has earned substantial amounts over the years. The *Business Week* article said Robertson acknowledged that he received about half of the firm's incentive fee, which in the firm's banner year of 1993 was said to have amounted to $300m, not counting any profits he may have gained from his personal holdings in the Tiger funds. Incentive fees are explained in more detail in Chapter 4. In the same year, George Soros was reputed to have earned more than $1bn.

More recently, things went less well. In August 1999, for example, Tiger said that it had changed its redemption period from quarterly to semi-annually, partly to protect itself against an outflow of 'hot money'. According to a report at the time in the *Wall Street Journal*, Tiger's assets then stood at $8bn compared to a peak a year previously of $20bn. Some $5bn of the drop was the result of withdrawals, and part of the remainder just poor performance, like the Soros funds, down to a misreading of the currency market. The remainder of the fall was the result of attempts to reduce the fund's borrowings.

Tiger's problems point up the double-edged nature of hedge fund performance fees. Though a lot of Tiger's investors were there for the long term, what proved to be the group's undoing was the presence of 'high water mark' rules, which mean that past underperformance must be recouped before the fund manager can go back to earning performance fees. These terms limited the fund's ability to pay bonuses and retain staff.

Robertson numbers Margaret Thatcher among his confidantes; she sat on the board of one of his funds. He frets about mortality. Ocelet, the last new fund launched by Tiger Management, contained the proviso that investors in the fund had to keep their money in it for five years, even if Robertson expired in the meantime. Robertson was then anxious to see his life's work survive him, instead of simply melting away into obscurity once he had reached a certain age. It is currently unclear whether recent events mean this is precisely what will happen, or whether Robertson will emerge in another guise in due course, especially now that value has reasserted itself as a factor in stock selection.

At the time Robertson was seemingly cheerful about the future and not too sorry to be out of the game. As he wrote to Tiger's investors, 'We are in a market where reason does not prevail.'

One hedge fund manager who simply folded his hand and walked away from the table was Michael Steinhardt. There are those who do not rule out his return to the fray, pointing to a temporary year's sabbatical Steinhardt took in the 1970s after a very bad year.

But five years on from winding up his empire, Steinhardt shows no signs of returning. What may be at work here, however, is a simple case of a lengthy spell of the pressure cooker environment of managing a hedge fund gradually wearing down a manager's resolve to keep coming back for more. Steinhardt himself speaks of the intensity needed to manage money successfully. He started in business on his own in 1967 and may have concluded that nearly thirty years was enough.

Interviewed in Jack Schwager's book *Market Wizards*, Steinhardt says that his interest in the stock market dated back to his bar mitzvah, when his father gave him 200 shares as a present After this he became something of an addict for the atmosphere of broker's offices, watching the ticker tape with old fogies while his friends played sport.

In contrast to late developer Robertson, Steinhardt was exceptionally bright. He grew up in a conventional Jewish home in Bensonhurst, a predominantly Jewish and Italian neighbourhood in Brooklyn. He graduated from high school aged 16 and from Wharton in 1960 at the unusually early age of 19. He then headed off for a career on Wall Street as an analyst. Between then and starting his own firm in 1967 at the age of 26, Steinhardt worked not only as an analyst but also as a financial journalist.

Like Robertson, Steinhardt is something of a rugged individualist. Although he started his fund management business with two partners – the original name of Steinhardt Partners was Steinhardt, Fine & Berkovitz – they left the business in the late 1970s. This is not to say, however, that the success of the firm was a completely solo performance, although some accounts of the Steinhardt method suggest that he had the ultimate say on whether or not a position was taken and he directed his staff – like Captain Ahab, according to one observer – from a desk shaped like the bow of ship.

Though given latitude in trading, Steinhardt's traders were required to justify their positions if necessary; or if they caused concern, Steinhardt would override the trader and sell out if he felt strongly enough that this was the right thing to do. This scrutiny did not sit well with some traders, of course, and a number left the firm over the years to move to places where accountability was less strict. As an aside, one suspects that some bank proprietary trading operations might have done well to adopt the Steinhardt style of control.

Steinhardt is described by Schwager in *Market Wizards* as 'relaxed, soft-spoken, patient and good-humoured' and something of a practical joker who was given to phoning up friends impersonating an IRS (Inland Revenue) inspector, or plaguing brokers with deliberately mumbled fictitious orders.

One thing that appears to have marked Steinhardt out from other hedge fund managers was the ability to be flexible in the style of trading he adopted and to be candid about admitting mistakes as soon as they happened. He did, however, tend towards adopting a contrarian approach, taking long-term positions when perceptions were out of line with reality. One point Schwager alludes to is Steinhardt's mental fortitude. He notes: 'Conviction is an important quality for any trader, but it is essential to the contrarian trader. Steinhardt has repeatedly demonstrated amazing resolve in maintaining large positions in difficult times, as long as he was convinced he was right.'

Perhaps the ultimate contrary view taken by Steinhardt was to announce in October 1995 that he was to dismantle his fund empire, at that time amounting to $4bn spread across four vehicles, and return the proceeds to investors. This followed an exceptionally bad performance in 1994, when his funds lost 28%, and a performance the following year barely in line with the market.

Steinhardt's stated intention was to devote his energy to Jewish charities and Democratic politics (Chapter 4). Lest one feel that Steinhardt is a has-been who has lost his nerve, it is worth remembering that he claims to have averaged a return for his investors of over

30% a year for more than twenty-eight years and exited from the stage at a time *before* other managers experienced less than buoyant returns. One is tempted to view Steinhardt as having quit while he was ahead, and the others as lingering at the table a little too long.

* * *

Bruce Kovner achieved fame and fortune during a remarkable ten-year spell investing in the interbank currency and currency futures markets, during which he realised returns of 87% per annum compound, a record which would have turned an investment of $2000 made in 1978 into $1m ten years later.

Kovner is intensely shy of publicity and there are only sketchy details of his career. It is known, however, that unusually for a hedge fund manager, he started out as an academic. He taught at Harvard, where he graduated, and also at the University of Pennsylvania. His subject was political science. Born in New York City he had earlier attended public schools in New York and Los Angeles.

He is said to have liked teaching but was less than enamoured over the race to publish that is part of an academic's life. In the early 1970s he turned from theory to practice, running a number of political campaigns with the idea of using this as a springboard to running for office. But he abandoned politics because, by his own admission, he lacked the funds to run for office and the will to work his way up the political ladder even had he been successful. For a time he did consulting work for the US Congress, the National Science Foundation, the Council of Environmental Advisers for the State of New York, and the University of Pennsylvania.

In the mid 1970s Kovner gravitated towards the idea of trading in financial markets, and approached the task with an academically rigorous approach to detail, studying several aspects of the markets intensively, notably interest rate theory. This led to the notion of trading the then relatively new markets in interest rate futures. He joined the Princeton, New Jersey, trading firm of Commodities Corporation in 1977.

Because of their relative novelty, interest rate futures markets were not traded actively by the big financial houses and hence possessed anomalies and arbitrage opportunities that an intelligent trader could spot and exploit. Kovner later switched to trading commodities and then currencies, his trades always backed up by an argument based around fundamentals and undertaken with strict trading discipline. In 1983 he left Commodities Corporation to start his own fund.

His vehicle, Caxton Corporation, returned more than 30% a year for its investors in its first twelve years of existence, faltering in 1994. In June 1995 Caxton returned $1.2bn of cash to investors, two-thirds of the money managed at the time. One reason for the move was the conviction that the $2bn Kovner then managed was too large an amount to operate effectively in the markets. A more recent move, however, has seen Caxton attempting to capitalise on its brand name recognition and move into the equities arena. In late 1998 Kovner recruited Kurt Feuerman, a former Morgan Stanley research analyst turned portfolio manager to launch a fund to invest in US stocks and market under the Caxton banner. A postscript: Kovner's fund turned in the best performance among his peer group in 2000, returning around 30%.

*   *   *

Of the hedge fund managers described previously, few have run funds that are single-mindedly dedicated to pursuing the philosophy first articulated by Alfred Winslow Jones. But pursuing the Jones philosophy does not necessarily mean sacrificing good performance, as a couple of examples show. The partnership of Martin Zweig and Joe DiMenna has been one of the most consistently successful in the hedge fund arena, and is based around the classic Alfred Winslow Jones long/short stock-picking model described in Chapter 1.

Martin Zweig started out with a doctorate in finance from Michigan State University and taught finance for a time. He hired Joe DiMenna, then still a college student, after receiving his request for a reference. DiMenna had a relatively modest background, the son of a school principal and a nurse. Impressed, however, by the fact that he was a high school chess champion, Zweig offered him a summer job, and then hired him full-time when he graduated three years later in 1980.

In 1984 the duo started a hedge fund with just $2.5m of capital; it is now one of the largest. DiMenna proved to be a superb stock picker, described Jones-like by one observer as 'the best stock picker no one's ever heard of'. DiMenna's stock-picking ability is complemented by Zweig's strategic feel, based around a very cautious approach which shuns bold moves and tends to limit market exposure to a net 65–70%, but balancing the long and short side of the fund exactly – or even erring to net short if the market looks expensive.

Zweig is also strongly wedded to quantitative investment techniques, employing researchers to comb statistical data on markets and the financial and economic background for any significant new relationship that might serve as a guide to the future market direction. Most of his work is based around the direction and level of interest rates, and the things that govern the supply and demand for money. He also uses a number of more arcane technical indicators related to the stock market and the volume of shares being traded.

Obsessive about losses, Zweig–DiMenna has consistently made accurate calls on market direction since its inception and was one of the few hedge funds to go up in value in the crash year of 1987. On so-called Black Monday, the Zweig fund actually rose by 9% on a day the market as a whole fell by nearly 23%. In 1998, when in the wake of the LTCM debacle the average return across the hedge fund spectrum was 7%, Zweig–DiMenna earned 26%. In 2000 they fared less well: returns were –10%.

Zweig–DiMenna is known for active, flexible trading and for a relatively lean approach to the business. Contrast the approach of Julian Robertson's Tiger, for example, with staff running at over the 200 mark: Zweig's outfit functions with what are reputed to be just two other partners in addition to DiMenna, five analysts researching stocks and market calls and a sales staff of nine ministering to the (mainly institutional) client base of the firm.

Zweig is also unusual among hedge fund managers – for whom paranoid secrecy is the norm – in that he has a range of other public activities. A mutual fund business he owned was recently sold, but Zweig still pens successful newsletters and is an author and a regular broadcaster.

In the same mould as Zweig–DiMenna is Lee Ainslie's Maverick Capital, with more than $2bn under management. Ainslie is 34 and married with one child. He is described by some in the business as the best conservative Jones model hedge fund manager bar none. Ainslie had been keen on the investment business since joining an investment club at school, but describes his big break as being hired by Julian Robertson when he completed his business degree.

Maverick Capital began life as a conventional 'family office' investment business, set up to manage the assets of the wealthy Wyly family in 1990. By 1993, having achieved returns of more than 40% a year, it was decided to turn this into a business and seek outside investors, at which point Ainslie joined them to become the sole fund manager of the two Maverick funds. He operates them independently according to a philosophy that stresses preservation and growth of capital, and is based on a stock-picking philosophy rather than making macro bets.

The fund is specifically dedicated to long/short equity investment and does not invest in bonds, commodities, futures, currencies or any other instruments. It typically has a net market exposure of between 20% and 60%. The fund focuses strongly on stock picking and has had very good results. Every year since its inception, stocks selected for long positions have outperformed and stocks selected as shorts have underperformed. Ainslie describes the 'vast bulk of his net worth' being invested in the fund he manages. This clearly concentrates the mind. Even in the difficult year of 1998, Maverick produced a return of around 20%.

*   *   *

Several large hedge funds are based around the trading of futures, options and commodities according to strictly defined systems generated by complex computer models. If done properly, this so-called quantitative, or quant, investing produces reliable returns with highly controlled levels of risk.

Along with Paul Tudor Jones (see below) and Bruce Kovner, Monroe Trout's success has been based around the highly specialised game of trading futures and options and commodities. Like Zweig and Kovner, Trout has an outstanding academic background but is probably closer to the 'rocket scientist' mould than either of the other two. Still only in his late thirties, Trout graduated with high honours from Harvard in 1984 in economics, and for the first two years of his career worked for NCZ Commodities, a proprietary commodities trading firm in New York, forming his own business in 1986 at the age of 24.

His style of trading is based around computing power, with complex quantitative models designed to spot emerging patterns in any of the 150 markets he monitors actively. The placing of geared-up bets on these patterns is complemented by exceptionally efficient risk control, and close attention to minimising transaction costs, producing good returns with low volatility.

Trout is known to favour the Sharpe ratio as the ideal benchmark for measuring the success or otherwise of a trader. Interviewed in Jack Schwager's book *The New Market Wizards*, he says, 'I sincerely believe that the person who has the best daily Sharpe ratio at the end of the year is the best trader.' Exceptionally tall and captain of his college basketball team, Trout now attends sporting events to relax and he reads widely, mainly in the areas of philosophy and psychology. But Trout is a realist about markets. He realises they can be dangerous places, full of traps for the unwary.

As Schwager notes: 'Trout's basic message is twofold. First, you have to have an edge to beat the markets. Everything else is secondary. You can have great money management, but if you don't have an edge then you can't win. . . . Second, assuming you have an edge, you must exercise rigid risk control to protect against those infrequent events that cause enormous, abrupt price moves that can decimate overleveraged accounts. And, as demonstrated by Trout's own graduate thesis, the possibility of sharp price moves is far greater than suggested by standard statistical assumptions.' Trout's funds returned 18% in 2000.

Rather like Martin Zweig, Paul Tudor Jones appears to have an instinctive feel for when markets can turn bad. He attracted publicity from the fact that in October 1987 his fund registered a 62% return.

Something of a contrarian, as he believes all traders must be, Jones has performed a variety of roles in his trading career. He first got interested in trading during his time in college, after reading an article about another famous trader, Richard Dennis, and went to work, initially for a friend of his uncle, as a broker on the floor of the New York Cotton Exchange.

After a particularly bad trade in 1979, Jones has always emphasised the importance of risk control, cutting losses early and not trying to, as he puts it, 'play macho man with the market'. Jones abandoned floor trading for professional fund management in 1984, launching the Tudor Futures Fund in September of that year with just $1.5m under management. In the first four years of the fund's existence, its value rose 17-fold, and the total amount under management increased more than 200-fold.

Jones is another trader who believes it is possible for hedge funds to become inefficient when they manage too much money: his fund closed to new money in 1987 and in 1994 reduced the size of the fund by around one-third, giving back close to $700m to investors. A private person, like most hedge fund managers, Jones has a mansion on Chesapeake Bay and owns a 3000-acre wildlife reserve; he has been active on the charitable front.

Unlike the eponymous hero of American legend, John Henry is not a steel drivin' man, but probably the largest fund manager involved in pure futures trading with, according to some sources, more than $2bn under management for institutions, private individuals and even broking firms such as Merrill Lynch and Salomon Smith Barney, who might have been supposed to have home-grown talent of their own. Henry's method is a so-called black box trend-following system based around quantitative analysis of markets. But he also has a longer time horizon than many other fund managers in this arena, with positions kept open for up to two or three months.

Henry set up shop in 1981. A second fund, using a different quantitative model, was launched in 1988; it is said to generate monthly positive returns more than 60% of the time and to produce a compound annual return of more than 27%. In 1992 Henry launched a financial fund that focuses on global currencies, interest rates, stock indices and commodities.

Note that, although Henry is looking for long-term market movements, the fund is not taking the sort of bets that have characterised players like Soros or Robertson, and the trades are generated by a systematic approach rather than by the intuitive judgements of a head 'trigger puller'. The annual compound return across all of the company's funds over the long term is close to 25%, despite a torrid year in 1992 when the company's risk control went badly awry after some stunning early gains. Henry's performance is said to have suffered in the past year or so from directionless markets. Fund withdrawals were also high, prompting the firm to cut back staff and adjust its fee structure – reducing management charges and increasing the performance-based element.

Though not the John Henry of American legend, the other John Henry is nonetheless bidding for a stake in Americana. He recently bought the Florida Marlins baseball team.

*   *   *

Many other hedge fund managers choose to keep very quiet indeed about their activities. Even conducting widely ranging computer searches fails to dig up any significant mentions of either their name or the activities of their funds. Among those maintaining an exceptionally low profile is Louis Bacon, who runs Moore Capital (Moore is Bacon's middle name), currently the largest of the global macro fund groups. Bacon's fund appears conservatively managed, however, showing returns of around 20% even in the torrid year of 1998. Returns in 2000 were flat.

In the wake of the withdrawal of both Tiger and Soros from the macro-trading arena, Moore Capital has in effect become the largest fund managed on a macro-trading strategy. Bacon is well aware of the pitfalls. In a speech in London in spring 2000, Bacon confessed that what macro funds had to do was to avoid having positions so large that other funds could see them coming and could trade against them. He said, 'There are those who know that they are in the game; there are those who don't know they are in the game; and there are those who don't know they are in the game and have become the game.'

Moore recently returned capital to investors to avoid precisely this fate. As Bacon says, 'Size matters. It is the bane of the successful money manager.'

Another large hedge fund group, Omega Advisers, is run by Leon Cooperman, a former Goldman Sachs partner and also, perhaps not surprisingly in view of the culture of his former employers, somewhat publicity shy. Cooperman gained an MBA from New York's Columbia Business School in 1967. During his time at Goldman Sachs he rose to become head of its influential investment policy committee. Since leaving Goldman to start Omega, Cooperman has also been involved in other seminal deals, including a leveraged buyout of the Samsonite luggage business; this was along with a couple of other heavy-hitting investors.

Not all Cooperman's deals go well. There is the strange case of $125m worth of investment vouchers in potential privatisation stocks in Azerbaijan. Omega and AIG bought the vouchers and related certificates required by foreign investors through Viktor Kozeny, a Czech intermediary. Kozeny had proposed sharing the profits from the eventual privatisation with his investors. However, the deal went sour, according to Kozeny because Azeri officials wanted to be cut in on the deal. The deal is currently the subject of a $160m lawsuit by Omega and AIG, who dispute Kozeny's version of events and are seeking the return of their investment, interest and legal costs.

Cooperman has not commented on the deal, his most recent generally reported public comment being a pained denial at the time of the LTCM debacle that his fund had financial problems. While this was wholly vindicated, nonetheless his fund did not have a happy time in 1998, ending the year down 8%. In 2000 Omega reportedly had a return of 8%.

*   *   *

Whether or not you consider the hedge fund managers described earlier in this chapter as an engaging bunch you might just like to meet in a bar or join for a round of golf, it is clear they are a varied collection of individuals. Personalities vary from the scientific to the more intuitive, from the cultured to the brusque, from the buccaneering to the cautious.

More important than the outward appearance they project or even the evidence of their fund's performance – that after all can change – is to look in more detail at what really makes them tick as individuals, their approach to risk, and their capacity for greed on the one hand and generosity on the other. This is the subject of a later chapter. But first we need to look at the different types of hedge fund and how they work.

3

Speculators and hedgers

Roughly speaking, the financial world is divided up into speculators and hedgers
Paul Wilmott, *Derivatives*

Today's courtesans of capitalism, have they irredeemably tainted the hedge fund ideal articulated by Alfred Jones? Yes and no. To understand why, one needs to examine and distinguish between different types of hedge fund and the way they operate. Just as investing in different types of companies can produce wildly different outcomes – investing in a boring utility company is different to investing in a highly geared small company – so the same is true of hedge funds.

Journalists being what they are, the funds that get the most column inches of publicity are often the biggest and most volatile. There are plenty of smaller hedge fund managers who conform closely to the Jones model, but it is the big funds that can pose the greatest danger to the functioning of the global financial system and individual economies within it.

* * *

Classifying different types of hedge fund, dividing them up into their respective categories, can be a complex business. In all, funds come in more than twenty principal styles. Each has its particular risk and return characteristics, its star managers, its triumphs and disasters, and its investor devotees. Some managers use subtle combinations of styles, or switch periodically from one to another.

The starting point is the Alfred Jones type of fund outlined in Chapter 1. This fund includes both long and short positions, it employs leverage to enhance returns, and it remunerates managers via fees linked to performance. While there are some hedge funds that satisfy all three of these criteria, in many instances this simple idea has been compromised. Hedge funds, as has been shown by some prominent players, need not necessarily hedge. Equally, they may hedge but use excessive leverage to boost returns and hence their remunerations. There have been instances of leveraged 'long-only' funds, although few survive market corrections.

A fund can usually style itself a hedge fund if it satisfies two out of the three conditions. Since fees are sacrosanct, if compromises are made, it often means that the long/short characteristic of the classic hedge fund structure is abandoned. I'll explore the potentially hazardous effects of incentive-based payment and leverage in later chapters, but abandoning the long/short method in itself has some consequences. Put simply, Jones's model suggested that combining long and short positions controlled or neutralised market risk. The result was that it produced a return based partly on the manager's stock-picking skills and partly on enhancing returns through relatively modest borrowing.

The concept worked best when the fund was small, because it allowed dealing to take place without market impact (the impact of a fund's buy or sell order moving the price against it). The manager could pick stocks in companies of any size (even quite small ones) and take positions in them with relative ease. In the Jones model, the fund's manager would seek out stocks that were either sharply undervalued or overvalued by the market. One reason for this could have been because they were comparatively small and therefore underresearched.

Now take away the notion of a mixture of long and short investments in a fund. Substitute instead the idea of either long or short investment, magnified by a level of leverage that may be far from modest. What you get is a vehicle that exaggerates risk rather than neutralises it. One example: the sharp deterioration in many US technology-orientated hedge funds in the wake of the sharp fall in the technology-heavy Nasdaq market from March 2000 onwards.

Another characteristic of the Jones style of operation was anonymity. Jones pursued his activities for many years until his secrets were revealed. The examples of high-profile hedge funds have shown that, as well as straying from the Jones model, courting publicity can be a double-edged sword, leading to a fund's performance being affected by the reaction of others in the market to news of the fund's strategy.

The issue of leverage, liquidity (the capacity of a market to absorb large-scale buying or selling without undue price changes) and this 'market impact' effect is more complex than these simple examples would suggest. In general terms, though, the key for managers is to play the game rather than to become the game that everyone else is playing.

As they have grown in size, some of the largest hedge funds have moved away, either intentionally or through necessity, from the Jones vision of a low-risk model to one that is risk seeking. Or they have moved to one where the investment returns of a fund that adopts an inherently low-risk strategy can only be raised to acceptable levels through the employment of levels of leverage that contribute to risk. In so doing, some have fallen victim to size and, in Louis Bacon's phrase, they have 'become the game'.

In these cases, why did risk seeking become so important? In part, because the biggest hedge funds are so big that the only bets available are big ones, and partly because of the bias towards risk taking and leverage induced by potentially huge performance-linked rewards for the managers concerned. Many large risk-seeking funds still operate: it is simply that they are more secretive than some of their contemporaries.

*   *   *

From this need for secrecy flow several other consequences. Although some hedge fund managers periodically court publicity, especially when their strategies are successful, generally they do the reverse. Many hedge fund managers have long had a horror of speaking to the press. Yet they are as sensitive as anyone about their public image, even though they do not generally raise funds from the average investor. As described in Chapter 2, in 1996 hedge fund manager Julian Robertson, who has since retired from the fray, sued *Business Week* magazine for suggesting that he might have lost his stock-picking touch.

There are legitimate reasons for some aspects of secrecy. Hedge funds live or die by their trading performance, and compete aggressively with each other. Any information about trading strategies leaking out of an organisation at the wrong time can be and is used against it by its competitors in the market, whether they are other hedge funds or banks' own trading desks, themselves organised along hedge fund lines.

Though secrecy may be sought, it is hard for a hedge fund to keep its trades a secret from the investment banks executing them. This was one reason for the LTCM debacle in 1998. Because it was held in such awe, its trades were mimicked and it became the game.

But whether it is essential or practical, or not, the secrecy extends into other areas. It is necessary, for example, for US-based hedge funds to avoid being categorised as mutual funds. The reason is that were they to be categorised as such, this would affect both their ability to borrow, the trading strategies they could pursue, and the frequency with which they would have to report, all of which are anathema to hedge fund managers.

For example, most US mutual funds can only borrow against up to one-third of their assets at any one time. This restriction has a knock-on effect, in effect prohibiting certain types of trading strategies involving short selling and other financing techniques. There are also restrictions on the degree to which mutual funds can invest in illiquid securities.

As the example of LTCM has shown, almost any investment can become illiquid if market conditions are wrong and the position held is big enough. But leaving this particular point aside, in practical terms what this means is that mutual funds are unable to invest in the types of tailor-made derivatives that hedge funds sometimes use. More potent, however, is the simple fact that mutual fund prospectuses must contain 'health warnings', and that the rules place obligations on their directors to ensure that assets are properly valued.

The result is that hedge funds typically locate themselves, for administrative purposes, in offshore domiciles and take other steps to avoid coming under the aegis of US federal securities legislation. Two-thirds of hedge funds locate themselves in tax havens, even though nine-tenths of hedge fund managers are domiciled in the United States. A Cayman Islands fund domicile is the most popular, but the British Virgin Islands, Bermuda and the Bahamas also have their adherents. Many managers not running their funds in the United States locate in low-tax areas like Ireland, the Channel Islands, the Netherlands Antilles and Luxembourg.

Equally important is that hedge funds do not raise funds via public offerings of their securities, do not advertise broadly, or generally solicit. To continue the courtesan metaphor, it is the difference between streetwalking and the discreet telephone call to a luxury apartment.

There are other concerns over this penchant for secrecy and the choice of domicile that goes with it. Tax havens and secrecy are a hallmark of another industry: drug cartels and related money laundering activity. While I am not suggesting for a minute that some hedge fund investors and money launderers are one and the same, or that hedge funds knowingly let money launderers invest in their funds, the plain fact is that they inevitably rub shoulders in tax havens.

The vast majority of hedge funds perform extensive due diligence on their investors, but inevitably rely on advisers, bankers and other intermediaries to a degree in this area. Technically, too, it is worth pointing out that hedge fund managers are strictly only 'advisers' to the funds they run, whose custodians and administrators act as cutouts, ensuring that the investment management process and the movement of funds are kept strictly separate. Nonetheless, it would be a brave individual who could suggest with any confidence that illicit cash had never found its way into a hedge fund, albeit perhaps without the knowledge of the manager.

Most hedge funds have to have a limited number of investors. These can be either investing institutions, such as pension funds or college endowments, other hedge funds, or (more usually) wealthy individuals. To ensure their exemption from the relevant legislation, mainly the Investment Company Act 1940, most hedge funds have a maximum of 100 investors and require potential investors, especially individual investors, to demonstrate that they are suitably qualified.

Note that to be suitably qualified, an investor does not necessarily need to be acutely aware of the risks involved, but only that he or she satisfies minimum standards in terms of net worth and income. This being US regulation, it is presumed – though often far from obvious – that if investors are rich, they cannot also be stupid.

Without sensationalising too much, then, the typical hedge fund is characterised by having either long or short positions in virtually any type of security or market, and occasionally (if the manager is particularly risk averse) both. It has leverage and performance-based fees for the manager. It tries to operate in relative secrecy, has an offshore domicile, and a limited number of rich investors who might variously be described as either greedy or risk seeking, depending on your perspective.

To this roster of attributes, one can add another. This is the limited liquidity that hedge funds usually have. Hedge fund investors can only cash in their chips infrequently and at predetermined times. The ostensible reason for this is to avoid disrupting intricate trading strategies by inconvenient, ill-timed redemptions. So-called liquidity days – the occasions when investors can sell – vary from fund to fund. Some allow the opportunity for redemption every quarter, some annually, usually with a 30-day notice period. Most impose what is known as a lock-up period, a period after the initial investment during which no withdrawals of capital can be made.

The extent to which a fund manager can get away with imposing a long initial lock-up period and still raise substantial funds depends on his or her reputation, another reason why hedge fund managers are acutely sensitive of their press image. LTCM's John Meriwether, at the time one of Wall Street's leading 'Masters of the Universe', asked for (and got) a three-year lock-up period from his investors, as well as management fees above the norm for the industry. Chapter 5 looks in more detail at the demise of LTCM and the lessons to be drawn from it.

The point about illiquidity, though, is a central one. Most conventional stock and bond market investments have instant liquidity. If you need to sell them you can, at a price which may be only marginally less. In bank savings accounts, absence of liquidity is normally compensated by a higher return, to reflect what economists call the time value of money. A 90-day notice account will carry a higher rate of interest than an on-demand deposit account.

So it's not unknown for investors to get a bad bargain in hedge funds: illiquidity on the one hand; and on the other a return, especially on a risk-adjusted basis, no better than the market average. Speculation, leverage, secrecy, investor illiquidity. It is a cocktail of characteristics that has at various times produced huge returns. But, despite what hedge fund advocates might have you believe, at other times it has meant a total wipeout for participating investors, dislocation to the smooth running of securities and currency markets, and adverse economic consequences. To say that it won't happen again is to take too much on trust.

To understand the way hedge funds work, in all their infinite variety, you need to strip away the veil of euphemism that is often used to describe their activities. Proprietary trading, for instance, is better described as out-and-out leveraged speculation conducted by your bank with your money. LTCM's initials stood for Long Term Capital Management, the opposite of rapid capital losses that actually resulted from its strategies in the end.

LTCM also would have been categorised, and categorised itself as a market-neutral or relative value fund. It sounds innocuous but this did not prevent its near collapse from threatening the global financial system. It was hardly market-neutral in its effect. There are other examples of these mild forms of doublespeak. The words may not always mean what you think they should.

One of the more lucid classifications of hedge fund styles is a report published by the investment bank Goldman Sachs. Entitled *Hedge Funds Demystified*, it was intended for consumption by pension funds, some of whom have indeed since decided that investing in such funds is a legitimate way of investing the contributions of their future pensioners. The report was published in conjunction with Financial Risk Management. Goldman trades actively on its own account (so-called proprietary trading), and so is no stranger to hedge fund techniques, so much so that the ranks of hedge fund managers contain several former Goldman traders.

One particularly piquant aspect of the report is the fact that it was published in July 1998, before the autumn debacle of LTCM. This was an event that, far from demystifying hedge funds, may have done precisely the opposite, or at the very least given would-be investors pause for thought. It is perhaps worth stressing that the Goldman document did not recommend particular hedge funds or hedge fund styles. It simply described the methods they employ and how to build up and monitor a collection of hedge fund investments. As such, the report provides a clear statement of the methods and objectives of different hedge fund styles.

Goldman divides hedge funds into four broad groups: market-neutral, event-driven, equity long/short and tactical trading.

* * *

Market-neutral, or relative value strategies are those pursued by funds that buy and sell a range of investments (typically bonds or shares) but are not dependent on the movement in the market to generate their return. Indeed they actually go out of their way to avoid being dependent on the market return. This is like the Jones model, only more so. Jones tended to have a bias towards expecting the market to go up. In this instance, however, long positions are exactly matched by short sales.

In theory this is a highly conservative strategy, with relatively low returns (typically 10–15% per annum). Managers of funds like this are looking to identify and exploit market inefficiencies, but that is all.

They do this by looking for disparities in the way very similar investments are valued by the market, or in the way in which closely related securities (e.g. government bonds in different jurisdictions, or a convertible bond and the underlying share into which it is convertible) trade relative to each other.

In the jargon we used earlier, the managers seek to identify alpha – in this case the return generated by waiting for the disparity to correct itself. The funds employ sophisticated computer programs that measure the behaviour of markets when similar anomalies have arisen in the past. They remove beta (any dependence on the market movement) by balancing a long exposure with equally weighted short positions. A trader might, for example, buy a convertible bond, but sell short the equivalent amount of the underlying shares. Or buy a British thirty-year government bond and sell short a similar US Treasury bond.

The common name for this type of activity is arbitrage, and it takes several guises. Because these strategies essentially often depend on ironing out very small disparities, the return on each individual trade tends to be small, hence the temptation for managers to seek to enhance it using leverage. In so doing, they court disaster if a sudden external shock causes the prices of the securities being traded to do odd things.

We will explore the intricacies of arbitrage in more detail in a later chapter. But for now it is worth noting that strategies of this type come in several different varieties. These include fixed-income arbitrage, convertible bond arbitrage, derivatives arbitrage, mortgage-backed securities arbitrage, and so on. Each of these is subtly different, and each subgroup has its specialists and its own subset of successes and failures.

These market-neutral strategies also include funds, typically in the equity market, which conform to the Jones model in almost every respect. They are orientated toward stock picking – buying undervalued stocks and shorting overvalued ones – and are constructed so as to have absolutely no market bias at all.

* * *

Arbitrage of one form or another is at the heart of all types of investment activity, although sometimes the form it takes is less obvious than the examples described previously. A conventional investment, buying shares, is usually based on a form of arbitrage. The investor, consciously or otherwise, is attempting to arbitrage the difference between the price of the share and its intrinsic value. Intrinsic value may be something you simply feel instinctively. Or it can be expressed with greater supposed precision as the discounted value of the future dividends or expected cash flows. Eventually, so the argument goes, the price of the share will rise to its intrinsic value.

Similarly, private equity or venture funds make their return, in effect, by arbitraging the lower value placed on small private companies and the higher value placed on them by trade buyers or by the stock market once they have gone public. Arbitrage of this sort is only one facet of investment. Another facet is, to use the jargon, event driven. Results, company news and other events may prompt investigation of a potential investment, and a subsequent purchase or sale.

Used in the hedge fund sense, however, 'event driven' means something altogether more specific. Event-driven funds pursue strategies that are unaffected by the direction of the markets in which they operate, but have defined events as their trigger points. Returns from funds like this can be in the region of 15–25% per year, albeit with some risk of loss.

By convention these funds fall into two main categories, each of which is related to some extreme form of corporate upheaval. Normally this means either a takeover or a bankruptcy. In each case the hedge fund manager will use in-depth analysis to analyse where any anomalies might occur and seek to profit from them.

So-called risk arbitrage, for example, sometimes known as merger arbitrage, was raised to an art form in the 1980s. This was the era of junk bond financing. Junk bonds, or high-yield bonds, rest on the principle that as long as the yield is high enough, investors will buy them. Junk bond finance allowed astute financial entrepreneurs to raise capital to mount audacious takeovers of sleepy, asset-rich companies, with the bonds subsequently repaid from the sale of surplus assets, leaving the entrepreneurs in control of a slimmed-down, debt-free company.

Merger or risk arbitrage was a part of this revolution, but continued to be practised long after the junk bond takeover boom faded. It stems from the principle that, in any takeover situation, the price of the bidding company will tend to fall and the target company rise, even after a takeover has been announced.

You might think that if this were all there was to it, everyone would be doing it. But this is not so. The reason the opportunity for profit arises in this situation is because other market participants are unwilling to take on the risk that a deal may fail to be consummated. Takeovers fail to happen for several reasons. Often it is because the authorities view the deal as anticompetitive. Or it might be because the terms are insufficiently attractive to shareholders, who withhold their approval. Or else (in the junk bond scenario) it could be that funds cannot be raised to finance it.

The key parameters a risk arbitrageur needs to fix are the probability of the deal going through, the eventual price and the timing of its final consummation. Risk arbitrageurs have a number of things going for them, however. One is that statistically most agreed takeovers are consummated at the initial terms or better.

The second is that arbitrageurs like this specialise in evaluating the intricacies of competition policy and regulation and so, in theory at least, they can make better judgements on this aspect of the equation than the market as a whole. This does not stop the risk arbitrage community from getting its fingers burnt from time to time when takeovers fall through.

The third point is that the entire arbitrage community tends to act in the same way in respect of the same target. Although they are competitors for investors' funds, their interests are often aligned and they frequently represent a large percentage of the shares in any take-over situation, particularly a hostile one. This enables them to influence the outcome of a bid by negotiating improved terms with a bidder, or seeking an alternative higher offer.

Because of their focus on several different transactions at any one time, their risk can be diversified by industry, geography, type of transaction (hostile, agreed or otherwise), or by the degree to which regulatory risk is involved.

However, this is not to give the impression that risk arbitrage players (often simply known as arbs in market jargon) solely invest in announced situations or exist as a homogeneous category. Some are more tolerant of regulatory risk than others, while some will also invest in situations where a takeover is little more than rumour, attempting by their actions to put a company 'in play'.

Like his screen equivalent Gordon Gecko in the film *Wall Street*, Ivan Boesky, the doyen of the 1980s 'risk arbs', took this process one stage further by taking his arbitrage positions based on inside information. These days risk arbitrage is somewhat less buccaneering and more scientific.

There are a number of ways that risk arbitrage players capture their returns. These depend on the nature of the transaction involved. In the case of a cash offer, it could normally be simply by taking a long position (i.e. buying shares) in the target company. In the case of a share-for-share merger, the method would be to buy the shares of the target but to sell short an equivalent money amount of the shares in the bidder, benefiting from the convergence in the price of the two as the merger approaches completion.

Because buying call options (options to buy) or put options (options to sell) gives a geared-up exposure to the underlying stocks, in some instances either or both sides of the transaction will be accomplished via the options market to add additional leverage. Options are particularly suitable for use in this way because they tend to behave in mathematically precise ways to the underlying shares and because they operate for a defined time period that can be aligned with the fixed timetable of a takeover transaction.

Where necessary too, the arbs hedge, or insure, against a general fall in the market by buying index put options, which rise disproportionately in value if the benchmark index drops. Put options in the target's shares can be used as a way of hedging against a takeover not going through. How this works in practice is sometimes more opaque than you might think, so don't try it at home! For example, a sharp fall in the market may have the effect of making one category of takeover (especially those involving cash rather than shares in the bidding company as the currency) more likely to succeed than another.

Investors feel better about a fixed amount of cash than about getting or keeping shares (either in the bidder or the target) whose future value is uncertain. Market volatility can play havoc with the precise calculations involved in trying to insure against these events.

The other category of event-driven strategies relates to so-called distressed securities. While this may conjure up the image of delicate Victorian ladies in need of smelling salts, in reality what is needed in these situations is a dose of legal action rather than the sal volatile. Some experts believe that the origin of funds of this type actually dates back more than a century to the 1890s. At that time, a five-year slump led to major restructuring in the US railroad industry, with around a quarter of the companies in the industry going bust and their assets being restructured.

In this situation the debt of the bankrupt companies was often exchanged for a combination of debt in a new vehicle, plus some preferred stock (a slightly safer form of equity, but with a fixed return) and some ordinary shares, known in the US as common stock. Because of the complexity of the transactions, some knowledgeable speculators were able to calculate that the new combination of securities would be worth more than the old, and would buy the old debt, convert it into the new, which they would then sell later at a profit.

Today, despite computer-driven investment decision making through which market inefficiencies like this would supposedly be ironed out, distressed securities traders make money consistently. That said, their profits accrue less consistently in times of rampant bull markets than at other times.

The reason the strategies can be profitable is that often the prices of distressed securities are unduly depressed because of adverse sentiment (the stigma of potential bankruptcy), because of a lack of liquidity, or because there are forced sellers. This happens because institutional investors are often not allowed to hold these types of securities in their portfolio and must sell them if the company concerned enters this category.

The way the managers operating funds of this type look at these situations is to work out the value of the security in a worst-case scenario (usually the company going into some form of liquidation), and working out the value of the different types of security under different outcomes. For instance, bonds usually have a claim on the assets of the company ranking ahead of preference capital, which in turn ranks higher in the pecking order than ordinary shares. The trader in these securities needs an in-depth knowledge of the bankruptcy laws in the jurisdiction of the company's legal domicile. Traders have to take into account the extent to which reconstructions are permitted, and the rights attaching to different types of security. These can differ significantly from case to case.

Different funds specialise in investing in different aspects of the distressed firm's capital structure, in the stage of the restructuring process at which they get involved, and in the degree to which they get actively involved in negotiations with banks and other creditors.

Usually a key element in the involvement is buying enough of a particular type of debt, for example, to get a seat on the creditors committee. Funds also differ in the degree to which they diversify, and the degree of ingenuity they employ in controlling risk. Normally the strategies involved are relatively simple, involving nothing more complex than buying the type of security considered most attractive.

However, two characteristics of all funds of this type are patience and flexibility. Creditors may not have the patience to wait out a restructuring, pension funds may be barred from holding securities like this, and banks may be keen to sell off their claims for cash to remove an embarrassing loan from their books.

In short, the distressed securities fund manager buys at deep discounts from those who can't wait or don't want to wait for a restructuring to be completed. And in the end, this type of trading is another variant of the risk and return dichotomy that underlies all forms of investment.

It's a complicated form of common sense. In a distressed situation, senior mortgage bonds, which are secured on a company's properties, may sell at closer to their face value than a more junior bond priced at 50% of face value. Here there may be no formal collateral. There will therefore be more uncertainty about whether enough cash will be left over to redeem the bond in full or, if it is repaid in part, what percentage of its value will eventually be paid. This type of bond is likely to offer more risk, but a higher potential return.

Distressed securities traders also have to make a calculation of the likely time a restructuring will take to complete, and relate this to the cost of having the funds tied up, or risk-free interest lost, for that length of time.

What also frequently happens in the restructurings that accompany bankruptcies (especially in the US system known as Chapter 11 bankruptcies, where bankrupt companies are granted protection from their creditors and time to arrange a restructuring) is that a company is recapitalised, with new securities issued in place of the old ones. Often one resulting component of these new structures is a new class of shares, often known as orphan equity, because it is generally unwanted and unappreciated.

Often creditors and some former bondholders issued with orphan equity in settlement of their claims on the company will sell as soon as they receive it, driving the price down to bargain levels. At this point it offers little downside risk to investors with the stomach to buy and hold it for a time. A judgement needs of course to be made about the long-term viability of the business. Utilities and businesses in stable basic industries can often prove surprisingly good stores of value in this respect.

Merger arbitrage and distressed securities investing are grouped together because they have a number of things in common. With distressed securities trading, the situation is analogous to a merger proposal. The same questions need to be asked about the probability of the deal going through, the eventual value to be realised, and the time taken for the deal to be completed; and decisions over risk and return need to be made quickly and accurately.

In distressed securities, however, the analytical aspect probably comes uppermost, as issue prospectuses, balance sheets, and the small print of covenants need to be carefully studied. In both types of strategy, however, negotiation plays a big part, whether with banks and other creditors and bondholders, or (in merger arbitrage) with bidders and potential bidders. For this reason, some managers have quite successfully practised both strategies simultaneously, or they alternate between the two. Since they are to some degree at the extreme end of the investment spectrum (bid euphoria on the one hand and the depression that might accompany bankruptcy on the other), in themselves they provide a natural form of diversification for the hedge fund manager.

*   *   *

Though the nature of what the funds do means that they attract least publicity, there is no question that the classic Jones-style long/short investment policy has remained durable and popular. In terms of numbers of funds rather than size, it is probably the most common style of hedge fund operation. The distinction between these types of funds and others that fall into the market-neutral category is the extent to which the long and short positions are balanced. In the Jones model, a view is taken on the likely trend in the market. The proportion of the fund 'outside the hedge' is the element that reflects this view.

Funds like this, in the Jones mould, earn their return by stock picking. The difference between them and, for example, an actively managed unit trust or mutual fund is that as well as picking undervalued stocks to buy, the manager also picks overvalued stocks to sell. Stock selection in these instances is made in both directions. The method uses fundamental analysis of a company's business, its prospects and its finances. Analysis of the past history of the share price (usually known as technical analysis) plays a secondary role, often only used for the timing of purchases and sales.

Some funds of this type may take a particular stylistic approach. They might either look for growth stories or buy shares on recovery or value-investing criteria. Some specialise by sector. Many use the smaller-sized quoted companies (the so-called small-cap sector) as their hunting ground, because stocks like this are often under-researched and consequently sometimes significantly undervalued or overvalued by the market.

Investing in funds of this type requires care from investors, because managers have different approaches to the issue of leverage and to how often and by how much the fund's overall exposure to the direction of the market changes. Many funds are consistently net 'long'; that is, allowing for leverage, more heavily invested in shares expected to rise than they are short of those picked to fall. The advent of derivatives, particularly index and stock options, has also meant that the net stance of a portfolio and leverage involved in its positions can be changed very quickly in response to perceived market opportunities.

* * *

The big beasts in the hedge fund jungle are what Goldman's *Hedge Funds Demystified* rather coyly calls 'tactical traders'. These are more commonly known, depending on your bias, as either global macro funds or simply as speculators. Dion Friedland, chairman of Magnum Funds, describes them as the grizzly bear in the hedge fund animal kingdom, 'mammoth and quick, keen and powerful, sudden and aggressive; they go for the kill, they want it all, not content with only a mere morsel of their prey.'

One can call funds like this speculative not necessarily out of any sense of moral outrage, although there are perhaps instances where such a tone could and should be adopted. The reason for the 'speculator' tag is simply that while some funds of this type use a proprietary system to generate their trades, others – and some of the biggest – fly by the seat of their pants. On occasion some macro funds are doing little more than backing hunches. They are large leveraged bets that are as often as not unhedged. They therefore qualify for the description 'speculative', simply by virtue of being large, highly leveraged and unhedged.

The so-called system traders in the global macro community generally use computer-generated models to identify trading opportunities, frequently using the futures markets to take positions because of the leverage that can be obtained. They make their returns by attempting, through statistical analysis, to spot recurring patterns, especially longer-term trends in the prices of particular currencies, stock market indices and commodities.

Such systems are based around the idea that most investor behaviour is irrational and causes distortions in the market, that different investments have an underlying value which in the longer term the price will reflect, and that share price patterns tend to regress to the mean. In other words, a price driven a long way away from the average will tend over time to move back towards it. So traders like this may buy when adverse sentiment has driven the security value well below its mean trend, and sell when euphoria has driven it above.

In this instance the bets being made are gambling on a move in a particular direction. But risk can be controlled, although not wholly eliminated, by making sure that each large trade is in a different unrelated area. This means that if one goes wrong, another will not, and may in fact offset it. Risk control is also introduced by having 'stop-loss' points, so that when absolute or percentage money losses above a certain amount are incurred, a trade is automatically 'closed'.

While macro speculators may use either simple hunch, a feel for market conditions, or some form of computer system, monetary analysis or geopolitical viewpoint for deciding what trades to place and when, the difference between these and the true 'system traders' is that in the former case the 'system' does not make the decision. The manager is the ultimate trigger puller and acts at his or her discretion.

These more speculative funds, of which the Soros group in its former guise is perhaps the classic example, will typically invest in different markets, financial instruments, commodities and currencies. Their trades will be based around forecasts of trends in these markets, interest rate trends, movements in the general flow of investment funds, political changes, government intervention and other external factors.

Large macro bets have been placed, for example, buying UK government securities in the late 1970s, selling sterling at the time of the ERM debacle in 1992, buying Deutschmarks following reunification in 1989, selling gold in 1998 and 1999 ahead of central bank sales, and on numerous other occasions.

* * * .

These descriptions of hedge fund styles by no means cover all of the permutations. Some of the other styles (especially those involved in arbitrage and those involved in emerging markets) will be covered in later chapters. But the four-way split outlined by the Goldman Sachs report is a good starting point, without complicating things unduly with definitions and descriptions of hedge fund subgroups.

Global macro investing, for example, which the Goldman report describes as tactical trading, is multifaceted. It can also encompass – if the definition is employed in a slightly looser way – a number of other styles of global investing. It can take in, for instance, funds that invest globally but specialise by sector or by geographical territory. Examples might be perhaps those investing in emerging markets or in global telecoms stocks.

Analyses of funds under management change dramatically, but the activities of the global macro funds have, until recently at least, tended to dominate the industry, especially in terms of the publicity they receive. Now they probably represent less than a fifth of the industry's total assets. Global macro managers saw a substantial outflow of funds from mid 1998 onwards

Though a minority in this sense, the significant point is that their power is concentrated in relatively few hands. It is a mistake to assume that macro investing is dead: it is simply now in the hands of players who adopt a markedly lower profile than its previous leading exponents.

The big gainers in this environment have been those operating the classic long/short equity style. The segment has had a cumulative inflow of money in the recent past almost equivalent to the amount lost by the global macro players in aggregate, although it is spread over a much greater number of funds. The other gainer in terms of inflows of funds recently has been the event-driven style.

There are some disparities in the numbers produced between competing organisations measuring hedge fund performance. Some analyses, for example, include funds of funds, which are hybrids investing across a range of styles and managers in order to generate more predictable returns and lower risk. There is unanimity, however, that the global macro segment has decreased in terms of total share of the hedge fund market, partly because of recent high-profile exits like Soros and Tiger.

One important point is that however meaningful or otherwise these figures are, they are dwarfed by the capital committed by the proprietary trading arms of large investment banks and commercial banks. These employ a range of the trading strategies described previously in order to produce dealing profits (or losses) in their profit and loss accounts. They are the 'hedge fund in your bank', whether you like the idea or not.

The figures in Table 3.1 reveal the variability of returns between different styles, especially when compared with the relative degree of risk run by the investor (or in the case of the bank proprietary trader, borne unwittingly by the bank's shareholders), as measured by the standard deviation of the returns. They show the returns on a broad selection of funds in the four main styles calculated for the five-year period from the beginning of 1994 to halfway through 2000, the drawdown, the standard deviation and the Sharpe ratio.

Remember that the returns from the hedge fund investments are calculated net of the management and incentive fees paid to the managers. It is nonetheless striking that for most of the period, the absolute return generated for investors by macro funds was actually lower than produced by the S&P500 index, the standard broad US stock market benchmark. The standard deviation of the return is only marginally less than that of the index, producing an almost identical Sharpe ratio. In other words, macro managers produce better returns than the index, only when their fees are excluded.

Table 3.1 Returns and other performance data analysed by style

Style type	1994	1995	1996	1997	1998	1999	2000	Overall	Drawdown	Std dev	Sharpe
Convertible arbitrage	-8.07	16.57	17.87	14.48	-4.41	16.04	19.84	10.44	-12.03	5.2	1.04
Dedicated short	14.91	-7.35	-5.48	0.42	-6.00	-14.22	-6.70	-4.09	-41.93	18.2	-0.50
Emerging markets	12.51	-16.91	34.50	26.59	-37.66	44.82	1.05	5.83	-45.14	20.8	0.04
Equity market neutral	-2.00	11.04	16.60	14.83	13.31	15.33	10.87	12.02	-3.54	3.5	1.98
Event driven	0.75	18.34	23.06	19.96	-4.87	22.26	5.23	12.36	-16.05	6.8	1.08
Fixed-income arbitrage	0.31	12.50	15.93	9.34	-8.16	12.11	3.44	6.60	-12.48	4.5	0.34
Global macro	5.72	30.67	25.58	37.11	-3.64	5.81	-0.07	12.31	-26.79	14.6	0.49
Long/short equity	-8.10	23.03	17.12	21.46	17.18	47.23	1.08	16.96	-14.21	12.7	0.94
Total	-4.36	21.69	22.22	25.94	-0.36	23.43	1.86	13.06	-13.81	10.1	0.79

Source: Hedge Index

The Jones-style equity long/short strategy produces a better return for significantly less risk. Equity market neutral strategies produce the best and most consistent returns per unit of risk, followed by event-driven and convertible arbitrage. Even here, though, it is worth remembering that the trade-off for these higher risk adjusted returns is loss of liquidity, since hedge fund investments cannot be cashed in with the same degree of alacrity as conventional mutual funds or other direct stock market investments such as shares or bonds.

These figures are only averages, however. They iron out differences between managers. So individual managers may do better or worse than these figures. And the figures are rich in ironic touches. The irony of the global macro fund managers is that seemingly, for all the philosophical musing and geopolitical analysis they undertake, investors would have been equally well off (and would have had more liquidity) investing in a low-load tracker fund replicating the standard US market benchmark. The irony of the superior risk performance of the equity market neutral funds is that it was a market-neutral bond fund, LTCM, which nearly blew apart the global financial system in 1998.

Hedge Fund Research produces a range of performance indices subdivided in the various styles described earlier in the chapter. The indices are unweighted for the size of the funds in the sample. Among its figures it records yearly returns from macro funds as a whole, ranging from as high as 30% in 1995 to as low as 6% in 1998. The figure for 1999 was 17.6% but slightly negative in 2000.

Equity hedge funds (the conventional Jones style) have generally shown returns in the range of 20–30% per annum, give or take a point or two either side, although 1999 was a banner year, with a return of over 40%. Distressed securities funds returns have generally ranged from 15–20% but actually went negative in 1998. The following year saw a rebound to a return of nearly 17%. Merger arbitrage funds showed returns in the mid teens in 1995, 1996 and 1997 but only high single-figure returns in 1998. Figures in 1999 and 2000 were back around the 14% mark.

Fixed-income arbitrage, a big component of the market-neutral segment, again showed returns largely in the high single-figure area with the exception of 1998, when the LTCM situation produced very poor returns in the September–October period of that year and left the total return for the year as a negative 10%. A fairly typical 7% or so was record in 1999.

Who are the big players in each of these segments? Some are famous and some not so well known. In the global macro sphere, according to recent figures, Moore Capital is the single largest fund group with assets around the $9bn area. In the past this would have been followed by Tiger, the Julian Robertson vehicle. The brace of Soros funds (Quantum and Quota) have assets around the $3bn mark currently. Tiger has now been wound up and Soros has markedly changed tack.

Among leading managers in the event-driven style are Perry Partners, whose two funds combined have a value of more than $2bn, Cerberus International, with around $1.2bn at the last count, and Westgate International, with more than $800m under management.

In arbitrage and relative value categories, the relative anonymity of some leading managers becomes even more apparent. A big player in convertible arbitrage, for example, is Highbridge Capital with some $1400m under management. CDC Gamma is a large bond arbitrage business with $1100m while rising star Pequot had, at the time of writing, one fund with $1800m under management in the long/short equity style and three further ones with $1200m each. Big equity market neutral funds include Fairfield Sentry with $2700m and Kingate Global with $1100m.

But hedge fund investment is driven as much by the reputation of the manager as the returns generated by their funds. Despite the secrecy that attends the methods used by some of their funds, many hedge fund managers have become, through choice or otherwise, figures with a high public profile. Among the big names are George Soros, John Meriwether, Louis Bacon and Julian Robertson of course. But there are also lesser-known luminaries such as Bruce Kovner, Nick Roditi, Martin Zweig, Michael Steinhardt, Monroe Trout, John

Henry, Paul Tudor Jones, Leon Cooperman and Crispin Odey, most of whom are still actively involved in the industry.

The next chapter looks at the way in which the courtesans of capitalism are incentivised. In particular, it looks at whether the re-muneration structure common in the industry contributes to excessive risk taking, both among independent hedge funds and in-house hedge funds within the banking system, and it looks at the personal enthusiasms of some of these individual managers.

4

Rogues, philosophers and philanthropists

The world is too much with us; late and soon, getting and spending we lay waste our powers

William Wordsworth

Like the activities of the world's famous courtesans, the life of hedge fund managers and their clients is a complex balance of risk and reward, remuneration and calculation. At the centre of the whole process is the issue of personal wealth and the incentive to perform, and what happens to remuneration if the performance is substandard.

Hedge fund managers have often graduated to that role by way of senior positions in another fund management company or in a bank's proprietary trading operation. Because they are perceived to be 'best of breed' in this environment, and awarded fat bonuses, if they then go on to become successful hedge fund managers there is a consequence. Not generally individuals for whom humility is seen as a positive quality, they can become insufferably egotistical.

But do they, like Tom Wolfe's characters in his book *The Bonfire of the Vanities*, see themselves as 'Masters of the Universe', superior to mere mortals, able to make or break currencies and bring down governments on a whim? Do the risks they take invariably pay off, bringing great wealth to them and their investors? And once they have generated that wealth, what do they do with it?

In his 1995 book *A Fool and His Money*, author Martin Baker sums it up by saying of hedge funds: 'Take a speculative cocktail shaker. Add four parts public ignorance to 33 parts greed. Toss in a little perceived genius. If you don't have any freshly ground perceived genius to hand, a little dried guru status will do. Season generously with mystique. Add apparent publicity shyness to taste. Serve in opaque tumblers of awed, ill-informed media coverage.'

This type of comment sets the scene for any discussion about hedge fund managers and their remuneration. And, as Baker suggests, we need to guard against being too awestruck by hedge fund managers and the returns they make for investors and themselves. There is, in fact, good reason to be sceptical.

Even in a strict statistical sense, one must take into account an element of what is commonly known as survivorship bias, and adjust the calculations of the returns that hedge funds make as a group to allow for those that fail. The hedge fund managers we hear about and their successes become public knowledge precisely because they are successful. Failures that lead to poor performance, the disappearance of hedge funds and losses for their investors rarely make the papers, unless they are colossal like LTCM.

*   *   *

One contributory factor to hedge fund managers' feelings of superiority to the rest of the human race lies in the earning power they have, which is inherent in the fee structure that underlies all hedge funds. While a conventional fund manager might typically take around 1% of the funds under management and no more, hedge funds take this (and more) plus a 20% (or more) share of any gains made in the fund. But, and this is the important point, there is no cash penalty for, or participation in, losses incurred by the fund. A recent *Financial Times* article suggested that many funds are now charging appreciably more than this and cites Moore Capital (3% and 25%) as an example.

Some institutional investors in hedge funds, actual or potential, find fees like this hard to take. Even allowing for discounts on fees related to the size of investment being made, and for the fact that published returns are usually calculated net of fees, investing in hedge funds is not for the faint-hearted.

Managers seem to get away with fee arrangements like this because of a carefully cultivated perception that they are the best, a perception that (certainly on a risk-adjusted basis) may not be entirely correct. Their hand is strengthened because, despite the fact that the industry has $400bn under management, capacity is claimed to be limited. Hedge funds operate best when they are of relatively modest size and can operate unobtrusively. Larger fees limit the number of investors to the real enthusiasts.

But the fee structure loads the hedge fund dice in favour of risk taking, even if a manager themself has a substantial investment in the fund. As a footnote here, it is not unknown for managers to exaggerate the size of their own involvement in a fund. But assume for a moment that the manager in the example that follows is scrupulously honest about the scale of their investment. He or she still has a reason to take excessive risks.

Take a $100m fund in which a manager has a 5% ($5m) investment. Say the fund's entire capital is placed in an investment that has a 50% chance of making a loss of 20% and a 50% chance of making a return of 20%. If the investment makes a loss, the hedge fund manager will make simply the management fee of the fund and his or her net worth in the fund will fall from $5m to $4m. The management fee of $1m makes up the loss. If the investment pays off, the performance fee will be $4m and the managers' net worth will increase from $5m to $10m.

If instead, the fund's capital were to be placed in a risk-free investment yielding 5%, the performance fee would be $1m on top of the management fee and net worth would rise from $5m to $7m. If an investment had a 50% change of halving in value and a 50% chance of rising 50% in value, the range of possibilities for the manager's net worth would be a drop from $5m to $3.5m on the downside or a rise from $5m to $18.5m. If the manager's investment in the fund had hypothetically been 10% rather than 5%, the spread of rewards in this example would still have been a loss of $4m on the downside versus a gain of $16m on the upside.

This is a fairly simple example, and a modest fee level by some hedge fund standards, but what it shows is that in theory the fee structure inherent in hedge funds not only encourages high-risk investment as opposed to risk-free investment, as might be supposed, but more particularly it encourages larger risks to be taken. The profit consequences for a manager of a risky investment that pays off are likely to be substantially higher than the possible losses if things go wrong, even if the manager has a significant investment in the fund.

Things are not quite as clear-cut as this in real life. Most hedge fund managers want to be in business to carry on collecting hefty fees for a lengthy period of time, so they might not seek to boost one year's fees in a risk that might sacrifice the possibility of several more years of lucrative remuneration.

In the Jones model of hedge fund remuneration, the performance fee was in part spent on administration and employee costs, and some hedge fund managers also pay a percentage of the performance back to intermediaries who may have procured large investors for them.

The costs of running a fund vary considerably. At one end of the spectrum a global macro fund may have several hundred employees and offices around the world, while the classic hedge fund in the Jones style can be run by a couple of individuals working from home. Either way, most hedge fund managers will budget to pay the administration costs of the fund from the annual 1% fee.

As far as the performance fee is concerned, if a fund underperforms, the value lost has to be recouped before the manager can resume earning performance-related fees; that is to say, the previous 'high water mark' has to be surpassed before the incentive fees kick in again. Some funds, especially those in which institutional investors are heavily invested, have more complex performance-based fee structures, structured around the manager beating an agreed benchmark by a margin specified in advance.

However, the key point is that although the interests of the fund and its investors are aligned in the sense of moving in the same direction, the alignment is neither precise nor perfect. In other words, the fee structure tends to mean that for any given risk taken, the manager's percentage loss will be less than the investor's if the investment goes wrong, and more than the investor's if it goes right.

* * *

A bias in favour of risk taking may of course be precisely what investors are paying for, but while there is every encouragement for investors to perform due diligence on funds they invest in, it is a moot point whether many really examine the imbalance in incentives that arrangements like this produce.

The fee structure in hedge funds is a mild form of what it generally known as moral hazard by economists and those who specialise in behavioural finance. The textbook definition of moral hazard is a situation where one party to a contract has an incentive after the contract is made to alter his or her behaviour in such a way that can harm the other party to the contract. Or, put simply, that people behave in ways to satisfy themselves, but don't bear the full cost (or indeed any cost in some instances) if that behaviour is to the detriment of others.

The simplest example is usually taken from the world of insurance. As a motorist, I have less incentive to be careful with my car knowing that it is insured than I would have if it weren't. It is a fact the insurance companies counter by making the claims procedure as awkward as possible, and by adding an excess (or deductible) to the policy. By doing this, it ensures that I have a certain financial loss to bear as well if I precipitate a claim.

A better example may be my son, who was a student at the time this book was written. If he knows that I will bail him out if he spends all his allowance before term's end, then there is less incentive on him to control his spending and hence a greater likelihood that I will be called on to act as a lender of last resort. In other words, if it persists, moral hazard can create lasting damage to a financial system (in this case mine), distort the measurement of risk, and encourage risk-taking or profligate behaviour.

Moral hazard normally comes into play in situations where there is a bailout of some description, whether it is my free-spending son, a sovereign government which knows that it can rely on the fact that others in the international community will come to its aid, or lenders to a hedge fund that previous actions have demonstrated may be viewed by the authorities as too big to fail.

The damage in this comes not just from the influence on the behaviour of the individuals concerned, but on the signal it sends to other similar institutions. In the case of LTCM, the bailout orchestrated by the Federal Reserve may have been necessary to prevent systemic collapse in the financial system, but it hardly led to the conclusion that excessive risk taking or massive leverage was being punished as it should. Holman Jenkins, writing in the *Wall Street Journal* in the immediate aftermath of the LTCM debacle, noted: 'Would hedge funds even exist without a fatty dollop of moral hazard somewhere along the great protein chain of lending?'

I said earlier that moral hazard was present in a mild form in hedge fund remuneration. One reason it is a mild form is that the egotism present in a great many of the higher-profile managers, and the desire of, say, the better-known macro managers to outperform their peer group and justify the publicity they attract, is a powerful incentive to make the right judgement calls in the markets. Hedge fund remuneration is so lucrative that managers want to continue to collect for many years, and not sacrifice their business on one throw of the dice, however lucrative the return might be.

* * *

A more pernicious form of moral hazard is present in the often much larger, internal hedge funds operated by large global commercial and investment banks, otherwise called their proprietary trading desks. Here the moral hazard arises because of the way traders are remunerated. If a team of traders are successful, they will probably be remunerated by a bonus linked either to the performance of the team or to themselves as individuals. The bonus will be linked directly to the profit they make for the firm that employs them.

If they are successful, their chances of being poached by a rival firm increase and their bosses, fearing this, will take pains to ensure their remuneration reflects their value to the firm. If they are less successful, the chances are they may lose their jobs, but that is all that will happen to them and, provided they as individuals manage the process correctly, they may well find employment fairly easily at another firm.

This ˙creates a culture that nurtures egotism and fosters excessive risk taking. The culture lacks even the checks that are normally present in an externally managed hedge fund where the manager may have his or her own money at risk in the fund. The upside for a bank proprietary trader is a bonus directly linked to the profitability of the trading desk team. The downside is being asked to find another job, possibly accompanied by some form of compensation; it depends on the contractual terms involved.

As an investment bank insider puts it, 'Proprietary traders have one client, and no transparency.' A fund of funds manager observes, 'The problem with proprietary traders is that they never have their own money invested.'

In turn this fosters what might be known as the 'rogue trader' syndrome, where trading profits are either fraudulently created or losses covered up, in order to maximise bonus payments, usually with disastrous results. This happened most notably in the instance of Barings, the long-standing and illustrious British merchant bank, brought down by a combination of failures of management and financial control, and by the incompetent trading of one Nick Leeson.

Here another more subtle layer of moral hazard showed up, because the profits being generated by Leeson's supposed risk-free arbitrage trading were also producing large bonuses for his superiors at the bank, who should more prudently have been questioning the 'too good to be true' nature of the returns being made. In such cases the losses that result are borne by a bank's shareholders and even, as with Barings, its bondholders who, it is a fair bet, will not even have known the risks were being run. Barings was, in the wake of this episode and the refusal of the Bank of England to countenance a bailout, sold to the Dutch investment bank ING for a nominal £1.

Another more complex case of moral hazard occurred in the case of Kidder Peabody, a venerable Wall Street house laid low by the activities of Joe Jett. Jett was blamed for faking profits amounting to

$339m on his complex arbitrage-style trading in the US government bond market. As with Leeson, both Jett and his bosses benefited from bonuses generated as a result of the profits he made.

In the end, Jett was cleared on fraud charges but fined for false record keeping and made to repay $8m in bonuses. The case was complicated because Jett was a black employee in a predominantly white business. After seeing another black trader fired for what he regarded as a trumped-up and rather vague charge of sexual harassment, Jett took to responding to even the mildest pleasantries from female members of Kidder's staff with the retort 'Discipline must be maintained,' a catchphrase which he also inscribed in signed copies of the book that resulted from his experiences. Jett is now at work in New York City – running a hedge fund.

These experiences raise the issue of whether or not traders' bonuses themselves exert a destabilising influence on behaviour. Central banks, which generally act as the supervisory authority for their own commercial banking systems and other financial institutions, are known to be concerned at the way in which trader remuneration skews risk taking in bank proprietary trading, but they have found little way of preventing it.

The introduction of methods such as tying traders' bonuses to long-term performance, or granting bonus payments in shares or share options that can only be cashed in at a later date have been thwarted because, where they have been attempted, traders themselves simply migrate to firms paying bonuses in the normal way. Strict risk management controls are the only answer.

Rogue traders, and rogue hedge fund managers, are not confined solely to the internal hedge funds operated by banks and other financial institutions. There have been a number of noted examples where the incentives involved have led to outright fraud on the part of hedge fund operators or their employees.

Most scams that do come to light tend to be based around fraudulent performance claims, allowing managers to claim performance rewards that they do not merit. In one recent incident a fund promoter concocted three-year performance figures to sell the fund to investors, even though the fund had not been in existence for that length of time. Investors in it subsequently lost two-thirds of their investment and took the manager to court.

In another case the fund promoter misrepresented not just the performance of the fund, but its very existence, pocketing most of the money raised from investors. The scam was discovered when an alert adviser of one of the fund's investors checked the address of the fund's accountant and discovered that it was a sandwich bar in a Los Angeles subway station.

A more recent case of outright greed concerned the chief financial officer of a hedge fund, who allegedly cost his firm $5m by trading his personal account through the fund and allocating winning trades to his own account and losing ones to the fund.

In another case in July 2000 Michael Higgins, a 36-year-old hedge fund manager for Ballybunion Capital Partners, pleaded guilty to defrauding investors of performance fees by falsely overstating the fund's performance, a deception brought to light only when an alert investor requested independent verification of the fund's performance. Higgins sent the investor a performance report purporting to come from an independent accountant, but when the investor contacted the accounting firm directly, they denied any knowledge of the report.

Also in July 2000 a group of investors sued Blue Water Fund's portfolio manager, Jonathan Iseson, claiming that the fund's superior first-quarter performance figures were only achieved through manipulating the price of NetSol, a thinly traded stock of which Blue Water owns 25%. In October 2000 Lehman Brothers sued Mark Yagalla of Ashberry Capital Management, a short-selling fund. The suit alleged that Yagalla had misused investors' capital to fund a lavish lifestyle, collecting performance fees while running a fund that was all but defunct. At the end of 2000, Michael Smirlock of Laser Advisers, and a former Goldman Sachs partner, was indicted in a Manhattan federal court for covering up $71m in losses by overstating the value of the fund's portfolio by 17% and charging fees commensurately. The case brought to five the number of major hedge fund fraud cases prosecuted in a one-year period.

It is straining credibility to the limit for hedge fund apologists to claim that these types of case are not caused by the presence of incentive fees that reward managers very highly indeed for good performance.

*　　*　　*

Hedge fund managers show considerable variation in their responses to the pressured environment of constant trading and dealing with issues of risk control, as well as some of the moral and ethical dilemmas the more sensitive among them may face. In some it finds its outlet in religion, in some in philosophy and more often than not also in philanthropy, which cynics might be tempted to see as a way of assuaging subconscious guilt.

David Weill, for example, probably one of the few fund managers to be a practising Buddhist, was a shooting star of the hedge fund business. Naming his fund Vairocana, a Sanskrit word for 'great conqueror', Weill raised money after attracting verbal backing from a prominent London banker. His investors were rewarded with a return of 63% in 1993.

Weill's deep interest in Buddhism and other oriental philosophies did not, however, save him from nemesis in the markets. As a bet on European interest rates went badly wrong, Weill's fund halved in value in a matter of weeks, forcing Weill to shut down the fund and repay his backers. He subsequently left for an extended sabbatical visiting ashrams in India.

George Soros, on the other hand, has been careful to separate his philosophical musings and his philanthropic endeavours from his market dealings, most noticeably by employing others to place a check on his wilder flights of fancy. Although Soros's books are often attacked as banal, Soros is seemingly modest about his philosophical accomplishments, on occasions describing himself as a 'failed philosopher who happens to be a speculator'.

When admitted to the Court of Benefactors of Oxford University in 1992, ironically at around the time his funds were described as 'breaking the Bank of England', Soros asked to be viewed as a financial and philosophical speculator. According to Robert Slater's unauthorised biography, Soros says, 'I would really like to be recognised as a practical philosopher, but I am quite happy to be recognised as a philosopher manqué.'

The centrepiece of Soros's philosophy is his theory of reflexivity, that the biases and flawed perception of the participants in historical events, whether they be stock market booms and busts or other sets of circumstances, themselves affect the eventual outcome. Some say this is analogous to Heisenberg's uncertainty principle. Commenting on Soros's book *The Crisis of Global Capitalism*, one reviewer threw out this challenge: try to find someone who denies this is the case.

It is clear that Soros has thought deeply and at length about his own beliefs and his own fallibility: it is perhaps impossible to play the markets year after year without coming to painful conclusions about one's own fallibility. Soros's strength is that in recognising his own fallibility he can try, not always successfully, to avoid or rectify the mistakes this produces.

There are plenty of paradoxes in Soros's thinking. One is that he acknowledges that a major influence on his thinking has been the logical positivism articulated by Karl Popper. But unlike the positivists, Soros believes there are not only true and false statements, but also reflexive ones. Since positivists hold that those statements that are not true or false are meaningless, Soros has to diverge from them at this point. Soros thus rejects the axiomatic systems of logic and mathematics, claiming that they cannot be applied correctly to the behaviour of human beings.

Monroe Trout is another hedge fund manager who has based his personal life and trading around an offbeat philosopher. In this instance the guru figure is not Popper, but the cult author Ayn Rand (of whom, it is said, Fed Chairman Alan Greenspan is also a disciple). Rand's philosophy of objectivism espouses the strengths of individual virtue and accomplishment as the foundation of achievements or, put less kindly, selfishness is okay and self-sacrifice is for the birds.

Trout has even gone so far as to name a futures brokerage business in which he is involved as Rand Financial Services. The objectivism – a rejection of philosophical speculation in favour of basing one's actions on observable fact – is even extended to the operations of this firm and imbues some of Trout's senior colleagues within it. Introduced to the works of Rand by Victor Niederhoffer, another fund manager, Trout's adoption of this philosophy has, it is said, caused a messy rift with his younger brother who worked at Trout Trading for a spell.

Timothy Trout parted company from his brother in 1999 with a substantial financial settlement and now lives in Monaco, although he has later sued, claiming that his compensation should be substantially greater and that he should be awarded punitive damages because of the circumstances of his departure. Trout Trading has countersued and attempts at settlement have collapsed, not least because of the animosity between the two.

For Michael Steinhardt, Judaism has long been a source of both comfort and perplexity to him. It has sometimes been said of him that it is only when faced with challenges and risk that he feels most intensely his Jewishness. Though a self-confessed atheist and an advocate of secular living, he has nonetheless, according to reports, spent a lifetime seeking spiritual enlightenment and given heavily to both secular and Orthodox Jewish charities. 'I find joy and meaning in the hope that I contribute something to a renaissance in the non-Orthodox Jewish world,' he has said, 'The values of our community are the best that humankind has created, and to perpetuate it is, I think, worthwhile.'

*   *   *

The philanthropic impulse is strong among the ranks of hedge fund managers, but whether or not it is a response to feelings of guilt over their contribution to the misfortunes of others is perhaps another matter. Hedge fund manager Michael Lewitt at Harch Capital says, 'There is a strong impulse bred of the ego that results from financial success to think that you can change the world and be remembered for more than just making money.' An investment banker who deals with hedge funds says, 'The charitable impulse results from the fact that they are deep thinkers about the world and what makes it tick. It is inevitable that they give. A lot of them are real softies underneath.'

Most macro traders probably take the view that the situations they exploit would be exploited by others if they did not, and that forcing governments to see sense can sometimes have a positively beneficial effect on their subjects. Hedge fund manager Paul Tudor Jones, for example, writing in a foreword to a George Soros book, described his unceremonious ejection of sterling from the European exchange rate mechanism in September 1992 as 'saving the British people from recession', a remark not so far from the truth.

A British hedge fund manager says, 'Macro managers in particular do have a cosmopolitan outlook and a global vision that has identified an equality of opportunity. Many treat their bonuses as scorecards, rather than having a real wish to use the money themselves to change their lifestyle.' Again ruminating on the influence of Soros and his peers, former Quantum Fund employee Rob Johnson, in an interview on America's PBS network, gave this description of hedge fund managers and how their minds work:

> The more sensitive you are, the more you can take on board in terms of awareness, the capacity to anticipate change and therefore make money. On the other hand, the more sensitive you are to pain and suffering and other dilemmas of how the world operates, the more it fatigues you. . . .
>
> People often talk about 'do people feel guilty?' There's a difference between feeling guilty and feeling a sense of empathy, tragedy and shame when people in Indonesia are suffering like they're suffering right now. People who can stay within the video game [of trading] might be quite resilient and not care and not understand what's happening in the world.
>
> Those people lack a certain sensitivity, an awareness that may cause them to miss a lot of opportunity. A man like Soros is fabulously sensitive to the consequences of his actions and the market's actions and the impact on humanity, and that's both his ability and his burden.

But perhaps the more common motive for philanthropic work derives from the relatively humble background of many hedge fund managers.

Indeed it might almost be the case that those for whom philanthropic effort is not a feature of their lives are those whose own backgrounds were relatively comfortable and whose extra-curricular interests reveal more of, say, hobby interests (however expensive) or a passion for collecting.

There could be other motives too. Famous courtesans of history craved one thing above all others: respectability and acceptance by polite society. The courtesans of capitalism doubtless feel the same impulse, attempting to gain favour among the great and the good by charitable acts, much as was attempted by Odette de Crécy, a former 'society beauty' who became Charles Swann's wife in Marcel Proust's great novel *Remembrance of Things Past*. Whatever the motivation, there is no doubt that the philanthropic impulse beats strongly in the breast of many a hedge fund manager. The examples are legion.

The ubiquitous Soros is of course the grandaddy of all hedge fund donors, scoring points also for outright eccentricity, not to say wackiness, in the causes he espouses. Among the oddest perhaps is a $15m donation to Project Death in America (PDIA) that seeks to promote greater understanding of the so-called end of life experience. As the *Philanthropy News Digest* reported in 1997: 'America is awash with scholarly projects on death. There are now seminars, debates, books, articles, college classes, courses for screenwriters, exhibitions, films, TV programmes and web sites on death, as well as grass roots projects aimed at enabling Americans to die more gracefully and in less pain.'

PDIA is one of the latter, dedicated to 'the creation of innovative models of care and the development of new curricula on dying', shorthand perhaps for the promotion of assisted suicides or at the very least the avoidance of unnecessary life-prolonging medical interventions. Soros's involvement in this area is actually less curious than it might seem. His father died a painful, lingering death from cancer and his mother, who it turns out was a member of the Hemlock Society, committed suicide.

Soros also espouses a long list of liberal causes in the United States, including drug decriminalisation. He has lent his name, credibility and hard cash to political campaigns in a number of states towards this end. Among other classic liberal causes he supports are vocational training for immigrants applying for naturalisation; abortion and birth control to combat teenage pregnancy; prisoners' charities; and inner-city schools. Soros is privately scathing about large, long-established charities and the giving policies they adopt, and also refuses to place money with established cultural organisations such as the Met or the Lincoln Center.

Outside of the United States, Soros has been active for much longer, establishing his so-called Open Society Foundation to channel donations into a variety of worthy projects in Central and Eastern Europe and elsewhere. From the mid 1980s onwards, successive foundations were opened up in Hungary, Russia, Poland, Czechoslovakia Romania and the Baltic States, many pre-dating the final death throes of communism.

Projects have ranged from textbooks for schoolchildren in Russia, to courses for investigative journalists in Hungary, to grants for scientists, management training, and many others in between. Some have failed, some got bogged down in bureaucracy or fell foul of corrupt governments or officialdom. In Russia, for example, his charities have undergone successive reorganisations as, unknown to Soros, funds were illegally siphoned off by crooked employees. Soros has also been critical of successive US administrations' failures to take advantage of the fall of communism by allocating cash for the establishment of stable political institutions in these countries.

Some sources hint darkly that Soros has less than altruistic motives in supporting Eastern European economies and institutions, that the encouragement of 'shock therapy' economic policies is part of a plot to allow Soros and his cronies to buy valuable state assets on the cheap. The reality is, one suspects, much more mundane, but it is undeniable that his charitable activities have given him access to senior politicians in the countries in which he invests and probably enabled him to make better judgements on their economic performance.

Soros eschews having the institutions he funds, such as libraries and colleges, bear his name, claiming that he wants rather to make a difference to the here and now, not perpetuate his name. Others have less grandiose ideas, but do like permanent memorials. Take Tiger Management's Julian Robertson. In 1997 Robertson gave $15m to his home town of Salisbury, North Carolina, as a contribution to a fund previously set up by his parents. They themselves were also generous donors from money made through involvement in the textile industry in the state. No strings were attached to the gift, but Robertson said at the time that he hoped the money would go towards remedying the social problems of the town, including race relations.

On a more artistic note, Robertson gave $25m in 1998 to the Lincoln Center for the Performing Arts in New York City, the largest ever given by an individual. Of the $25m, some $10m was used to create the Josie Robertson Fund for the Lincoln Center (named after Robertson's wife) but Robertson placed no conditions on how the money should be used. At the time of the gift, Robertson said that he intended it as a surprise for his wife, in whose honour the centre's fountain plaza has been renamed.

Paul Tudor Jones is also active in a number of areas. Among his past interests is funding the Save Our Everglades movement, a campaign to make sugar companies pay more towards the cost of cleaning up the Everglades pollution resulting from their activities. Records dating from 1996 show that Jones had contributed to this cause to the tune of some $4m at that time, something of an irony for a man whose activities are so closely associated with commodities trading.

Jones has also given money to other causes, notably the I Have A Dream Foundation, while his Robin Hood Foundation – to which George Soros has also made donations – gives money to dozens of New York City worthy causes, provided they pass a rigorous examination of their managerial skills and financial health by the foundation's hit squad of accountants and MBAs. According to an article in the *New York Times*, the foundation's executive director David Saltzman claims, 'We perform due diligence on our projects that you can compare with the best investment houses. We have a venture capital attitude towards charity.' Outsiders describe it as 'tough love' charity.

Moore Capital's Louis Bacon does not feature too prominently on the list of charitable givers, but is on record in 1996 as having given some $200 000 to the Republican Party. Zack Bacon, also director of Moore Capital Management, serves on the board of World TEAM Sports, a charity created to encourage, promote and develop opportunities in sport, especially for people with disabilities.

Fellow low-profile hedge-funder Leon Cooperman is similarly reticent about his charitable activities. But there are signs of his charitable generosity. The Cooperman Foundation of Short Hills, New Jersey, in conjunction with Toby and Leon Cooperman is recorded as being a member of the ADDA100 Club, a charity supporting treatment of attention deficiency disorder. Its members donate at least $100 to the organisation.

Oddly for a self-confessed atheist, Michael Steinhardt still adheres strongly to Jewish tradition, celebrating the sabbath with his family in the traditional manner. And he has been notably generous with his money in support of Jewish causes, including a plan to provide a free trip to Israel for any young Jewish person who wishes to take advantage of the offer.

Steinhardt made it a condition of his Project Birthright that the cash would be available to any Jew wherever they lived, whether or not they practised their religion, and irrespective of their family means. Steinhardt was also closely associated with Shlomo Carlebach, a charismatic and controversial Orthodox (but anti-establishment) rabbi, and he underwrote several of Carlebach's projects in an association spanning several decades.

More recently he has spent some $25m getting an organisation called the Jewish Life Network off the ground. This is a foundation intended to develop a Jewish centre in Manhattan to attract the unaffiliated by helping them (American psychobabble never being far away) 'to connect positively with their Jewishness'. Steinhardt has also backed a Jewish chaplaincy in New York to train carers for the terminally ill, and has also donated money to the National Jewish Outreach Project and other Orthodox Jewish charities.

He also has his eccentric touches. Owner of a 51-acre estate, he has been busy filling it with a menagerie of animals, including an attempt to collect every variety of duck and swan in the world, as well as wallabies, zebras and llamas. Steinhardt and his wife, Judith, also collect Judaica, modern art, antiquities and textiles from areas as far afield as Asia and Peru. A grand conservatory in the Brooklyn Botanic Garden is named after the Steinhardts, following a $3m donation some years ago.

Caxton Corporation's Bruce Kovner is arguably one of the more active hedge fund managers when it comes to charitable giving. Kovner has been active, for example, in backing a private voucher scheme to enable children from low-income families to attend a better school than they would normally have the opportunity to. Kovner's contribution in this respect was the School Choice Scholarships Foundation, a New York City charity that is the second largest private educational voucher scheme in the United States. When it began in 1997 it had an initial fund of $6m but this has increased significantly since then, enabling thousands of children each year to choose from a range of participating private schools to attend instead of their existing one.

Among Kovner's other interests are board membership of the Thomas B. Fordham Foundation, which supports research, publications and action projects of national signficance in elementary and secondary education reform, as well as specific educational work in Dayton, Ohio, and its vicinity. In the political sphere Caxton is represented (as is the Soros group) on the Council on Foreign Relations, a Washington DC pressure group designed to keep America's foreign policy outward looking rather than protectionist. Kovner has also personally been a large donor in the past to the Republican National Committee.

Among other projects that Kovner has donated money to more recently, and in which he is actively involved as a fundraiser, is the Juilliard School. Kovner is chairman of The Campaign for Juilliard, an ambitious plan to raise $100m for the conservatoire over five years. Its purpose is to increase scholarship and faculty salaries, commission and produce new works, renovate the Juilliard's buildings and expand and enrich the school's curriculum. Kovner has been a trustee of the

Juilliard since 1995. He is also a board member of the Philharmonic Society of New York, of the American Enterprise Institute and the Manhattan Institute.

*   *   *

The roster of Steinhardt's and Kovner's charitable activities is undeniably impressive. But there is a darker side to the duo's activities that helps to put it into context. In December 1994 Steinhardt Management and Caxton Corporation were obliged to make what were undoubtedly less welcome and certainly involuntary 'donations' to the government in order to settle antitrust and securities charges brought by the Department of Justice (DoJ) and the Securities and Exchange Commission.

According to DoJ documents, the two agreed to a settlement that involved the payment by them of some $76m, split roughly equally. The case revolved around an attempt to corner the market in a two-year Treasury note issue in April 1991, forcing other investors to pay inflated prices for the stock over a period of several months in the spring and summer of 1991. It seems Caxton and Steinhardt coordinated their trading and bought a combined position of $20bn in the issue, compared to the more than $12bn of bonds actually issued, a feat made possible because some investors were selling the issue short.

Some hedge fund managers confine their giving to more hobbyist pursuits. Baseball fan John Henry liked the Florida Marlins so much that he bought the team, lock stock and barrel, for $150m from previous owner Wayne Huizenga. When asked by a *Fortune* reporter how he actually paid for it, cash or cheque, he is said to have replied 'probably a wire'. As *Fortune* reported, the word 'probably' was the interesting part of the reply. It noted, 'In Henry's league, wealth is measured by the details that don't concern you.'

Finally, a heart-rending tale. Victor Niederhoffer's hedge fund went bust in spectacular fashion. A former squash champion, Niederhoffer had spent twenty years collecting sporting memorabilia and antiques with a sporting theme. In December 1998, in the wake of the fund's collapse, they went under the hammer.

The proudest piece in the collection was a five foot tall 4000-ounce silver sculptural group depicting Victory, her wings outstretched, riding on the back of an eagle and holding a wreath. The piece was made by Meissner in Paris for a Brazilian nobleman to help celebrate his part in the overthrow of the monarchy and the establishment of the Brazilian Republic in 1889. Among the sporting trophies were a brace of yacht racing cups and several horse racing trophies, including the 1929 Ascot Gold Cup.

One of the more unusual pieces, leaving aside the musical tugboat, was a silver gilt inkstand made in London in 1842 with two horse-hoof inkwells and a tripod holding a bullet. The inscription read, 'In memory of an exceptional war horse who in his youth received a grave wound at the battle of Waterloo; you see here the bullet taken from his testicles at death and two of his hooves.' Old George, as the horse was remembered, lived until the age of 33 and was buried with full military honours.

As Niederhoffer said at the time, 'Once I started collecting, I pursued it with a passion and if a piece was heroic, historic or unique, I bid on it.' The circumstances befalling Niederhoffer and how he came to have to sell his prized collection were, however, minor by comparison with the damage wrought by leverage and misjudged speculation that brought down LTCM, whose story is told in the next chapter.

5

The Archimedes of Greenwich

A company for carrying on an undertaking of great advantage, but nobody to know what it is
Company prospectus around the time of the South Sea bubble

Courtesans gain notoriety at their peril, and with it come the seeds of destruction. In the space of a few days in September 1998, John Meriwether went from being little known, outside the select circles of the American financial community, to being very public property indeed. His fund, Long Term Capital Management (LTCM), became a symbol of the damage that hedge funds could wreak on the lives of ordinary individuals. If, that is, they were left to their own devices.

LTCM is an example of what can go wrong, and how big a crash can be. As such it is important for all those who choose to invest in hedge funds, and for those who might want to regulate them. And even for those who might want to try to eliminate them altogether.

Inevitably much of the press comment that accompanied the fall of LTCM was misguided, the result of a lack of understanding mixed with envy and a dash of Schadenfreude. Delight at the misfortunes of the wealthy is an understandable emotion, especially if the individuals concerned are seen either as brainy, arrogant or secretive. Before its fall, LTCM was regarded as one of the most beautiful and mysterious of the courtesans of capitalism. As was the case with the courtesans of centuries ago, her enemies greeted her downfall with glee, while the curious just looked on bemused.

One might have expected those who could have been in a similar position to be sympathetic. But this is not necessarily so. Even John

Meriwether's peers in the hedge fund community were prone to some wry comments about his fate, and more particularly that of his backers. Interviewed in *Forbes* magazine, Michael Steinhardt, then retired but in his time no angel when it came to moving financial markets, said 'So the brokerages lost a lot of money. It's not one of life's great tragedies. What's the saying? Live by the sword, die by the sword.'

There are many ironies in the LTCM story. One is the fact that because Meriwether and his team were viewed as highly skilled individuals among the cognoscenti of the bond markets, their reputation actually contributed to the fund's downfall. The reason for this was simple: Meriwether's trades produced hordes of imitators, contributing to a disastrous panic when things turned sour. Another is that despite employing the best theoretical minds in finance, including two Nobel prizewinners, LTCM was floored by a market phenomenon by no means unknown – a 'flight to quality' in moments of high uncertainty.

Combine this with high levels of leverage and the cocktail becomes a lethal one. The leverage aspect of all this is one of the most interesting features, because the attitudes to leverage of so-called financial sophisticates are different to those held by the rest of us.

Financial theory does not look at leverage as those in the real world do. Intuitive commonsense notions of what might or might not be prudent are thrown out of the window in favour of the appropriate levels of leverage being related to complex calculations about the structure and cost of different forms of capital (equity and debt and the many variations in between) and the volatility of the underlying asset – the violence with which its price swings around day by day and week by week. One theory is that if the price tends to be less volatile, higher levels of leverage might be appropriate.

In the case of LTCM, human nature or, to be more realistic, ego also entered into the calculations. Meriwether's reputation was riding high, and LTCM's early returns were spectacular. Rather than risk the market believing he had lost his touch, Meriwether appears to have sanctioned greater use of leverage in order to make the fund's complex – and theoretically low-risk – strategies produce the returns the market had come to expect.

LTCM's undoing was analogous in some ways to the experience of Barings' Nick Leeson. The comparison may not seem obvious, and one should state clearly that there was no illegality about the way LTCM or its employees functioned. But in both cases at a crucial time, what intervened was an unexpected external shock. In Leeson's case this was the Kobe earthquake, in LTCM's the Russian default in August 1998. Both events made the markets behave differently to the textbooks. In many other ways the Leeson case was different, because Leeson had been misinforming his employers about the scale of the positions being held, and committing the classic error of doubling up losing trades to get out of the hole.

Yet there are other similarities. These boil down to one simple fact: for all the sophistication of financial theory, cash is still king. One reason cash holds sway in financial markets is because of margin. Short selling and derivatives trading require margin deposits to be made. These are cash deposits designed to be a precautionary offset against adverse market movements. If prices move in the wrong direction, brokers and other counterparties can call for additional margin to be deposited.

Calls to top up margin deposits by sizeable amounts indicated what was going wrong at Barings. The same was true in a different way at LTCM. Margin calls are a routine part of professional stock market trading. But it is when a large trader fails to meet a margin call that fear sweeps the market. Once LTCM's trades started to go wrong, its lenders realised their funds were at risk, and its imitators realised that their own trades were going wrong too and began to unwind them, worsening the position. LTCM's massive levels of leverage essentially meant that it ran out of cash to meet the required margin calls, and was forced to seek a bailout.

The saving grace of the banks which imitated its trades and who also executed trades on its behalf was that they had more cash and broader streams of income, even if they were just as leveraged. The Federal Reserve claims that the bailout was organised not because LTCM itself was too big to fail, but because its failure and the impact this would have on its imitators meant there was a probability of the financial system seizing up. The distinction may be valid, but it is a hard one to grasp for the person in the street.

Despite the many acres of newsprint published about LTCM and excellent books by Nicholas Dunbar (*Inventing Money*, published by John Wiley) and Roger Lowenstein (*When Genius Failed*, published by Random House) about the firm and its history, there are still unanswered questions and intriguing relationships to explore. One issue partly contradicts Dunbar's evocative description of the crashed LTCM as like an alien spacecraft being crawled over by puny earthlings while the dazed and shell-shocked 'Masters of the Universe' looked on. The fact was that the strategies being pursued by LTCM were often known about or guessed at, albeit imperfectly, by proprietary traders at investment banks. How did that knowledge leak out?

Why were the conventional credit limit disciplines imposed by otherwise hard-nosed investment banks waived where LTCM was concerned, allowing it to build up hitherto unheard of levels of leverage? And what about the personal investments said to have been held in the fund by senior investment bankers who themselves negotiated the rescue package? Was this moral hazard writ large? What of Meriwether's claims in the heat of the crisis that there was a conspiracy at work to deliberately drive the firm out of business? Will it be harder for America to preach financial discipline to poor countries coming cap in hand for loans in future after a bailout many felt should be described as the ultimate in crony capitalism?

To answer these questions, and arrive at what the LTCM lesson means for hedge funds, we need to look at several aspects of the LTCM saga: the personalities involved, LTCM's ethos, the nature of the trades the firm made, how the leverage they used worked, and why lack of financial market liquidity was so deadly to them.

*   *   *

John Meriwether was born in 1947 and grew up in Roseland, on the south side of Chicago. The family were Catholics of Irish descent. Meriwether is also said by some still to keep rosary beads close at hand, but like so many stories about him, this could be apocryphal, flourishing, as such stories do, because of the privacy with which he has always surrounded himself. With privacy comes secrecy. Meriwether has always operated by building up a close-knit team of people, in whom he inspires great loyalty and from whom he expects loyalty in return and also a code of silence and secrecy where the outside world is concerned.

After a conventional education, Meriwether graduated from Northwestern University in 1969 and was destined for a career as a teacher. His mother was a school administrator and wanted her son to remain part of Chicago's tight-knit Catholic community. However, all accounts of Meriwether suggest that he is temperamentally unsuited to the teaching profession. Shy and polite, it follows that he would have intensely disliked the macho style of a Wall Street trading floor too, a distaste that perhaps provides one explanation for what came later.

In 1971 Meriwether left his teaching job and enrolled as an MBA at the University of Chicago Business School, a faculty at that time stuffed with leading figures in financial economics: Merton Miller, Eugene Fama, Fischer Black and others. Again it is speculation, but one must presume that his early stock market trading habit, investing money he had earned as a caddy at a local country club, may have helped pay for this venture. Miller can probably claim the credit for introducing Meriwether to the concept of arbitrage.

After Chicago, Meriwether headed more or less straight for Wall Street and to the bond trading desk at Salomon Brothers. But his ideas on arbitraging the bond market were less than enthusiastically received by more traditionally minded colleagues at Salomon. In 1974, when Meriwether joined Salomon, traders contented themselves with less mathematically intensive methods of trying to exploit the markets, using their instincts rather than complex computer models – seat-of-the-pants flying not fly-by-wire.

But times were changing. Meriwether's major leap forward at Salomon came with the introduction of futures contracts on the thirty-year Treasury bond in 1977. This opened up the possibility of exploiting small discrepancies between the prices of underlying bonds and the futures. Futures allow traders to buy or sell an underlying bond or basket of bonds for future delivery at a specified time. But their importance rests on the fact that large numbers of bonds can be bought and sold very quickly for a low initial outlay, facilitating arbitrage.

Meriwether saw the potential that this offered. At his urging, Salomon set up a specialist bond arbitrage desk. Meriwether increased the scale of his trading and started to make big profits. But an essential part of the game was that no one should know what he and his team were doing, lest others exploit the tiny margins before he did. Meriwether was made a partner in Salomon in 1980.

The activities of the team gradually evolved into a series of specially designed complex arbitrage plays which brought in leverage and also allowed them to exploit hidden options within bonds and other instruments, whose true value could be accurately assessed by the financial wizards Meriwether had at his disposal. Because of the intricacies of the instruments and the abstruse nature of the theories, few understood that there were bonds in which hidden options existed which were often either ignored or at best badly priced by the market's seat-of-the-pants traders.

Meriwether's edge by contrast was the high-powered mathematicians and financial economists he gathered round him. Michael Lewis, whose sojourn at Salomon Brothers was turned into the best-selling book *Liar's Poker*, described Meriwether later as having an 'underground railroad' spiriting out the bright students from finance graduate schools around the country to work at Salomon, a reference to the informal network that grew up in the nineteenth century to ensure escaping slaves safe passage north. It is just one of a series of images that he has conjured up about his former colleague. Lewis also describes Meriwether's outbluffing of Salomon chief John Gutfreund in the famous 'liar's poker' incident.

Invited by Gutfreund to play a hand of the gambling game (betting on the serial numbers of banknotes) for a million dollars, Meriwether challenged Gutfreund to raise the stakes to $10m before he would play. Gutfreund walked away. The point, as Lewis observes, was not that Meriwether wanted to play, but simply by raising the stakes to a point where even Gutfruend would think twice, he extricated himself from a stupid financial risk. Gutfreund's high-profile social life and free-spending lifestyle – or more particularly that of his wife – meant that it was easy for Meriwether to calculate how much the Salomon chief would baulk at losing. Then again, there are those who claim the incident did not involve Meriwether at all, but another Salomon partner.

But more turbulent events were to come, for both Meriwether and Salomon. In the wake of the much publicised Treasury bond auction scandal, where another Salomon colleague had been caught trying to rig the periodic auction of US government bonds by submitting bogus bids on behalf of a client, Meriwether (even though his involvement in the scandal was non-existent) left Salomon in disgust. He re-emerged shortly afterwards to found Long Term Capital Management (LTCM), based in the leafy Connecticut suburb of Greenwich, its office complete with tranquil views across Long Island Sound.

Meriwether and the team he assembled, many of which were former Salomon colleagues, wanted to run the fund away from Wall Street. This was partly in order to cultivate a more detached cerebral approach to their trading, and partly to get away from the yahoos and philistines they believed populated the trading floors of Lower Manhattan. This is confirmed by Michael Lewis. *Liar's Poker* contains another interesting description of Meriwether:

> He had an ability, rare among people and treasured by traders, to hide his state of mind. Most traders divulge whether they are making or losing money by the way they speak or move. They are either overly easy or overly tense. With Meriwether, you could never, ever tell. He wore the same blank, half-tense expression when he won as when he lost.
>
> He had, I think, the profound ability to control the two emotions that commonly destroy traders (fear and greed) and it made him as noble as a man who so fiercely pursues his own self-interest can be.

The reason for Meriwether's detachment is obvious, of course. He is and was fascinated by the idea of arbitrage, the idea that profits can be made from market inefficiencies in a riskless manner simply by superior reasoning and a scientific approach. The macho swaggering of the seat-of-the-pants traders is anathema to him. Recent descriptions of Meriwether are fleeting but illuminating. Here are Lewis's observations in a long newspaper article written during the wake of the LTCM collapse:

> His movements are quick and so is his talk. He speaks in fragments and moves rapidly from one idea to the next, leaving behind a trail of untidy thoughts. He shapes other people more completely than he does himself.

He is also uncomfortable with the first person and, says Lewis, seeks privacy because he is uncomfortable with public attention. He has, it is frequently said, a phobia about public speaking and is even reticent in social gatherings. 'Meriwether sought power in a different form,' says Lewis, 'through the markets.'

For much of the time Meriwether's New York lifestyle was relatively modest: a bachelor apartment with two friends in York Avenue on the Upper East Side. He lived there for twelve years, from 1981 to 1993. In the early days in New York, reports suggest he roomed at a Manhattan athletics club and was slow to make friends.

Meriwether's interests have always revolved around golf, horses and the science of betting. An accomplished golfer even at high school, he caddied in his youth to make money, and made carefully calculated bets on Chicago Cubs baseball games (studying weather reports in great detail, for example, prior to placing his stake). He liked to bet on horses. Often his arbitrage group would take sojourns at the Meadowlands track across the river in New Jersey.

Even during his period rooming in the Upper East Side, however, Meriwether indulged his passion for golf (his handicap is reputed to be around six) and became a member of three prestigious clubs: Shinnecock Hills in Eastern Long Island, Winged Foot Golf Club in Westchester County in upstate New York, and Cypress Point in California. At a later date he and a group of partners at Salomon actually bought a golf course, in Waterville, County Kerry, on the West Coast of Ireland. Golf in the 'old country' was a treat for him and the arbitrage team and a successful week-long outing there one year developed into a regular tradition.

Meriwether's interest in horses extends to owning thoroughbreds. He owns a large 43-acre property in northern Westchester County. His wife, the former Mimi Murray, whom he married in the late 1980s, was an Olympic-level equestrienne. The estate has a large covered paddock. Meriwether is a trustee of the New York Racing Association, which operates the racetracks at Belmont Park, Aqueduct and Saratoga Springs.

Aside from this, like many other arbitrageurs who are less prone to the grand gesture than the larger than life macro traders, there is little documentary evidence of any other charitable works. Always open to new ideas, however, Meriwether never took the credit for those proposed by his subordinates and is remembered by Salomon colleagues for his integrity, even down to remembering to pay off old bets long since forgotten by the other party.

If there is or was a weakness in Meriwether's ideas, and those around him, it seems it may have been a quite simple one. The Achilles heel of LTCM seems to have been a failure to give due weighting to the fact that markets, even though they are generally efficient, can occasionally be illogical for short periods. In turn, they and the human nature of the participants can produce reactions to external events that are out of proportion to what is required or appropriate.

In 1987 and arguably in the bond market sell-off in 1994, Meriwether and his team had been exposed to the market's illogicality but had overcome the difficulties because liquidity – the ability to do large deals without moving the price of the stock being traded – was always present in sufficient quantity at the right time to enable them to exploit the market's illogicality to the full.

LTCM's downfall came about in part because of an undue reliance on mathematics at the expense of market nous, in part because of huge leverage (gearing to small price movements), in part because of lack of liquidity, in part because of a random external shock, and in part because it had become too influential and too much imitated. It may also have been that, located in Greenwich and highly secretive and inward looking, there was no opportunity or room for any challenging or criticism of the methods being used.

* * *

Carol Loomis, regarded as something of an authority in hedge funds after her seminal article on Alfred Winslow Jones, has described leverage in the context of LTCM as 'an addiction to the oldest and most famously addictive drug in finance'. The average person might think of leverage in terms of borrowing from a bank. Large numbers of middle-aged and middle-class homeowners in the UK, for example, have become wealthy beyond their expectations because of leveraged investment in property made through the medium of mortgages and inflation in property prices.

If you put a £10 000 deposit on a house worth £100 000, and borrow the remaining 90%, you are leveraging 9:1. If the value of the property rises by just 10%, your net worth has increased from £10 000 to £20 000. Multiply these numbers by a million, imagine that you are performing the trick with other people's money as well as your own, then add in the fact that you are likely to receive an incentive bonus of 20% of the gain, and it is easy to see why the hedge fund style of leverage could become addictive.

LTCM was leveraged to a much greater level than the average householder with a mortgage. Estimates vary, but at the time of its collapse it was by some margin the most highly leveraged hedge fund. Guesses suggest that its leverage was upwards of 25:1, equivalent to our householder putting up a deposit of less than £4000 on the £100 000 property.

The reason for the leverage was that the fluctuations in value of many of the firm's investments were likely to be relatively small. LTCM was primarily investing in government bonds, securities backed by mortgages, corporate bonds, emerging market bonds, and so on, often using arbitrage strategies that meant the tiniest of margins on trades which were nonetheless designed to be free from risk.

The concept of arbitrage is reasonably easy to grasp. To give a simple example, let's say you have two nearly identical assets priced respectively at £499 and £501, whose value ought to converge to £500. Selling the more expensive and buying the cheaper of the two suggests that you could make a return of £2 on assets with a combined value of £1000. The sale of one asset will finance the purchase of the other, although some capital may have been used to acquire the asset in the first place.

The returns look better if you can employ a little leverage. If you do not own the asset your are selling, and have to borrow it to sell it (this is called selling short), then you will be expected to put up an insurance deposit (known as margin) with your broker to allow for the fact that the asset you sell might in fact go up in price, forcing you to buy it back at a loss. If the trade goes the right way, all is well and good. If your short sale rises by more than a certain amount, however, an additional call for margin might be made. In the meantime the asset you bought may have fallen in price.

The fact that these movements may be contrary to logic and may only persist for a short time does not alter the fact of the immediate demands for cash that unsuccessful trades will generate. This highlights the essential problem with much riskier forms of arbitrage trading, and the next chapter explores it in more detail.

It may be regarded as somewhat simplistic to say so, but the introduction of leverage – even into arbitrage trading of the least volatile assets – immediately introduces an extra element of risk, because the terms of the leverage (such as a margin call) may necessitate a forced sale at a loss in order to raise cash.

In other words, this type of leverage is different to the straightforward leverage represented by a mortgage loan secured on a property. In this case, provided the borrower can continue to service the loan, the lender does not call it in, because the property acts as collateral. In securities market leverage, the emergence of anything remotely approaching 'negative equity' immediately produces a demand for cash to make up the difference. The simple example described above of short selling to produce cash to finance a straightforward purchase of a bond would seem dangerous enough to the layperson. In fact, it is minor by comparison with what actually goes on.

Gearing is ratcheted up essentially because leverage in the securities markets is acquired in ways other than straightforward borrowing. The two principal ways in bond arbitrage are through the repo market and via the use of futures and options. Repo markets are crucial to the smooth running of the financial system, but they also allow traders to build up leverage. Typically operating in government bond markets, they are effectively a system of collateralised loans.

A repo is shorthand for 'repurchase agreement' and works like this. If a dealer wishes to buy a large quantity of a bond for a short-term trade, the repo allows them to avoid paying cash for it. A repo is a bilateral transaction, usually between two investment banks, whereby the buyer of the bond (who we'll call the dealer bank) will repo it – they enter into a sale and repurchase agreement with another bank (the repo bank).

In return for entering into the repo arrangement, the dealer bank has the economic interest in the bond, but finances the position in the bond by selling it in the short term to the repo bank in return for the funds required to buy the bond in the first place. The key point, though, is an undertaking to buy it back in, say, a day's or a week's time for the amount of the loan plus interest. Result: the repo bank has the government-guaranteed bond as security for the loan; the dealer bank has the economic interest in the progress of the bond with only the cost of interest on the repo as the outlay.

If, for example, the dealer wishes to buy £100m of a UK government bond and the repo interest rate is 6%, then repoing the bond for a week will cost 0.115% of £100m or £115 000. If the bond appreciates 1% in price over the course of the week, the dealer will make a profit of £1m for an outlay of £115 000. Selling the bond will allow the collateralised loan to be repaid as agreed, and everyone will be happy.

As arbitrage trades of the sort LTCM was engaging in involve one category of bond being sold and another being bought, it is clear that this creates the capability for a double dose of leverage. Bonds that are to be bought can be repoed; bonds that are held are reverse repoed to produce cash. Alternatively bonds can be borrowed and sold short against margin.

The superficial rationale behind arbitrage is of course that however the trade is constructed, one transaction supposedly hedges the other. It is not the bonds themselves that are the attraction, but the spread (or yield difference) between them. However, if for whatever reason the bond being bought goes down and the bond being sold or sold short goes up, it is clear that the leverage works in reverse. In other words, if the spread between the two widens rather than narrows, the leverage involved means the loss can be huge.

There is a sort of loose control exercised in the repo market, known colloquially as the haircut. What the haircut means is that the repo bank financing a trader's position will not take the full value of the bond as collateral, but retain a small margin to cover any residual risk. Haircuts are based not only on the type of bond being repoed, but also on the supposed quality of the counterparty. It is significant that LTCM was at times able to repo its positions with no requirement for a haircut.

Another control is hypothecation, which means that the bond being repoed or reverse repoed is earmarked as collateral and cannot be used in another transaction (or rehypothecated) with a different counterparty. In LTCM's case too, rehypothecation was allowed.

Aside from repos and stock borrowing, leverage can also be obtained through the futures market, where the futures contracts may not themselves move by huge amounts in absolute terms, but are bought on margin, magnifying the potential gain or loss. They work like this. In financial futures markets, interest rate futures contracts of the sort dealt in by LTCM are priced on the basis of 100 minus the prevailing interest rate. Hence if rates go up, the price of the contract goes down.

A 4% prevailing rate of interest means the future is priced at 96, a 5% rate means the future is priced at 95, and so on. However, to take LIFFE's contract as the example, a single futures contract in the short sterling market worth £500 000 can be purchased by a trader for margin of £500, leverage of 1000:1. A half-point movement in interest rates would produce a change of £2500 in the value of the contract, five times the capital put up to buy it.

Once again, if you multiply this by the sheer size of the LTCM capital and asset base, it is easy to see how substantial leverage can be achieved.

The official US government investigation into the LTCM debacle recorded, for example, that LTCM held long and short positions and 'supported these positions in many cases through repo and reverse repo and securities lending agreements with a large number of other market participants.' It also, says the report, 'took on futures positions at about a dozen major futures exchanges worldwide, including some very size-able positions' and that it 'engaged in over the counter [that is, custom-tailored] derivatives contracts with several dozen counterparties.'

The report found that the fund had a staggering 60 000 trades on its books with long positions of over $50bn and short positions of an equivalent magnitude. It said that the fund's derivatives positions at the end of August 1998 exceeded $500bn on futures exchanges, over-the-counter (OTC) derivatives of $150bn and swap contracts of more than $750bn. At the end of August, the fund's total assets were some $125bn, but the equity capital in the fund was only $4.8bn and its cash resources even less.

While many of the positions were self-cancelling and arguably the numbers look worse than in reality, the fatal combination was the sheer size of the positions and the relatively low capital base that supported them. In normal circumstances, should it need to meet margin calls on certain trades, the fund would be able to cash in some of its other trades to provide liquid funds to satisfy the margin requirement. But in panic conditions, brought about as a result of the market shock administered by the Russian default, and with simultaneous margin calls on multiple trades and with the market well aware that the fund was facing diffi-culties, the liquid capital base of the fund was swamped.

*   *   *

Liquidity is one of the most important aspects of financial markets, as important as the indissoluble link between risk and return. LTCM's problem was that it didn't have enough of it. The arbitrage oppor-tunities being exploited by LTCM were present not just because of inefficient pricing by a market which did not understand how to value embedded option contracts in some securities but, in the simplest of arbitrage trades, because of the different levels of liquidity available in the different instruments.

A 30-year benchmark Treasury bond would have vastly more liquidity than the off-the-run 29-year bond, which has nominally almost the same characteristics but which is not regarded as a market benchmark. In ordinary arbitrage between the two, the liquidity issue would not matter, because both would have reasonable levels of liquidity. In a panic, however, the standard liquidity benchmark would be the bond that was sought, and the relative value of the more illiquid one would decline.

Looked at another way, LTCM's own trading activities, backed by its huge leverage, were pushing together the prices of bonds that normally would have been a little apart because of the relative differences in their normal liquidity. In these circumstances, if an external shock caused a dramatic market change, the liquidity argument worked in reverse, with LTCM's leverage making it forced to unwind its positions. If so, partly because of the sheer size of the holdings and partly because the fund tended by definition to be long of the less liquid securities and short of the more liquid securities, this meant the problem was compounded.

But even at the best of times, the sheer size of LTCM's positions in the market would have strained liquidity. The official report on the debacle notes for example that the fund's futures positions alone represented in some instances well above 10% of overall open interest (the value of positions that are not sold before the end of the trading day) in a particular contract, and were even larger in terms of the daily turnover of a particular market or contract.

In an abstract academic sense, leverage and liquidity can be treated logically as mere components of financial engineering. In the real world, when losses start to mount, concern grows at those who have supplied leverage, then issues of accountability come into play, along with sheer fear.

As it became clear that LTCM was seeking additional funding to cover its capital erosion, the margin calls and requests for collateral, which had once been flexible and informal, now grew formal and contentious. Alarms bells rang at lending institutions, and calculations started to be based on worst-case scenarios involving sudden liquidation of the collateral.

One element of the problem was what one might call 'me too' trading. Such was Meriwether and his team's reputation in the market that the proprietary traders in other large banks were to an extent imitating its techniques. Despite the fund's attempts at secrecy, LTCM's repo activities meant that the big banks' repo desks were able to, as it were, 'reverse engineer' and work out precisely what trades the firm was placing. Repo traders do talk to each other, and the market as a whole may have had an idea what LTCM was up to.

More than likely too, as each large investment bank was given a massive LTCM trade to execute and finance, it spotted and imitated the opportunity identified by Meriwether's team. What both they and, says Meriwether, LTCM itself did not know, however, was that this process of execution and imitation was being carried out at every other large investment bank. Only when LTCM's creditors sat around the table at the time of the debacle did they discover the extent of their collective exposure.

To the extent that the banks themselves consciously imitated LTCM's strategy, and they seem to have done, then there is an element of double risk involved here. Not only were the banks involved as counterparties to LTCM's repo trades, but they were attempting to replicate the same risks that LTCM was taking in their own trading books, magnifying the impact of these trades on the market, both in their effect when they were placed, and in the subsequent dash for the exit.

Moreover, the same banks' repo trading desks were exposed to LTCM as repo counterparties, where the values of the collateral they held as part of these agreements were dropping as a result of the fears for LTCM's financial health and the consequent likelihood that its collateral would be claimed and liquidated.

Guesswork may well have been involved in the 'me too' proprietary trading in the wider market, and it probably contributed to the uncertainty. LTCM went to considerable lengths to disguise its strategies in the market, at least from those not dealing on its behalf, but the success of its disguises is not at all clear. Myths abounded about where and on what scale LTCM had positions.

The point is summed up by the official investigations into the crash. According to a US Treasury report, the 'fund stood out with respect to its opaqueness and low degree of external monitoring, and its high degree of leverage. . . . Individual counterparties, partly because there were so many, were not necessarily aware of the depth of LTCM's liquidity problems.'

The report goes on rightly to blame the banks who dealt with LTCM as being as much to blame as the fund itself for the subsequent debacle because they 'exercised minimal scrutiny of the fund's risk management practices and risk profile. This insufficient monitoring arose because of LTCM's practice of disclosing only minimal information to these parties.'

LTCM got away with this, if that is the right phrase to use, because of the reputation of those involved, because it represented an attractive source of business for these institutions, and because LTCM was a risk-seeking provider of liquidity that made it an attractive partner with which the firms concerned could in theory hedge their own market exposure. In reality, they ended up redoubling it.

*   *   *

The circumstances of the LTCM bailout were well documented in the press at the time of the collapse of the fund, and have been aired in great detail in subsequent official reports. The technicalities are unimportant but there are some piquant little details that make the whole affair interesting.

One is that Warren Buffett, a byword for shrewd investing and, for all his folksy image, more interested in the hedge fund arena than is often supposed, made an offer to buy the fund's portfolio in its entirety. Buffett's involvement here is interesting for a couple of reasons. The so-called Sage of Omaha was involved in rescuing Salomon Brothers

from the crisis it became involved in at the time of the scandal over
the rigging of the US Treasury bond auctions, and he doubtless came
across Meriwether and his techniques at the time.

And Buffett, despite his public persona as an equity investor in
companies, has played extensively in other securities markets and in
commodities. In the bond market he has made substantial gains on a
large portfolio of US government zero-coupon bonds (these are bonds,
bought at a discount, whose return derives not from interest payments
but from the appreciation of the bonds as they move to maturity).

Because of the price discounts they are issued at – often a few cents
on the dollar if the maturity is a long one – the price of 'zeros' can
move up sharply if views on interest rates become more optimistic.
Bonds like this have built-in leverage, but they are a speculation on
the direction of the market rather than arbitrage.

Buffett's methods are also essentially contrarian. He is known for
ignoring short-term movements in the market. Buffett has huge liquidity – backed by the cash flow of the insurance company that is a
central part of his corporate group – and a reputation in the market
sufficient in itself to stem any problems of confidence. The Buffett
offer was also to be backed by Goldman Sachs and AIG, another
derivatives market specialist. Meriwether has since hinted darkly that
AIG had been part of a covert campaign to drive LTCM out of
business by bidding up the price of derivatives the fund was short of,
and vice versa.

Meriwether reportedly suggested that AIG wanted to see the fund
fail because it resented its power in a market in which it was ac-
customed to being a big player. There is little firm evidence of this
envy factor impinging significantly on LTCM's collapse, which was
brought about by other factors.

What is clear, however, was that while Buffett was clearly motivated
to participate in the rescue, and provide much of the capital, simply
because of the returns potentially on offer, Goldman and AIG had
other motives. They were more interested in gaining access to the
secrets of the LTCM portfolio and the techniques it used. Goldman's
then leading light, Jon Corzine (now a senator for New Jersey), was a

University of Chicago contemporary of Meriwether and had attempted to replicate his techniques in Goldman's own business.

Buffett, Goldman and AIG, however, saw no continuing role for Meriwether if they bought the business of LTCM. But Meriwether was aware, from the negotiations there had already been about a bailout, that the Federal Reserve was desperate to avoid a collapse. The result was that Meriwether was able, in true 'liar's poker' style, to refuse the Buffett offer on the grounds that investors in the fund had to be consulted before any deal was struck, in favour of a deal which offered the possibility of his retaining control over the way the fund was liquidated and the proprietary techniques it used.

Meriwether's hand was immeasurably strengthened because he realised that LTCM was essentially too big to be allowed to fail. Even if it did not bring down the financial system, a collapse might contribute to bringing down some of the senior individuals at the leading investment banks who were LTCM's counterparties in its deals. It was they who had sanctioned the involvement with the fund and allowed it to continue with inadequate monitoring and control. Moreover, imitating of LTCM's techniques by bank proprietary traders had resulted in losses that would steepen if the fund defaulted, further putting jobs on the line.

More interesting still, some of those senior bank executives were personal investors in the LTCM fund, not only negotiating the bailout, but also with substantial amounts of their own money at risk. Senior executives at Merrill Lynch, including CEO David Komansky, were said to have $20m in total at risk, and James Cayne of Bear Stearns and Donald Marron at Paine Webber were also cited in the Lowenstein book and elsewhere as having money invested.

In a way these investments should not be too surprising. Merrill in particular enjoyed a special relationship with LTCM, because it had been a key player in canvassing for investors in the fund when LTCM was set up in 1993. Banks have controls over how and in what circumstances their senior executives and other employees can invest, and there is no suggestion these guidelines were ever breached by any of these individuals. But the fact is that with personal money on the line and jobs at risk, the pressure on the bankers to negotiate a deal over LTCM was intense. While there is no suggestion that any of these investors acted in any way improperly, it is hard not to view the episode as giving moral hazard a subtle new twist.

Central bankers are normally the ones wont to preach about moral hazard. However, the curious might also wonder why the Bank of Italy invested in LTCM to the tune of $100m. It has been claimed that the bank's most senior managers did not realise LTCM was a hedge fund. According to Nick Dunbar, LTCM purchased cheap Italian government bonds over a long period. In doing so, it was ostensibly betting against the odds that Italy would be able to satisfy the Maastricht criteria. If it did, the yields on its bonds would converge with those on German ones, producing a big gain. This speculation proved to be correct. Indeed, some observers are convinced that LTCM's intervention alone allowed this to take place – the ultimate self-fulfilling prophecy.

It is probably overstating things to say that Meriwether and the other principals at LTCM deliberately courted personal investment by high-net-worth individuals in leading Wall Street firms, or the involvement of central banks, as an insurance policy or to use in arm-twisting if the going got tough. But whether or not that was what they did, that is what turned out to be the result.

*   *   *

There are lessons for hedge fund managers and investors in the story of LTCM and its demise. One cardinal point is that however sophisticated the financial mathematics used, the indissoluble link between risk and return is as strong as ever. If a fund is taking seemingly riskless trades and generating returns that amount to 40% a year (as in LTCM's case), then risk is present somewhere.

If a trade seems riskless, it is simply because risk has assumed another form that has not been recognised by the trader. I will look at these ideas in more detail in Chapter 9. In LTCM's case the guise that risk assumed was liquidity risk. Former LTCM partner and Nobel laureate Myron Scholes, having lost a portion of his net worth as a result of the debacle, retired to academia for a while and made a study of the possibility that such liquidity risk could be reduced by the introduction of liquidity options. More recent reports have him back in the fray managing money.

The Federal Reserve took Scholes's new idea of liquidity options on board at the turn of the millennium, in the sense of issuing some in order to guarantee the provision of liquidity necessary for the financial system in the event of Y2K problems. But note that issuing liquidity options does not eliminate liquidity risk; it merely transfers it from one party to another. The seller of the options might be just as likely to go bust if called upon to honour the contract in times of a far-reaching financial panic.

So far as leverage is concerned, banks have reputedly cut back their lending to highly leveraged institutions such as hedge funds for the time being, but all past evidence on the behaviour of the banking system suggests these enthusiasms will return somehow in due course. The mistake from the banks' standpoint was not in this instance the lending itself, although with hindsight that was incautious enough. It was the incomplete knowledge that all the banks had about the fund's strategies or the size of its total positions, and hence the incomplete knowledge of the banks' own overall exposure to the fund.

In other words, everybody has had a bit of a fright, but memories in the financial markets are notoriously short. In due course executives will assume power at these institutions who have had no first-hand experience of these events, and who are therefore capable of making the same mistakes again, perhaps in a subtly different form. The impact of the fright has also been softened by the fact that the orderly liquidation of the LTCM portfolio has now been completed and the bailout money returned to the lending banks, all of which reinforces the argument that moral hazard has been embedded in the system.

Meriwether's new fund, JWM, is employing the same techniques as before, albeit with lower leverage and more emphasis placed on liquidity. As one member of the banking consortium put it in an interview with the *Financial Times*, the relaunch 'illustrates the ongoing vitality of the Wall Street system.' Others might describe it as the triumph of hope over experience, although Meriwether is reportedly chastened because his new fund failed to raise a hoped-for $1bn.

The more piquant question relates to moral hazard in a personal sense, and should perhaps be addressed to regulators and the senior management at leading banks. It concerns whether bank employment contracts should be tightened to prevent executives investing in such a way that their independence of action could be compromised, or perceived so. In the LTCM situation it is arguably the case that the personal investments by senior Wall Street figures in the fund ultimately acted to produce the optimum outcome for all concerned, but that may have been as much by accident as by design.

If the size of the fund had been less life threatening to the stability of the financial system but the personal conflicts of interest had still been present, would the same appropriate decisions have been made? It is impossible to say. Another big question is whether or not the officially sanctioned bailout of LTCM has stripped the American banking sector of its claim to have the moral high ground when dealing with small debtor nations, especially when it urges them to show the transparency and discipline that have been all too absent in this case.

Arguably it has. It is perhaps part of a broader dilemma in the US financial system where the economic and stock market bubble fed by borrowing has assumed such proportions that to puncture it risks triggering a severe economic decline, while repairing the leak (through Fed action to cut interest rates) means that the bubble inflates even more dangerously. This scenario will play out, with almost certain negative consequences at some stage in the future. Whether or not the collapse in technology stocks from March 2000 onwards has let enough air out of the bubble remains to be seen.

Perhaps the best last word on the collapse comes from Lou Corrigan, writing on the Motley Fool internet bulletin board at the time:

> Alan Greenspan was mistaken in believing that that the largely unregulated hedge fund industry can be effectively controlled by regulating creditors. As we have seen time and time again, creditors can be just as prone to greed as the latest wizard of Wall Street, but they are often the last to understand the risks that would ordinarily help fear counterbalance greed.

Another Lou, Lou Margolis, well-known as a former Salomon Brothers proprietary trader, is reported to have said, 'Whenever there is a financial fire, the same two characters are involved: leverage and mortgage-backed securities. If I was an arson investigator, I'd know who to go after.' This perhaps highlights the fact that LTCM has not been the only financial disaster to hit the hedge fund industry in recent years. In looking at some of these, it becomes quite obvious that the notion of arbitrage as a risk-free activity needs to be exploded once and for all. Leverage alone is only one part of the equation: the nature of arbitrage and the techniques practised by arbitrage specialists are the subject of the next chapter.

6

Toxic waste and vultures

If you can keep your head when all about you are losing theirs and blaming it on you . . .
Rudyard Kipling

All the courtesans of history were different, even if the differences were subtle and secret. And if you investigate arbitrage for any length of time, it becomes clear that arbitrageurs are multifaceted personalities, and far from uniform in their attributes.

One face of arbitrage is that of John Meriwether, whose travails are described at some length in Chapter 5. He fits the classic mould of the arbitrageur. Cool, detached, unemotional, adept at calculating the odds and the percentages. Many arbitrageurs share similar characteristics. Yet despite the scientific detachment and the seemingly innocuous idea behind arbitrage, Meriwether and colleagues still managed to threaten the global financial system with collapse in 1998.

Another side of the split personality of arbitrage is the one typified by Ivan Boesky, the renowned risk arbitrageur of the 1980s. Boesky resorted to inside information to gain his market edge, and he finished up behind bars, emerging like some Old Testament prophet, with a flowing white beard and a haunted expression.

The third way is typified by Michael Vranos. Vranos is less of a household name, but no less entertaining. Far from being unemotional and detached, most reports have Vranos slamming down phones, smashing furniture and bawling out associates during a four-year period running Kidder Peabody's mortgage-backed securities operation in the early 1990s.

Kidder was of course also the workplace of one Joe Jett, the trader who left the firm after a little local difficulty over the valuing of his extensive, and seemingly highly profitable, government bond trading positions. The conglomerate GE at that time owned Kidder. They sold it to Paine Webber after Jett's activities resulted in a huge write-off for the firm.

Vranos's distinction, apart from having been a Mr Teen Connecticut and having a penchant for four-letter expletives, was that in one banner year for Kidder he emerged with a pay packet of $115m, comfortably more than his ultimate boss 'Neutron Jack' Welch. This was even though Welch has been touted by some as the best chief executive of all time for his efforts at extracting returns from shareholders in GE's diverse and stodgy businesses.

Vranos's speciality, however, and the reason for mentioning his name in this context is that he was, and still is, the undisputed king of the mortgage-backed securities market. He has, more than any other individual, mastered the complex art of trading securities like this. Yet time and again, in the hands of others, mortgage-backed securities emerge as one of the villains of the piece when it comes to financial market disasters, whether at hedge funds or elsewhere. Seemingly innocuous, they have the power to blow a hole in even the biggest balance sheet.

*   *   *

Arbitrage has a long and distinguished history, and sounds like a conservative sort of activity – something you wouldn't mind your son-in-law getting into. Just one step removed from being an actuary or an accountant. The reality is a little different. If one were to analyse the major difference between the personalities mentioned previously and why they behaved like they did, one could come up with a single answer to fit all three sets of circumstances. The word is frustration, or perhaps boredom combined with frustration.

Meriwether's downfall was precipitated by the colossal leverage taken on to make returns that might otherwise have seemed puny look exciting. Boesky tired of making respectable profits on some transactions and losses on others, and he concluded that the way to liven up the action was to get an extra edge through inside information. Vranos's aggression while at Kidder fits the behaviour of the person who doesn't get his own way often enough. Testimony perhaps to the point made earlier that the best hedge fund managers are often individuals who are ill at ease working in large institutions, however large the rewards.

For some, arbitrage as an activity can contain a self-destructive impulse born of the tedium of continually attempting to produce the returns that investors might value from only the tiniest of opportunities. Tedium is, however, the least likely adjective to be applied to mortgage-backed securities arbitrage, which is very definitely not for the faint-hearted investor. Nor indeed is it for those with a dislike of complexity.

So complex and potentially volatile are these instruments that they have occasionally been nicknamed 'toxic waste' by those on the receiving end of their potentially hazardous characteristics. As an aside, this is a distinction they share, pretty much uniquely, with early 2000 dotcom IPOs and Russian government bonds – also in the past potentially hazardous to financial health.

Mortgage-backed securities are a peculiar subset of the investment scene, based around the concept of securitisation. Securitisation is the collecting together of various forms of loans or other obligations and turning them into securities that can be bought and sold by investors. Exercises of this type have been done with various types of consumer debt, including mortgages, credit card payments and car hire purchase loans. In the context of mortgage-backed securities, it means taking a pool of individual mortages and working with their essential component parts, interest payment streams and repayable principal amounts.

It is mortgages that have proved the most popular area for securitisation, because of the sheer size of the mortgage market and its relatively predictable nature. The market's size means that the securities created have a reasonable degree of liquidity.

While the mortgage market as a whole may be relatively predictable, it does contain some quirky features which contribute to the volatility of mortgage-backed securities. One of these features is that the person who has taken out the mortgage may have the option to refinance it at a lower rate of interest under certain circumstances. Another is that the mortgage may be paid off early if they decide to move house or get divorced, or if they should die.

These events can be assumed to happen with a reasonable degree of statistical precision, hence they can be allowed for in the way a securitised bond is designed, but there is less predictability in the option to refinance if interest rates fall. First, it is uncertain whether or not interest rates will fall or rise at any moment, although securities traders are well used to making judgements about this. But it is also unclear how householders might respond, say, to small changes in interest rates. However, the option that the householder has to refinance is precisely that, an option capable of being valued with some degree of accuracy. This is the missing piece of the jigsaw that underlies all mortgage-backed securities arbitrage.

So how does it work? The method goes something like this. A normal mortgage-backed security is issued in the United States, typically by one of the federal government sponsored mortgage banks, such as the exotically named Fanny Mae (FNMA, Federal National Mortgage Association) or Ginny Mae (GNMA, like her cousin Fanny but government rather than federal) or their relative Freddie Mac (FHLMC, Federal Home Loan Mortgage Association). These quasi-governmental agencies have high credit ratings, but investment banks and housebuilders also create mortgage-backed securities too.

Yet it seems the arbitrage community finds all this a little too straightforward. The idea devised by the arbitrageurs is based around packaging together a group of bonds issued by agencies like those mentioned in the preceding paragraph into a synthetic bundle known as a collateralised mortgage obligation (CMO). This entity, essentially a derivative (because its value derives from that of the underlying bonds which comprise it), is then split into several different securities with varying characteristics; the idea is to release additional value and create opportunities for arbitrage. In his book about the fall of LTCM, *Inventing Money*, Nick Dunbar describes the process like this:

In the real market these hidden options [to refinance a mortgage] were overpriced. Not understanding the nature of the embedded options, investors demanded a higher yield from the issuers than they needed to. . . . LTCM would buy up mispriced mortgage-backs and replicate the bits and pieces inside them.

Once the pieces were assembled, the various risks inherent in the bonds were separated and identified: (1) interest rates would rise, (2) the yield curve would steepen (i.e. it would get relatively costlier to borrow for long periods than for shorter periods), and particularly (3) homeowners would exercise their option to repay the loan early.

Then using readily available securities, such as Treasury bonds, swaps and Treasury bond options, these risks were insured against, or 'hedged out'. Once the cost of the 'insurance' had been deducted, the extra value that remained could be quantified. This represented the potential profit for the arbitrageur, in this case LTCM.

While this sounds logical, even relatively simple, the mathematical problem for arbitrageurs and investors to solve when dealing in mortgage-backed securities is not a straightforward one. This is because, human ingenuity being what it is, a quest for returns has resulted in the creation of ever more exotic variations on them. Needless to say, the variants with the largest potential for arbitrage profit are also those that are the riskiest and most volatile.

To illustrate the Byzantine complexity of the mortgage-backed securities market, and why it tripped up even some of the supposedly most astute brains in the business, consider some of the securities that can be created from a group of common or garden home loans. In a collateralised mortgage obligation (CMO), for example, there can be sharp variations in the way in which risks and returns are allocated. A simple case might be that one class of bond might rank ahead of the rest for receiving principal repayments.

In a more complex scenario one class of stock might have to bear all of the early repayments up to a certain point, after which other classes have to take the brunt of them. Some securities are constituted as so-called strips, formed by carving up the bond's characteristics into two types of securities, one of which receives all the interest payments (interest-only, or IO), and the other just receives repayment of principal at the end of the bond's term (principal-only, or PO). POs are normally bought at a substantial discount to face value, receiving their return in the form of capital appreciation as redemption of the bonds nears. Other variants include inverse floaters (interest-only strips whose value paradoxically rises when interest rates fall) and other weird and wonderful stuff.

Frank Partnoy's book, *Fiasco*, about his experience of derivatives trading at Morgan Stanley, contains a wonderful description of so-called IO-ettes, another vicious beast in the mortgage-backed jungle. These securities were formed largely from IOs but had a tiny embedded sliver of POs. The complexities involved in creating them produced what was a stressful, complex but ultimately highly profitable trade for the bank. Because mortgage-backed securities trading is essentially a zero-sum game – one person's gain is another's loss – they were possibly a somewhat less exciting experience for those on the other side of the trade. Partnoy claims that in one of these trades alone, the bank made some $75m in fees and profits.

More generally, the underlying reason banks create this gamut of mortgage-backed securities, and find buyers for them, is because investors take different views about the risk of early repayment, and the risk of interest rates rising or falling. There is money to be made by mortgage-backed hedge fund arbitrageurs, because of the complexity of the instruments. For the most astute, the returns can be reasonably predictable and enhanced by the use of leverage. For others, disaster waits lurking in the wings.

The market is a tough one to call because not only are the securities involved complex, but their pricing is far from transparent. The banks that create the securities may be the only institutions prepared to deal in them, creating potential liquidity problems and, as a rash of scandals has attested, traders are apt in some instances to play fast and loose with their valuation models to flatter their own performance and improve their bonuses.

Last of all, the spread, or difference in yield, between the underlying mortgage bonds and the benchmark Treasury bonds with which they tend to be compared, ought to be consistent most of the time. But in times of crisis it is unlikely to be the case. And small movements in the spread with the equivalent Treasury bond can have major implications for the value of these exotic securities. Partnoy puts it like this:

> Every investment bank has multimillion dollar computer models for valuing CMO derivatives. Yet, even when modelled correctly, some of the most volatile CMOs can become worthless almost instantly. Victims of CMOs have ranged from tiny municipalities, who experimented with the exotic bonds, to the most sophisticated CMO funds.

Perhaps the most celebrated instance of death by toxic waste was Askin Capital Management.

*   *   *

David Askin ran a fund called Granite, the main constituent of the Askin Capital Management stable. Granite's performance was, however, far from rock-like. Worth around $600m in its heyday, the value of the fund went to zero almost overnight following the effect of toxic waste on its portfolio of mortgage-backed instruments. A mid-1998 article in *Worth* magazine offered this assessment: 'Askin doted on CMOs' most volatile bits, dubbed toxic waste by Wall Street wags. But in March 1994, following a string of interest rate hikes by the Federal Reserve, the value of that waste plummeted, and the Granite funds imploded.'

On the surface, it seems like a straightforward case of misreading the market, but according to *Fiasco*, there was an element of computer error as well: 'Askin based the value of its CMOs on what the computer model said they were worth, not what the market said they were worth. Unfortunately, its computer model was slightly inaccurate. With volatile CMOs, even a small error can be fatal, and for Askin it was.'

Askin, described at the time as scholarly, soft-spoken and egotistical, took over the Granite fund in 1990 after a successful career at Drexel Burnham & Lambert. The fund's parent at the time was Whitehead Sterling Advisers, a posh money management firm controlled at one time by a biomedical industrialist called Edwin Whitehead. The fund was sold to Askin following Whitehead's death.

More interesting perhaps is that Askin, clearly a persuasive individual, attracted an impressive list of investors in the fund. These included Nicholas J. Nicholas, former president of Time Warner, his colleague James Gray, David Chemerow, chief financial officer of Playboy Enterprises, and a partnership headed by Isadore Pines, a big cheese in kosher food and chairman of National Foods. Several institutional investors in the fund also lost money, including the 3M pension plan and Minnesota Power and Light. Why Askin had the knack of attracting institutions based in Minnesota is unclear.

Askin's problem may have been an unduly close relationship with the producers of the toxic waste in which he invested. Kidder Peabody, its mortgage desk at that time headed by Mike Vranos, Bear Stearns and Donaldson Lufkin all sold large amounts of CMOs to Askin. They subsequently seized and liquidated Granite's portfolios when it failed to meet margin calls. The whole affair then descended into a messy courtroom dispute in which allegations were made that the brokers had provided artificially high valuations for the securities in order to inflate Granite's performance.

There was a suggestion that Bear Stearns' dealing-room tapes were deliberately erased, in violation of a court order for their preservation as evidence. The broker claimed at the time that the tapes were erased accidentally by a junior employee while the executive responsible was away on holiday.

In the wake of the Askin debacle, and the resulting nuclear winter in the toxic waste market, Vranos left Kidder, reputedly having decided it was much better to be an investor than a dealer. It was an astute move, made at a time when the market was depressed. He set up Ellington Mortgage Partners with an initial $30m from a handful of investors. At the time of the LTCM debacle, there were rumours about the likely chances of Ellington's survival (or more precisely that it might not survive), but if indeed it ever was in danger, it appears to have pulled through. Ellington's two main funds are currently worth some $500m in total.

Subsequently, in mid 2000, Ellington filed a lawsuit against UBS Warburg, claiming that panic at the investment bank caused them to force Ellington to liquidate investments at a loss following the collapse of LTCM, contrary to the terms of repo contracts between the two. At the last count, the suit was being vigorously contested. Until this point, Ellington and Vranos must have been doing something right: the fund chalked up 32 consecutive monthly gains. It has also since gone from strength to strength. Ellington's edge is reckoned to be in its hedging expertise, crucial in a market like this, and founded on a band of high-powered mathematicians, many of which also previously worked at Kidder.

That it pulled through the LTCM crisis suggests its hedging policies – designed to lock in the arbitrage profit inherent in the bonds they trade – actually work, while the monthly income stream typically generated by the mortgage bonds produces much steadier returns than many other funds. In short, Vranos is someone you feel you should dislike for his reputed dealing-room histrionics, but a man who is actually running a fairly conservative operation with a technical edge over the rest of the market.

So perhaps, in fact, the toxic waste tag is something of a misnomer. Dion Friedland, chairman of Magnum Funds, a large fund of funds firm, writes in their favour. He says their attributes include a 1–2% advantage in yield over the equivalent Treasury bond, a wide range of products, high credit quality (deriving from the underlying agency which pools the mortgages), and liquidity. All of which goes to prove that it takes serious human ingenuity and mismanagement to turn products like this into a recipe for losing money fast.

Their drawback, which Friedland acknowledges, is unpredictable movement in the spread between them and Treasury bond benchmarks, as David Askin and his investors would bear out.

*   *   *

In the end, the downfall of all the arbitrageurs who have come to grief in the last few years amounts to much the same thing. This was an overreliance on suspect computer models and a lack of common sense in appreciating liquidity risk. David Shaw is another obsessively secretive computer whizz who ended up torpedoing the balance sheet of one of the largest banks in America.

Described in one newspaper article as a cross between Einstein, Midas and Rasputin, Shaw, a chiselled 48-year-old, was a Columbia University computer science professor before he got into the even more arcane world of finance and arbitrage. Shaw graduated from Stanford in 1980, where he rubbed shoulders with some of the hi-tech industry's elite. In the 'damning by faint praise' manner of some academics, he was considered bright and competent, but not outstanding.

Fresh from building supercomputers, Shaw embarked on an exploration of the world of statistical arbitrage, a technique that models the relationships between different types of securities and how they might be expected to behave over time. Subtly different from conventional arbitrage, which exploits *actual* price differences minute by minute, the Shaw method exploits the closing of gaps some way in the future – based on the statistical analysis of price performance of the securities concerned under similar circumstances in the past.

Whatever the technicalities, Shaw, like Askin, attracted a raft of affluent investors, among them a major insurance company. The firm set up shop in a loft in Greenwich Village. Ironically enough, for a firm that at its height used to account for more than 5% of the trading on the New York Stock Exchange, it was located above a communist bookstore. Over long periods, Shaw's fund earned annual returns consistently in the 18% area and by 1996 the fund had grown to around $600m, from $28m eight years previously.

One can speculate that if Shaw had simply stuck to proprietary hedge fund trading, things might have turned out differently. In fact, he added on software development to his list of accomplishments, and entered into a joint venture with Bank of America, supplying what appears to have been an outsourced proprietary trading and arbitrage service for the bank.

In 1998 the LTCM debacle and associated contagion in the markets meant that Shaw faced the possibility of going under. He chose to hand back the proprietary trading business's portfolio to Bank of America and wind down the joint venture. The bank, subsequently taken over by NationsBank, took a hit of some $370m on the nominal $20bn value of the positions Shaw had open at that time. The software businesses have been sold, one of them to Merrill Lynch.

Shaw is reportedly now content to run a hedge fund based around strict quantitative principles, and no less hostile to the idea of talking to the press. All employees sign non-disclosure agreements. Shaw admits that the problem he had not foreseen was liquidity risk. Quoted in a rare interview in the *Financial Times* in October 1998 he said, 'We were aware of this risk, but I don't think any of us realised just how bad the avalanche could be. . . . If we had known how bad things were going to get, we would have had smaller positions.'

* * *

In some senses the hedge fund community has it both ways. If dabbling in toxic waste blows such a hole in their balance sheet that it drives a bank into a shotgun wedding with a competitor, or a company to the brink of extinction, the vulture capitalists move in to make sure they make money too.

The mechanics of distressed security investing are described in an earlier chapter but a logical description of the techniques involved does not convey the full flavour of the market. Briefly to recap, distressed securities trading is usually grouped together in a hedge fund category euphemistically described as event-driven. One of the events is bankruptcy or near-bankruptcy and the other event is takeover arbitrage, two different but related extremes of the securities business. Returns from event-driven risk arbitrage are usually pretty reliable.

Bankruptcies (and takeovers for that matter) tend to follow distinct patterns and have defined risks to which can be assigned probabilities. Research improves the odds, and it is within the power of the players concerned to influence events their way. Takeover arbitrageurs gang up together to put pressure on bidders to sweeten the terms, for instance, while distressed debt traders attempt to influence creditor committees.

What distressed debt traders rely on is that most investors recoil from bankruptcies in horror, or are forced to do so by their trustees and investment committees. This forced selling of securities because of bankruptcy or pending bankruptcy produces anomalies that the patient and knowledgeable investor can exploit. Distressed debt traders are also adept at finding loopholes or hidden covenants in bond trust deeds and the like, anomalies which others have not spotted and which can influence the price of a security or the bargaining power of those who hold them.

Distressed debt traders, as well as doing their financial and legal homework, have to be pretty resilient and able to play rough if necessary. They are often also larger than life characters, on occasion keen to use the press to put their case across and influence events. Their names and exploits are well known in US financial circles. An excellent book, *The Vulture Investors* by Hilary Rosenberg, covers the area in some detail, outlining not only the character of those involved, but also their painstaking methods.

The names include Michael Price, the scourge of Chase Manhattan (now wedded to J. P. Morgan in a classic 'top of the market' merger), Ronald LaBow, closely involved in the restructuring of Wheeling Pittsburgh Steel, Japonica's Paul Kazarian, who made a tilt at the household goods conglomerate Allegheny International, Carl Icahn, a legendary corporate raider and a key player in deals over the insurer Reliance Group and the Trump casino empire, and Sam Zell, the self-styled 'grave dancer' whose speciality has been spotting overlooked value in the real-estate assets of bankrupt corporations.

A look at a couple of other players in the event-driven field illustrates how the game works.

*   *   *

The doyen of European distressed debt traders is (or was) undoubtedly Gary Klesch, a legendary operator who had the distinction of doing (or at least he claims to have done) the first leveraged buyout in Europe.

Over the years he has specialised both in vulture capitalism and venture capitalism. He was, for example, a thorn in the side of Eurotunnel in its attempts to restructure. Those with long memories for the detail of such things will recall that Klesch found an obscure clause in a bond trust deed which enabled him to extract a dramatically better price for the debt he had bought, by threatening to block an urgently needed proposed capital reconstruction. This left the French side of the Eurotunnel partnership aghast yet again at the antics of Anglo-Saxon capitalism.

Though resident in Europe for many years, Klesch is actually an American. The orphaned son of a professional boxer, Klesch began his career as a corporate vulture in the unlikely setting of Cleveland, Ohio, at McDonald & Co., a regional investment bank. A bright spark, he was made a partner in the firm at the age of 24.

He also worked in government, appointed by then President Gerald Ford as director of capital markets policy at the US Treasury, responsible for formulating policy on the future development of capital markets, including the deregulation of the financial markets in the United States in 1975. To those on the receiving end of the whirlwind this unleashed on Wall Street, it may seem like describing Stalin as a Russian politician – accurate but not quite conveying the full meaning. After sorting out Wall Street, Klesch was also involved in the reconstruction of the US railroad industry prompted by the collapse of Penn Central.

After this influential flirtation with public service, Mammon took the upper hand again and Klesch joined Smith Barney in Paris in 1978 and was later president of Dean Witter in London. He set up a leveraged buyout business, Quadrex, in 1983 and embarked on a series of deals, especially with companies in need of major reconstruction or, as the *Economist* put it in 1998, 'preying on Europe's troubled companies'. In recent years Quadrex has metamorphosed into Klesch & Company, primarily now a private equity fund based at a chichi town house in Mayfair, an upmarket London address, and Klesch has adopted more modest goals than some of his 1980s forays.

These earlier moves included trying to take over Olivetti's personal computer business and attempting to break up the media giant

Pearson, owner of the *Financial Times* and the *Economist*, among other organs. Styling himself a champion of shareholder rights in the face of incompetent management and City vested interests, he has brought back a number of companies from the dead. Of late his ventures have included a French shoe business, a Scottish book distributor, and a pair of financially threadbare lingerie companies.

Klesch is a unique animal in the hedge fund business: part company doctor, part distressed debt fund manager, part private equity entrepreneur. His hedge fund vehicle, Klesch Capital Partners, is based in Bermuda and has launched a number of funds aiming to invest in distressed companies in Europe, not least because returns are higher than is now the norm in the United States. Klesch welcomes the advent of the euro because it removes an element of foreign exchange risk for his operations and because it shines a spotlight on the corporate inefficiencies that have built up over decades, if not centuries, of statist-style cosseting and lax labour laws. Or, as Klesch might put it, it exposes companies with 'inefficient work practices and poor management, along with weak capital bases, and onerous debt burdens.'

As one might suppose, he is not universally popular although many, myself included, find him engaging and entertaining. Those who have run foul of his methods or accord him only grudging respect, like the author of an *Economist* profile on him, are wont to point out that one of his favourite books is a slim volume detailing the exceptions to the rules of golf. This, they might claim, is something of a commentary on the way he approaches the investigation of bankrupt company trust deeds.

*   *   *

Klesch is, however, not the only larger than life character among the ranks of vulture capitalists. Another is Leon Black. Black, according to an article a few years ago in *Business Week*, is universally dubbed Doctor No on Wall Street because he is notoriously picky about the deals he will invest in. One of his coups, and a measure of the man:

seizing control of some prestigious New York properties from the legendary Reichmann brothers in the wake of the reconstruction of Olympia & York (O&Y).

The Reichmanns have developed properties all over North America. Leading light Paul Reichmann was the visionary behind the construction of London's huge waterfront office development at Canary Wharf. But Black's New York deal with the Reichmanns was just as special and just as visionary in its own way. The deal was worth $100m in the autumn of 1996. Estimates of the buildings' value now are put at several times that figure. Black's company, Apollo Advisers, is arguably on the margins of the hedge fund universe. But it is nonetheless a huge business. Estimates suggest that Black at any one time has upwards of £1.5bn to invest, a sum he has recycled several times in recent years.

Black's deal-cutting skills were honed as head of mergers and acquisitions at Drexel Burnham, which achieved notoriety in the 1980s as the home of junk bond artist Mike Milken. He was, however, born with business genes. His father was Eli Black, a rabbi who turned businessman. Black Senior committed suicide by jumping from a 44th floor window in midtown Manhattan one day in February 1975, leaving his family if not destitute then at least less comfortable than they might have been.

Black was educated at the prestigious Dartmouth College, majoring in philosophy, and Harvard, which he says he loathed. He claims he learnt more about business from studying Shakespeare than from Harvard Business School. In the wake of the collapse of Drexel, few were in such a good position to evaluate the debt of the now somewhat distressed former corporate clients of Mike Milken's junk bond department, although Black has always vehemently denied that he capitalised on inside knowledge to get a head start for his firm. His edge actually comes from his slightly different style of doing business. Black is probably unique in his willingness to cooperate with creditors in the interests of getting a deal done, and willing to share some of his gains.

In the O&Y example, Apollo bought the debt being sold by those who wanted to exit, for 50% of its face value. He left himself with several options: one was a charge on and therefore possible ownership of the buildings; the second was that the coupon on the bonds was enhanced by the fact that it had been bought at half face value; a more remote option was that he might even gain total control of the portfolio. Any of the three events produced an attractive return, the only downside risk being a prolonged recession in the New York economy.

Black's due diligence paid off. He investigated the attitude of the buildings' tenants and a variety of other variables, arriving at the view that the buildings' rental stream was secure. Quoted in the *Business Week* article, an O&Y executive is reported as saying of Apollo's involvement, 'Everybody had the same opportunity they did. . . . But no one else had the guts to do it.' In the end, an agreement was reached to divide up the assets, with Black gaining the O&Y building at 245 Park Avenue and another large property, the Sperry building on the Avenue of the Americas.

The buildings themselves had been part of a property portfolio originally picked up by the Reichmanns in 1976 for a song (only a cash payment of $50m for eight mortgaged buildings). Known as the Uris package, from the original developers, the buildings were later acquired by Edward Minskoff, a real-estate broker. Though hawked around, they represented some of the best addresses in the city. For Black, the later deal was a textbook example of distressed debt trading. It probably also contained a heavy element of tragic irony for him. The buildings had been bought by the Reichmanns – later to be sold to Black – in the middle of the city's depression that had driven his own father to suicide.

Black has had his failures too. Notably there was a little local difficulty in the restaurant business when Apollo found itself owning a Mexican-style restaurant chain at a time when nutritionists slated Mexican food as unhealthy and temporarily decimated the customer base. The restaurant company's management then compounded the error by switching to blander alternatives that didn't have customer appeal either.

But the failures are outnumbered by the successes. More recently, in late 1999, Black scored a coup by acting as midwife to the birth of a major consolidation play in the building maintenance area. This story began in April 1999 when Apollo helped finance a highly leveraged recapitalisation of Building One, a Minneapolis-based 'janitorial services' business. As part of the deal, Apollo received $105m of convertible subordinated notes.

At the end of a complex series of manoeuvres, Apollo and Black ended up owning the rights to convert into around 22% of the enlarged company after Building One merged with the Houston-based Group Maintenance. His effective shareholding increased from the 15% it held in the smaller company. This deal followed quickly on the heels of Apollo's taking of a profit from the sale of Alliance Imaging, in which Apollo had folded its stake in another health-related business. Here Apollo's combined investment of $72m eventually produced a profit in the region of $200m after Kohlberg Kravis Roberts and several other private equity bidders ended up competing for the prize.

* * *

Black and Klesch, not to mention others like Sam Zell, Ronald LaBow and Carl Icahn, aren't the only players in this rather esoteric area. Another is Marc Lasry, who owns Amroc Investments. Amroc styles itself as America's largest independent broker of distressed bank loans and junk bonds. Lasry set up shop in 1988 with the backing of financier Robert Bass, whom he bought out in 1990, converting the firm from a conventional hedge fund into a broker.

Notwithstanding the highly publicised and, until recently, durable boom in the American economy, distressed debt is booming, with corporate defaults at an all-time high. This has arisen thanks to problems produced by the predilection for financing deals with copious amounts of leverage, share buy-backs draining cash, banks' habit of dumping bad loans, and other troubles. Even in the good times, a high proportion of leveraged buyouts (LBOs) end up in receivership, a fact not usually highlighted by those promoting them to corporate management teams.

Lasry estimates the volume of trading in dodgy debt is now 10 or 20 times what the firm saw at the start of the 1990s, thanks in part to a sixfold increase in the size of the junk bond market to around $750bn. Default rates are currently rocketing. The size of bank loans out to highly leveraged companies, and therefore susceptible to the attentions of distressed debt traders in extreme circumstances, could be as much as $1trn on top of $750bn junk bond piece. In another of the industry's dirty little secrets, Lasry reckons that around $25–50bn of this debt trades at a discount of anything up to 20%.

Amroc's role now is to service the needs of hedge funds investing in this area. Its competitors, few and far between at one time, are now the likes of Goldman Sachs, Merrill and Bear Stearns, and even some of the commercial banks responsible for the original loans – another neat, if ironic, twist of capital market logic.

Troubled LBOs seem to figure prominently in any list of distressed debt. When I wrote the first draft of this chapter, the classic play was in the trendy clothing maker Fruit of the Loom. The reason for the play's attraction sheds an interesting light on the way the market works. Fruit's loans in October 1999 were selling at around 65% of face value, the lenders having injected more money in July 1999 with the crucial proviso that the new money would be secured on the company's assets. Previous loans were unsecured and ranked alongside rather than ahead of the company's bonds in any liquidation.

By law, however, if the company were to file for bankruptcy within three months of the new loans being issued, secured status would be revoked. This shows the dilemma faced by distressed debt traders, or more particularly it shows where their specialist knowledge comes into play. Buyers of the debt were betting that the company would survive past this date without filing for bankruptcy. If it did survive then the loans, backed by security, would become worth close to par value. In the event, they did survive, but only for a time. Fruit of the Loom eventually went bankrupt in December 1999.

The real point is that distressed debt traders thrive when times are tough and when poorly managed companies get into trouble. Lasry says,

'When times are good we do well. When times are bad, we do extremely well. There aren't many asset classes you can say that about.'

Lasry's view raises an interesting question. If his business is booming now, what might happen to it in the wake of a recession-hit economy and a precipitous stock market collapse? Those with a long view might recall the depths of the early 1970s bear market in the UK, when convertible debt in the UK's Grand Metropolitan hotels and brewing group could have been picked up at a 50% discount to face value. What sellers of the bonds in this instance had overlooked was that, even if the implied call option represented by the conversion feature was worthless, the bonds were still secured on the company's assets and therefore likely to be paid out at par in the event of liquidation. It never came to that, and the bonds soared in price when the corner was turned.

* * *

Returns from the event-driven style of hedge fund have been fairly good on the whole. According to Hedge Fund Research, over an almost ten-year span to August 2000, distressed securities as a group showed an annualised return averaging around 20% with a standard deviation of under 6%. The years 1990, 1994 and 1998 itself (especially the end of 1998 with the LTCM problem) were 'off' years. In 1999 the return was some 17%. Returns at this level or better seem likely in the years ahead. Delight at the misfortunes of others is some-times considered a distasteful characteristic. But profiting from such human frailties as an addiction to leverage is surely a neat counter-point to the foibles of the rest of the hedge fund industry.

Profiting from the frailties and weakness of emerging economies, as so-called global macro funds have occasionally sought to do, has an altogether more controversial flavour. That is the subject of the next chapter.

7

Highwaymen of the global economy

Hedge funds have become the privileged children of the international financial scene, being entitled to the benefits of free markets without any of the responsibilities

Ian Macfarlane, Governor of the Reserve Bank of Australia

It can perhaps be disputed that the courtesans of history harmed the vulnerable. Hedge funds have a harder task disproving the theory that they damage those least able to care for themselves. Hedge funds are intertwined with global markets. While many hedge funds pursue their activities solely and quite profitably within the confines of the US securities markets, others see the world as their casino, with currencies, economies, stocks, commodities and other staples acting as the gambling chips.

Certain funds, mainly the so-called global macro funds – among the highest-profile examples were some of the funds operated by the Soros group and by Julian Robertson's Tiger Management – regard any market, wherever it might be located, as fair game for their activities. This includes shorting currencies perceived to be vulnerable and other practices that can have a brutal effect on the economies on the receiving end.

Now and again, the tables are turned and governments stand up to the bully-boy tactics of hedge funds and send them off with a bloody nose, as happened in the case of Hong Kong. Like bullies, there is evidence that hedge funds gang up on the seven-stone weakling economies to do their worst. Other hedge fund investors befriend the underdogs of global markets. These are more specialist funds and focus specifically on investing in emerging markets, generally acting as long-only investors attempting to spot value that may have been ignored by others because of the inadequate information available generally on these investments.

It is self-evident that the interests of these two categories of investor are not necessarily aligned, although emerging market specialists may be able to pick up stocks at bargain basement prices in the wake of the depredations wrought by macro funds on a currency and an economy. Generally they are patient long-term investors who ride out the volatility generated by the actions of others. Do these two groups talk to each other? Probably they don't.

Indeed emerging market funds have little for which to thank the big macro funds. In early May 2000 there was a bout of selling of emerging market debt attributed to the Soros group's decision to move away from risky macro investment. It came in the wake of decisions by several emerging market funds to wind up or restructure their portfolios. Emerging market economies are the poorer for the lack of involvement by mainstream funds investing in their securities: the volatility induced by the activities of the macro funds in the past may have been partly to blame.

As the demise of LTCM showed, the idea that markets can be insulated from each other is totally bogus. The collapse of a fund primarily invested in US fixed-income securities can affect emerging markets by triggering a flight to quality which will affect the securities denominated in emerging market currencies particularly acutely. Similarly, it is fair to say that it was events in emerging markets, notably the Russian default in August 1998, which triggered the LTCM debacle.

George Soros, doyen of hedge fund traders, philanthropist and self-styled philosopher, has said in evidence to official bodies that he does not believe individual hedge funds are sufficiently large to be able to influence currency markets other than in the very short term. At best this comment is disingenuous. Even in the short term a lot of damage can be done. Raids on currencies are typically over within a few days, as was the case with the ERM debacle in September 1992. The remark also does not take account of the fact that mounting a raid on sterling or the dollar might be difficult to pull off, but a similar raid on the more thinly traded currency of an emerging market economy is a different matter entirely.

Similarly, it is not unknown for hedge funds to hunt in packs, following each other into selling short a currency that the actions of one fund have highlighted to be vulnerable. Even if the collective financial muscle of the hedge funds themselves is not sufficient to tip the scale, larger institutions, such as the in-house trading desks of large global banks, often follow suit. Once a currency starts to crack, other effects make the process unstoppable, effects such as the calling in of loans by foreign lenders.

Encouraging others to follow suit is arguably essential to the way hedge funds function in markets like this. Through targeting markets that are small relative to their own size, and precipitating the collapse as other institutions follow suit, hedge funds can produce the desired effect, say a devaluation, while committing a position sufficiently modest to be reversed after the event with a reasonable degree of assurance that sufficient liquidity will be present.

Some call this the information cascade effect, where investors acting later do so because they assume that those preceding them (the hedge funds) may have better information, generating a self-fulfilling herd reaction. The hedge fund may then close the short position relatively early, buying back while the tail-enders are still selling, and unwittingly providing the necessary liquidity.

The case studies that follow show the way in which hedge funds have acted to put pressure on certain countries and currencies. The justification after the event is normally that they were only helping along what market forces would have accomplished anyway. Sometimes it is claimed that the resulting crisis had the effect of producing beneficial economic reform, or removing the cronyism and politically directed investment said to be rampant in these economies.

Though some minimise the extent of the lasting damage done by these actions, observation of the consequences, in terms of political instability and economic hardship for the person in the street, can scarcely be denied. Investment bankers and hedge fund managers are typically unsympathetic. One says, 'If you accept that an adjustment is necessary, hedge funds merely accelerate the process. Is that worse than a death by 1000 cuts?' A fund of funds manager observes more brutally, 'Markets can have no responsibility for unintended consequences. It's just the ecosystem. You have to accept it.'

The fact remains that, however necessary some form of economic reform may be, the impact of the actions of hedge funds in this manner typically exaggerates the process and makes it more brutal than it need be. Even if one accepts that the impact of hedge funds has beneficial effects by promoting much needed reform, it is hardly necessary or appropriate for them to take the credit for this, since this was scarcely their motivation at the outset.

The reality is that the effect of hedge fund raids on emerging currencies is damaging the prospects for the economy in the long term. It arguably raises the barriers to the country pursuing its future economic goals. It may drive it into a protectionist economic stance, or provide ammunition for political demagogues. In either case it can only damage future trade and so affect the rest of the world, albeit perhaps in a small way.

* * *

Opinions differ on the role of the hedge fund community, or rather certain of its more prominent funds, in precipitating the Asian currency crisis in 1997 and 1998. One can take one's choice as to which account is believed, but the evidence suggests that both hedge funds and bank proprietary trading desks actively speculated against the Thai baht in mid 1997 and later moved on to attack, unsuccessfully, the Hong Kong dollar. Consider this comment on the bulletin board at the Chapman Spira web site:

> Hedge funds are like sharks, touring the water looking towards the sick, the lame and dying for their next meal. The sharks do not pollute the waters in

which they live: that would affect them as well. They are among the oldest living creatures on earth and didn't earn their longevity by ignorance.

Hedge funds, much as sharks, are constantly chumming for currencies that are too high, governments that don't understand economics, banking infrastructures that allow bad loans to be treated as performing, places that reward incompetence and poor work ethic. Having fixed on a target they can be as unwavering as the shark.

The origins of the crisis arguably dated back to 1994, when the US government on the basis of some long-forgotten objective fostered a policy of encouraging foreign investment in the economies of East and Southeast Asia. Some $77bn in investment went into Asia in 1995 and a further $93bn in 1996. Countries were encouraged to peg their currencies to the dollar, allowing investors to invest and banks to lend money in the local currency with some perceived degree of security.

After the crash, the IMF and others castigated these countries for their profligacy, but one would have to conclude that they were considerably encouraged in this profligacy, if profligacy there was, and they could be forgiven for feeling a little piqued at the eventual outcome as the sharks began to circle.

The shark attack in Asia appears to have followed a sequence of events something like this. In 1996 and 1997 the bubbles – largely generated by a US-induced influx of foreign investment – burst in the Thai stock and property markets. Foreign banks were heavily exposed to Thailand, again having previously been encouraged in this position. As we have seen before, banks need few excuses to join a bandwagon, and this was one they joined as enthusiastically as ever.

Suddenly, the wheels began to come off. The banks realised that many of the loans they had were unprotected, should there be a devaluation of the baht. The profitability of the loans depended on the exchange value of the baht-holding firm. In other words, the maintenance of the peg to the dollar was vital. So, at the first sign of weakness in the currency, they were primed to head for the exit.

This is when the issue of hedge funds being able to influence markets comes into play. While they may or may not have had sufficient firepower to drive down the value of the currency for anything other than a short time, they were able to drive it down sufficiently to panic the banks in selling, quickly exhausting the country's foreign exchange reserves and precipitating the devaluation.

In fact, in the case of Thailand, the available reserves were much less than the market had been led to believe by the authorities, hence the currency was more vulnerable than it may have appeared at first sight. In Korea the same turned out to be the case, with some sources describing the misrepresentation by the authorities as being even more flagrant.

The IMF, which entered Thailand with a support package in August 1997, has minimised the role of the hedge funds in the collapse, saying that they were in the situation late and closed out their positions shortly after the collapse. In the light of subsequent comments by MIT professor Paul Krugman, comments from Tiger Management and general anecdotal evidence, this does seem unlikely.

The fact that the hedge funds closed out their positions shortly after the collapse of the baht is hardly evidence that they were not involved. Early closing is a natural precautionary measure for short sellers, who may be worried about the development of a classic 'short squeeze' (a sharp adverse price movement) if they delay the exit for too long.

In fact, not only has the IMF acted as a verbal defender of hedge funds, its own actions have been called into question. Jeffrey Sachs, professor of economics at Harvard, describes the IMF's heavy-handed measures in Thailand as the equivalent of 'screaming fire in the theatre', with the predictable effect of people getting trampled underfoot.

In October of that year, Taiwan instituted a relatively small devaluation, essentially as a precautionary measure (given its sizeable foreign currency reserves). But the measure had the effect of focusing attention on possible devaluation candidates elsewhere in East Asia (acting as a 'firebridge' in the evocative description of one commentator), with Korea and Hong Kong singled out as the obvious candidates. In effect, Taiwan's action was the conduit along which the problem spread from a localised Southeast Asian problem to affect the entire region.

The effect, in countries like Korea, was to see bankers attempt to liquidate their loans to prevent their being damaged by depreciation in the currency. The result of this action was that good firms as well as bad went under or else were forced to take extreme measures to raise cash to meet their obligations: withholding payments from suppliers, selling goods below cost, laying off employees.

Banks absolved themselves of responsibility for the mess by claiming that 'crony capitalism' was at fault. True up to a point, the position was also exaggerated by official misrepresentation about the country's foreign currency reserves. What may have been more at fault was the actions of the banks themselves first in lending so incautiously to these economies and denominating the loans in local currency, and then in allowing their investment banking arms to indirectly finance hedge fund short selling, a small dose of which in Thailand had the effect of triggering a domino effect across much of Asia.

The IMF, according to some of its many critics, essentially misdiagnosed the problem that many of these economies were experiencing. The problem was not a payments imbalance brought about by excessive consumption, but rather the reverse. Foreign loans had encouraged the creation of excess capacity and were causing debt deflation and a liquidity crisis triggered by externally created currency instability. In other words, hedge funds' destabilising of the currency made matters worse.

Because of the nature of the crisis, raising interest rates would not have the effect of reversing the capital flows into the country. Confidence was at such low ebb that no rate would be high enough to tempt investors back. At the same time, the IMF required a sharp rise in bank capital adequacy standards, the middle of a liquidity crisis hardly being the best time to contemplate such far-reaching reforms. The result of this was predictable: less credit and more bankruptcies.

Malaysia has had none of this. Its response, having seen the problems elsewhere, was to institute capital controls and effectively to take the ringgit out of the international currency trading system. Interestingly enough, Malaysia modelled these controls, which are designed to minimise short-term capital flows, explicitly on those adopted by

China. Malaysia may have seen the way in which China avoided any involvement in the Asian currency crisis, yet continued to attract substantial direct investment.

This is not to say that China has completely escaped the backwash from hedge fund activity. A mysterious event serves as an example. In early May 2000, Li Fuxiang, a protégé of the Chinese premier and a senior currency official, fell to his death from a window on the seventh floor of a hospital in Beijing. Reports in Chinese language newspapers in Hong Kong suggested that his apparent suicide might have been linked to 'inappropriate activities' at his office. Some observers connected the fact that his death occurred after a substantial correction in US equity markets and that Mr Li was personally acquainted with the managers of some US hedge funds.

Back in Malaysia, however, one of the reasons the country was able to turn away from the official financial community – much of which trilled its disapproval and predicted dire consequences (which have not materialised) – is that it has one of the highest savings ratios in the world. This is in sharp contrast to that bastion of capitalism, the United States. Hence Malaysia had little immediate need of external capital in either the short or the longer term. Foreign investors withdrew $2.6bn in the second half of 2000, but Malaysia's stock market is capitalised at $112bn or so.

Prime Minister Mahathir Mohamed's actions in Malaysia essentially pre-empted the hedge funds from doing their worst with the Malaysian currency. Hong Kong's situation was different. At the time of the raid on the baht, the Hong Kong dollar appeared on the face of it overexposed in the wake of the devaluation that had taken place elsewhere in the region. The obvious reason why things would not be the same in Hong Kong related to the accession of the territory to the Chinese. In the immediate aftermath of this event, the loss of face by the Chinese government that would have been entailed in surrender to Western currency speculators would have been too much to bear.

Eventually, after a torrid year, the government took steps to ease pressure on the currency by restricting dealing and at the same time stepped into the market to support the stocks and prevent short sellers from making money. For this to take place, without apology, in a territory hitherto regarded as a prime example of capitalism at work, shows the extent to which officials believed the speculative actions of the hedge funds were unjustifiably tainting their economy and currency.

Eventually the hedge funds backed off, taking big losses, and as little as a couple of months later, the LTCM crisis took over the limelight and removed the pressure. Ironically it also exposed the US government to its own charges of crony capitalism in fostering the bailing out of the stricken fund – in which leading bankers had personal investments – for the good of the markets and the health of the wider banking community.

As economist Robert Wade at Brown University notes, the tone of comments from the normally unflappable Alan Greenspan gets more heated when it comes to discussing capital controls. Greenspan predicts that such moves would leave the countries operating them as 'mired in a sub-optimal standard of living'. As Wade points out, the more real threat (and the reason for the comments) may be to the standard of living of low-saving Americans rather than high-saving Malaysians:

> [Greenspan] and other US officials see it as imperative to make sure that the troubles in Asia are blamed on the Asians and that free capital markets are seen as key to world economic recovery and advance; the idea that international capital markets are themselves the source of speculative dis-equilibria and retrogression must not be allowed to take root.

The previous pages explain in general terms the way the Asian crisis took hold and its underlying causes, but what about the specifics of individual country crises, and what about the parts played by the courtesans of capital?

*   *   *

In Thailand, hedge funds' direct forward sales of baht were reckoned to be in the region of $7bn compared to the total forward book of the

Bank of Thailand in the region of $28bn, estimates courtesy of the IMF. In an unconfirmed Reuters report, it was said that Tiger Management, then one of the largest global macro funds, may have spent as much as $3bn in an attack on the baht at the start of the Asian crisis between May and July 1997.

This may not tell the whole story, however. Hedge funds may also have sold baht forward through offshore intermediaries, onshore foreign banks and onshore domestic banks, all of which may then have hedged these positions by selling the exposure to the central bank. The IMF claims that hedge funds were not at the head of the selling, but the scale of the exposure seems to have been enough to unnerve domestic corporations, and domestic and international banks, who must have seen the speculative build-up of positions as a sure-fire indicator that a devaluation might be around the corner.

Though the reserves held by the Bank of Thailand were less than was generally assumed at the time, it had still managed to give the speculators a bloody nose initially. In fact in early 1997, when the first signs of selling pressure on the currency appeared, it responded by instituting a rule that prohibited banks from selling baht to foreigners other than in connection with documented trade transactions. Thus when the hedge funds and others needed baht to cover short positions, they were forced to buy offshore, where baht were scarce. On one occasion, the one-month offshore baht interest rate was as high as 100%.

It may have been revenge for this that provoked the hedge funds to renew their assault on the baht. According to the IMF, the baht was the only currency in which the hedge funds took short positions in the early summer, the spread of the crisis to other Asian countries having caught everyone by surprise. As well as being inconsistent, the IMF's view smacks of naivety. The resources of the hedge funds were concentrated at the weakest point in the chain. In the subsequent rout, hedge funds, say the IMF, took opportunist long positions in the Indonesian rupiah, which was deemed to have fallen too far too fast.

According to the IMF, the main players in the runs on the rupiah, the Malaysian ringgit and the Philippine peso, were commercial banks, investment banks and domestic investors, acting respectively to cover loan exposure, imitate the hedge funds in markets that had not been attacked, and as a means of precautionary capital protection. Some investors take issue with the portrayal of Thailand as the underdog suffering the depredations of the playground bully (or more accurately in this case a gang of them). Writing an open letter to the Thai government in his Applied Derivatives Trading online newsletter, trader Patrick Young puts it thus:

> While you were healthy, you reaped the rewards. You failed to take the hard decisions necessary to reform the economy. Then you tried to ignore the problem and desperately hoped that no-one would spot the difficulties. How foolish that you should think that the likes of the major hedge funds would view your success in one way, but yet not seek to prosper when you let things deteriorate.

* * *

Malaysia has had an appreciably stronger economy than Thailand and therefore did not suffer the effects of the currency crisis to the same degree, not least because it acted quickly and, as described above, decided to impose capital controls rather than place itself at the mercy of short-term capital flows.

Ironically enough, although Dr Mahathir has repeatedly blamed hedge funds for making the imposition of capital controls necessary, this does not appear to have been the case, at least according to the IMF. The main short sellers of the ringgit at the time were commercial and investment banks. Some hedge funds seem to have taken modest positions but none, says the IMF, 'appear to have ridden the ringgit for any substantial range of its fall from 2.5 to 3.5 to the US dollar.'

Mahathir may take the view that the identity of the speculators against the ringgit mattered little. In a bitter speech to a conference dedicated to managing the Asian financial crisis in November 1998, he suggested that while Korea may have practised crony capitalism and nepotism, other countries did not. This is what he said:

We know the countries of East Asia suddenly collapsed together. If it is not because of bad governments, their corruption, their crony capitalism and nepotism, then what? They collapsed because their wealth was taken away from them, through their money being devalued. They collapsed because they were suddenly made extremely poor.

Blaming currency traders for the collapse, Mahathir goes on:

It was greed; a kind of greed that cares nothing for the destruction caused, for the collapse of perfectly healthy and prosperous economies, greed that thrives on the misery of others.

These currency traders control, and manage huge funds invested by the very rich in the very rich countries. They are well connected. They are the cronies of the bankers who managed huge funds belonging to the public. They believe that if they are big, no-one can stop them manipulating the market any way they wish.

Mahathir goes on to point out, in similar vein, that the hedge funds he alludes to lacked any concern for the populations of the countries whose currencies they were shorting and that economies previously lauded for their economic growth were suddenly blamed for creating the loss of confidence themselves. Then, when their remedies failed, they were blamed, with no one apportioning the blame where it actually lay – at the feet of hedge funds and currency speculators. More significantly, and in a passage that has the ring of truth, he says:

Cronyism is extensive in the operations of the banks and the funds. They all know each other and talk all the time to each other. In many instances they had previously worked together in the same institutions or companies. Subscription to the funds is by invitation only and obviously those invited are known to the managers of the funds. Although the funds may compete with each other, there are also enough indications that they also collude.

Despite the ill-tempered nature of this rhetoric, an unbiased observer would have to admit that Mahathir had a point. Moreover, doubtless to the chagrin of hedge funds and the Western establishment alike, the much criticised capital controls appear to have worked. A partial relaxation was seen in mid 1999, allowing capital mobility after paying an exit tax, but even before this there had been virtually no let-up in foreign direct investment, and foreign portfolio investors are also testing the water in increasing numbers. The exit tax provision was later relaxed further.

Complete liberalisation may have to await a further rapprochement with the West, which the Malaysian government has tied to its inclusion in talks to reform the global financial system. Reported on Reuters in September 1999, the then deputy finance minister Nazri Aziz said that 'whatever is planned, it should take into consideration the views of countries that have seen the impact of the outflows of hot money.' This is a reference to Mahathir's often expressed, if simplistic, view that it is significant that the only countries that do not suffer in this way are those that the hedge fund managers operate from.

*   *   *

The theme of potential collusion between hedge funds in their mounting of speculative attacks is one that crops up again when one looks at the case of Hong Kong. The Hong Kong dollar has undergone periodic attacks from speculators since the territory reverted to China in mid 1997. The first serious attack took place in October 1997, in the wake of the crisis elsewhere in the region, with hedge funds allegedly selling short some US$5bn of Hong Kong currency.

Operating through the automatic checks and balances built into the currency board of the Hong Kong Monetary Authority (HKMA), short-term interest rates went as high as 280%. Since many of the associated speculators were local banks forced to borrow locally to fund short positions, they were forced to unwind their positions and took heavy losses. Related short positions in the stock market worked out better: the index tumbled in the course of the currency defence, more than offsetting the losses made elsewhere. But the hedge funds seemed to have stumbled across a foolproof way to make money.

The result was that a more concerted attack was made in August 1998 with over HK$30bn sold short on August 5, mainly through US investment banks accompanied by carefully placed rumours that the currency peg would fail and even that the Chinese external currency, the renminbi, would be devalued. The operation again resulted in sharp falls in the stock market, making this almost a carbon copy of the earlier attack.

At this point, however, government intervention took place on two fronts, buying the currency to flush out the short sellers, and also supporting the stock market through purchase of equities to ensure that hedge funds did not profit from their short positions on futures contracts. In total some HK$20 000 were spent for each man, woman and child in the territory but the government in the end had the last laugh, with the value of its holdings increasing by nearly 50% from the August low point.

Like Dr Mahathir of Malaysia, Hong Kong government officials – specifically Joseph Yam, head of the HKMA – have berated Western governments for not doing enough to regulate the activities of hedge funds. According to Mr Yam, while there may have been policy weaknesses in Asian countries, they did not deserve the market meltdown precipitated by the actions of hedge funds. Like the Malaysians, Mr Yam also complains that increasingly discussions about regulation of hedge funds have been pulled back under the G7 umbrella, rather than including representation from economies which had most recently suffered at the hands of the hedge funds.

*   *   *

Few disagree with the proposition that, like the humiliating withdrawal of sterling from the ERM in September 1992, the Asian currency crisis was precipitated by hedge funds. Arguments that benefits may eventually flow from this cut little ice, certainly with those on the receiving end. They have seen unemployment rocket, companies go bust or be taken over by foreign entities at a fraction of their true value, and have faced the withdrawal of their countries from normal economic activity, a process exacerbated by inappropriate policies dogmatically pursued by the IMF. The surprise is perhaps that more countries have not collapsed into anarchy as a result.

Even the IMF, generally an apologist for hedge fund community, appears to accept that hedge funds were responsible for at least some of the damage. But there are those around, and perhaps more level-headed voices than Malaysia's Mahathir Mohamed, who believe that collusion between different hedge funds was at the root of the problem.

Paul Krugman is a well-known commentator on economic affairs and an economics professor at MIT. He writes a widely read column in *Fortune* magazine. In an article after the crisis was over, Krugman wrote suggesting that collusion between hedge funds may have been a factor in it. He says that proving a conspiracy is difficult, because if it did occur, it would be hatched in secret inside the proverbial smoke-filled room or at a discreet restaurant table.

Krugman claims to have been told by government officials in Australia that they were steered towards a policy of benign neglect towards their exchange rate by hedge fund operators who claimed that the slide in their currency was part of a wider attack on all currencies in the region. The final surreal twist to the whole episode is that in March 2000, three years after the Asians' problems began, Soros Fund Management began the launch of a new investment drive in Asia, focusing among other things on real estate and distressed assets. Soros, it is said, suffered large losses in the Asian crisis, although these suggestions have never been convincingly demonstrated.

The losses may have occurred more in Hong Kong, Indonesia and Russia than in Thailand where Soros, along with Julian Robertson, was rumoured to be a large player behind the operation to drive down the value of the baht. In fact, Soros lost heavily on the Indonesian rupiah, heavily buying into the currency shortly before it went into free fall. He may have been more ready to release information on these losses than on the profits made elsewhere in the region during the crisis.

Perhaps as a postscript one should also record that painting the Asian nations as wholly innocent victims is just as misleading. As Nicholas Dunbar records in his book *Inventing Money*, property prices in certain parts of Australia increased sharply during the crisis, a phenomenon that was attributed to an influx of Asian 'funk money'.

*   *   *

If global macro funds are characterised as the villains of the piece when it comes to emerging markets, the guys in the white hats are surely the emerging market hedge funds, who attempt to profit from the undervaluation that arises from the uncertain investment climate in these markets.

All emerging market funds share several common features. The central theme is that the funds essentially make their returns from the fact that, in emerging markets, market mechanisms are inefficient and uncertainty rife, information hard to come by and frequently inaccurate, meaning that valuation anomalies crop up regularly and sometimes they are substantial. Different funds invest differently; some in single countries, some regionally, some in emerging markets as a category, wherever in the world the opportunities are seen to exist.

Through a presence on the ground and hence an intimate knowledge of local market conditions, emerging market long-only funds can profit when the bogus nature of the disparities is recognised and valuation levels return to normal. The process requires strong nerves, not least because of the marauding effects of the macro hedge funds described earlier in this chapter. Most successful investment, according to Hedge Fund Research's Joe Nicholas, takes place early in the transformation of the market concerned to a more mature market-based economy. The search is for fundamentally sound businesses whose activities may have been held back by lack of technology, or the lack of access to capital markets.

More often than not, emerging market hedge funds of this type have to generate their own sources of information, not only reading local sources, but also visiting companies and meeting managements and government officials in an attempt to untangle what makes a particular situation likely to generate a useful return. This is also likely to involve extremely rigorous financial analysis, not least because the accounting conventions that apply in a developing market may not be as robust or as consistently applied as in the United States or Western Europe.

The very evident risks that this approach brings with it can be controlled to some degree, partly by diversification, especially making sure that each stock held has different characteristics to the others in the portfolio. In the book *Investment Biker*, former hedge fund manager Jim Rogers describes how in each emerging market he would look for a bank, a brewery and a newspaper to invest in, which sums up the approach. The other element of risk control is simply the one that is inherent in buying good assets very cheaply, with a large margin of safety.

The bottom line is that these distortions, volatility, uncertainty and a lack of sophistication all create the ability for large businesses to be misunderstood by the market. This means that patient money can make substantial returns over time. The process is underpinned by the natural tendency of market ratings to rise and volatility to decrease as countries open up their capital markets and become more tied in to the international financial system.

That at least is the theory. Of course, participation in the international financial system can bring pain as well as pleasure. As a category, emerging market funds such as Banyan, Latinvest, Permal and others have shown marked movements in both directions. Emerging market funds, for example, showed spectacular returns in the early 1990s, peaking at around an annual return of 80% in 1993 but up around 45% in 1991 too, before dropping to more modest levels later.

In the aftermath of the Asian crisis the funds, which had suffered during the debacle, rebounded sharply, rising by perhaps 55% in 1999, according to Hedge Fund Research and depending on your choice of index. As a category, they exhibit both high returns and high levels of volatility, and this is likely to continue for as long as capital flows are allowed to disrupt the economies of emerging countries.

*   *   *

To some degree perhaps, the conditions that led to the Asian crisis and the role played by hedge funds were a one-off. It may be some time before the US government so overtly encourages commercial banks and others to invest in emerging economies with such alacrity, and some time before emerging market governments accept such largesse without mechanisms to ensure the money flows are somewhat less rapid in the opposite direction.

The experiences of Malaysia and Hong Kong have been an example to many that the sky does not necessarily fall, in economic terms, if you contemplate market intervention to thwart speculation, nor indeed does it collapse if you introduce capital controls to prevent short-term money flows. Though Asian economies are likely to show much slower growth in 2001, the cause of this is mainly sharply reduced export trade within the region itself.

Global macro funds, though still powerful, are not the force they were, particularly in the light of recent developments at Tiger and Soros, two of the key players in the Asian crisis. Some other funds have been caught up in the old economy–new economy stock market whipsaw and have become more interested, if not in this, in the merger arbitrage opportunities currently present in more mature markets.

This does not, however, mean that global macro funds have ceased to operate in emerging markets for good, simply that they may be less obtrusive about their trading in future. Nor does it invalidate the calls for greater disclosure and greater regulation of the activities of hedge funds, especially in respect of the deleterious and wholly unnecessary effects their speculative activities can produce in vulnerable economies.

It is patently unfair that such countries should be excluded from the process of reforming the hedge fund community. It is also paying too much lip service to capitalism and free markets to suggest that the violent consequences produced by the actions of hedge funds in emerging markets are the only way of effecting reform of crony capitalism and other undesirable attributes these economies may have.

The US government in particular, it can be argued, needs to weigh much more carefully the consequences of actions it takes in the emerging market sphere. As the LTCM debacle proved, it is all too ready to intervene in the workings of the free markets when the need arises, yet prone to castigating others when they seek to do the same.

Countries like Malaysia, with a relatively resilient and self-sufficient people, a disciplined way of life and a high savings ratio have every right to be irritated. But as one observer pointed out, honest disciplined people have sometimes not been led by equally honest and disciplined governments. One investment banker says, 'It's not hedge funds that damage emerging markets, it's their governments that do so.'

Yet in the United States, for example, it may be the other way round. Those in emerging markets may get a little tetchy when American politicians and government officials preach restraint to them while presiding over an economy where savings rates are non-existent and excessive amounts of wealth are gambled in geared-up investment on the stock market, with a bailout round the corner if the market turns sour.

8

The hedge fund in your bank

Banking is not a field for weaklings
Frank Vanderlip

Banks are courtesans of capitalism in disguise. We know the names of the famous courtesan/hedge fund managers, but proprietary traders at leading banks are anonymous figures.

Banks and bankers are a breed apart. They often make it very difficult for the rest of us to have a very high opinion of them. The LTCM debacle and the roles that large US banks played in it, in the collapse of Barings, and in a number of other episodes are revealing. They suggest that banks are neither the conservative institutions they like to pretend, nor sometimes are they particularly good at assessing risk.

Anyone who knows the history of finance in the post-war era will realise that banks are prone to rushes of enthusiasm that seemingly blind their senior executives – often temporarily, sometimes permanently or fatally – to the most elementary notions of risk management. The record speaks for itself and is often the reason why big banks get taken over.

Henry Kaufmann, a former head of research at Salomon and known universally as Dr Doom for his pessimistic view of the markets, calls this (tongue in cheek) 'entrepreneurship in banking', referring to the aggressive so-called liability management practices first introduced to the world by former Citibank chief executive Walter Wriston.

UK banks have simply contented themselves with allowing their overheads to grow and alienated their users with poor service or insensitive treatment of long-standing customers. US, and indeed

European, banks have been more adventurous. Think, for example, of the involvement of Credit Lyonnais in acquiring a well-known film studio. A massive bailout had to be engineered. Or reflect on the risk that Deutsche Bank took, in haste to become a big player on Wall Street, by buying Bankers Trust. This venerable US bank so completely changed its spots as to become a byword for overly aggressive marketing of derivatives. While these products were supposedly custom-tailored for the needs of the bank's corporate clients, in the end some of them turned out to be simply custom-tailored for depleting the recipients' balance sheet.

UBS's involvement in the LTCM debacle is another case in point. Here we have an ostensibly conservative Swiss bank so desperate to be seen at the cutting edge of financial rocket science that it ended up losing nearly $700m in a joint venture option deal with John Meriwether's men. The moral of the story: don't buy a product from someone who knows more about what is being sold than you do. These latest escapades are only the most recent in a string of ill-judged lending decisions by banks on a global basis over several decades. The other exhibits are familiar enough.

*   *   *

It seemed like a good idea to lend to sovereign governments in underdeveloped countries in the 1970s, until governments started defaulting on their debt in the wake of the oil crisis. This was sorted out thanks to the ingenuity of US Treasury secretary Nicholas Brady, inventor of the Brady bond. Brady bonds allowed cash-strapped governments to exchange their doubtful bonds for new ones backed by US dollars. This was self-interest on the part of the US Treasury. US banks had bought so many of the original bonds that their collapse threatened to blow some big US banking names out of the water.

Yet no sooner had this bailout been arranged than banks began to get keen on lending to highly leveraged management buyouts. This trend reached its high point in the United States with a blockbuster bid for RJR Nabisco, a deal which brought out the worst in Wall

Street. In the UK the high water mark was reached with the takeover of the Gateway supermarket group, a company that all but went bust on its backers a few years later. Those seeking an instance of why banks and leveraged buyouts don't mix could do worse than read *Barbarians at the Gate*, the best-selling account of the RJR saga, written by two US business journalists.

Quite apart from the 1990s vogue for backing hedge funds in various guises, if one were looking for examples of the collective madness returning, one might cite the more recent trend towards blue-chip banks allowing (even encouraging) their venture capital offshoots to back flimsy internet vehicles. This has even gone so far as creating proprietary private equity funds to invest in internet start-ups and allowing staff members a carried interest in the funds. Predictably, it has ended in tears. The justification for these actions is familiar. It is usually based on the notion that, if there is a bandwagon rolling and one bank decides to jump on it, competitors will follow without examining the logic for doing so too closely.

There have been, of course, other equally egregious instances. These include the savings and loan debacle in the United States, where the unscrupulous exploited loopholes in the law to fleece investors and the financial community. There is the lending to property developers in California just before the peace dividend decimated the West Coast defence industry, and lending to oil and gas businesses in Texas, just as the oil price started heading south. Then again, there is the whole sorry saga of the Japanese banking industry, too lengthy and complex to go into here. The latest enthusiasm: telecoms industry debt.

According to Kaufmann, regulation is incapable of restraining the banks. The rules are out of date and take insufficient account of many of the financial 'innovations' that markets have developed, while regulators themselves are both underpaid and underpowered.

The activities of the banks in their external investments and lending often pale into insignificance beside the in-house, so-called proprietary trading that many of them indulge in, in foreign exchange markets, derivatives and other instruments. While banks need to offer a dealing service in these products to their corporate customers, the turnover that banks generate goes far beyond their customers' needs and far beyond the notion of doing what is needed to keep a liquid market going.

Proprietary trading is no more or no less than banks' own trading with the accumulated funds of shareholders and depositors – for which read 'your money'. It has reached a level where, in some instances, it dwarfs conventional lending and contributes to a marked volatility in banking profits. Why trade in this way? Quite simply, bank managements find it exciting and, of course, everyone else is doing it.

The central point is that banks, whether European or American or indeed Japanese, and whether conventional banks or investment banks, do not have a particularly good record when it comes to keeping a disciplined approach to lending, trading or other moneymaking activities. The banks' involvement over the years with the hedge fund community bears testimony to these lemming-like tendencies.

Yet speak to any bank account holder in Europe or the United States and it's a fair bet that they are blissfully unaware that the operator of their local bank branch or the provider of the ATM in the shopping mall is also wheeling and dealing in the markets with their money – and not always doing a particularly good job. All the customer was looking for was a reasonably safe home for his or her money. They may get that, but often in spite of the efforts of the bank depleting capital in injudicious trading.

Bank management teams tend to be secretive about what they do in the proprietary trading area, ostensibly because they regard such information as trade secrets that might be of use to their competitors. It may also be because they fear that account holders might revolt if they knew exactly how much of their wealth was being risked in this way.

In fact, the risk taking represents another form of moral hazard. The bank executives responsible for proprietary trading, and their bosses who sanction it, stand to earn large bonuses if it goes well. If not, the losses can usually be buried. Most large banks know that if depositors' funds were seriously at risk, in other words if the losses were just too big to be buried, the financial system would not let them fail. Hence excessive risk taking, which might be rewarded by higher returns and higher bonuses, is hardly discouraged.

*   *   *

Why banks indulge in proprietary trading and other high-risk forms of activity is because commercial lending has become a commodity business, or at least one on which the volumes have shrunk and the margins are low.

Custody and portfolio administration to some extent compensated for a while. But the technological scale required to win business in this area, and downward pressure on fees as a result of competition between large banks as the industry has consolidated, has made this a difficult area for some banks to make an adequate return. And besides, custody and securities administration is, on the whole, intrinsically an even more boring business than commercial lending.

The result: proprietary trading, for a time, and especially when markets were rising, has been both a by-product of other parts of many a bank's business and, at the same time, a way of bank executives doing something exciting and earning hefty bonuses into the bargain.

Almost the only exception to this rule has been Citigroup. Following the merger that created the banking and insurance giant, steps were taken to sharply curtail proprietary trading at the investment banking subsidiary Salomon Smith Barney. Citigroup's recent acquisitions have been in much more prosaic areas of consumer financing, and probably none the worse for that.

But as the Barings example showed, some bankers fail to appreciate that the high returns which generate big bonuses also produce high risks. This gets to the essence of moral hazard. Because of the way traders' bonus schemes are constructed, the personal returns from adopting a risky strategy are much higher than the risks run if the strategy fails.

While the Barings executives clearly did not plan the outcome from the start, consider what happened to Nick Leeson and his bosses. Leeson's trading brought Barings to the point of extinction and some executives were carpeted, but only Leeson himself went to prison, and it was a condition of the sale of the bank to ING that the Barings bankers still got their annual bonuses, even ranking ahead of the bondholders when it came to getting their hands on the limited spoils available. It would take a heart of stone not to feel that this was rough justice all round. For Leeson, a jail cell in Singapore, cancer and the break-up of his marriage; for Barings' higher echelons, not exactly a happy ever after but not too much pain either.

Why proprietary trading is a banking by-product stems in part from what banks do and the way capital markets have changed. Dealing in foreign exchange for corporate clients has led to proprietary activity in this area. Skills in dealing in foreign exchange for customers led banks to the view that trading on their own account would benefit from the market knowledge they had gained. As the foreign exchange markets developed futures and options products, these began to be traded too.

Because they lend, many banks have a view about interest rates, trends in the yield curve, and the tone of the bond markets. In turn this has led on to trading in interest rate futures and options over and above the basic needs of the investment or banking clients. Because banks serve up big corporations with commercial loans, treasury services and all manner of other products, they have a tailor-made customer list. Each customer's requirements are different, in the sense that they may have, for example, a mismatch of their assets and liabilities in different currencies.

This leads to demand for the hedging of currency risk and to differing requirements for fixed-rate and floating-rate loans. The result has been the creation of the swaps market, essentially a simple way of meeting these requirements. But it is a market in which banks have found a whole new area for earning fees, trading, and custom tailoring derivative products for specific corporate needs, either real or imaginary.

*　　*　　*

The result, however, has been the creation within investment banks of what amount to large internal hedge funds. And since now any large money centre bank worth its salt owns an investment bank, then hedge funds are a piece, perhaps a modest one, but nonetheless a piece of the bank that processes your cheques and that you rely on to keep your money safe.

The hedge fund in your bank would be all well and good, were banking not the very antithesis of the hedge fund culture. When hedge fund style risk-seeking individuals meet an ossified, or at least inflexible and bureaucratic corporate culture, accidents are likely to happen. Traders being what they are, that is used to sizing up a market and opting for the most attractive return on offer, the best traders will tend to go and work for independent hedge fund groups, because that is where the best rewards are.

Hence when bank traders try to mimic what the best of the hedge funds do, it can be disastrous. The best traders work for the hedge funds, the second best traders for the banks. The differences may be small, even imperceptible, but there is plenty of evidence to suggest that this makes a difference. In an attempt to compensate and to juice up their bonuses, bank traders get high on the potent drug of leverage.

The report from the General Accounting Office (GAO) in the wake of the LTCM debacle provided some interesting statistics on the risk profiles adopted by LTCM. LTCM was a large hedge fund castigated for having assumed huge levels of leverage. But you might imagine that the cadre of big investment banks with which it dealt, with blue-chip reputations to protect, would be more restrained in the levels of risk they sought. In fact, they had even higher levels of debt.

The GAO report showed, for example, that the leverage adopted by several other investment banks, including Goldman Sachs and Merrill Lynch, matched or exceeded the leverage adopted by LTCM at the time of its collapse. The figures for these two respectively were 34:1 and 30:1 compared with LTCM's 28:1. Remember that these figures adjust for the different sizes of capital base. The absolute numbers were markedly larger than LTCM's.

So rather alarmingly, though there was much publicity given to the fact that LTCM had been able to accumulate notional positions in derivatives contracts totalling $1.4trn, few people picked up that the positions of Goldman Sachs and Merrill Lynch at that time were no less than $3.4trn.

Notional derivatives outstandings arguably look somewhat scarier than they are in reality because they are bought on margin. The banks mentioned are somewhat better capitalised than LTCM turned out to be, and hence better able to ride out market volatility. But perhaps more worrying are the orders of magnitude involved and the key position these banks play in the global financial system. And the record shows that these institutions themselves, learning of the scale of LTCM's positions, were undoubtedly worried.

Forget LTCM and the pickle the big investment banks got themselves into, and look for a moment at more mainstream banking institutions. It is also fair to say that the scale of the proprietary positions taken by many big banks is larger than we might be comfortable with. Not only this, but are we confident that some of the banks' traders are sufficiently adept at controlling risk?

In fact Barclays, despite having sold its investment banking business, still ended up as one of the creditors in the LTCM debacle, evidence perhaps that the absence of investment banking is itself no guarantee that there will be no exposure to so-called highly leveraged institutions (as if, of course, the big banks did not themselves fall into this category).

Some mainstream banks, many of them the sort that you and I use, have racked up some pretty impressive losses from trading in recent years. The numbers are opaque, of course, buried within much broader categories within banks' balance sheets. Here are just a few examples:

- Salomon Smith Barney, part of Citigroup, saw revenue from principal trading in fixed income fall from $1882m in 1997 to a loss of $869m in 1998 and then back up to $1378m in 1999.
- Over the same period Goldman Sach's overall revenue from principal investments went from just short of $300m to $146m and back up to $950m.
- Credit Suisse saw trading investment gains halve in 1998 from SFr 3.3bn to SFr 1.45bn and then go back up to SFr 4.8bn.
- UBS saw its unrealised investment losses rise from SFr 10m to SFr 556m in 1998, while at the same time writing off SFr 106m of trading fixed assets.
- NatWest, now no longer independent, had a track record that showed a steady pattern of trading investment gains, but with

almost £800m of exceptional charges buried in the notes of the accounts in 1996 and 1997.

- Barclays follows a similar pattern: modest realised investment gains but a big exceptional charge of some £400m in 1997 and trading investment gains showing a negative of £133m in 1998.
- Commerzbank recently lost some DM 90m in short order on a portfolio of long-dated zero-coupon bonds bought for its proprietary trading book as a speculation that Eurozone interest rates would remain low. The loss was only discovered after a new boss at the bank ordered an audit of the bond trading book.
- Nomura Securities, admittedly more a mainstream investment house than a conventional bank, showed a $726m loss on fixed-income trading and a whopping $1.2bn deficit on mortgage-backed securities in the year to March 1999.

Nomura's report makes interesting reading. Curiously enough, the details behind the losses are buried in the detail, the bank referring only to the sale of certain proprietary trading activates in mortgage-backed securities in the United States. The bank also alludes to 'mark-to-market' losses in Russian government bonds.

The term 'marking to market' means valuing a trading position at the current market price rather than its book cost. The company adopted a 'new business plan' in the wake of the LTCM debacle. A new risk management policy, adopted (surprise, surprise) in October 1998, rates a page and a half in the 1999 annual report.

Trading investments show the size of the banks' exposure to the markets. Here are some examples of the size of trading activities. In each case the comparison is with the bank's total assets. Bank shareholders' funds are usually a small fraction of their balance sheet totals.

- J.P. Morgan's trading investments in 1999 represented $152bn out of assets of $260bn. J.P. Morgan recently merged with Chase, a move some observers interpret as producing an undue degree of concentration in some aspects of the financial markets.

- At Morgan Stanley, trading investments are $112bn out of assets of $366bn.
- At Citigroup a measure of the change in style alluded to previously has been that trading investments as a proportion of total assets dropped from a quarter to a seventh between 1997 and 1999.
- Deutsche Bank's takeover of Banker's Trust showed the reverse – trading investments rising from a fifth of total assets to more than a quarter over the same period.
- At Nomura Securities, trading investments in the year to March 1998 were Y8.9trn out of Y20trn, and in the year to March 2000 Y4.8trn out of Y14.5trn.
- UBS's trading investments were SFr 212bn out of SFr 982bn in the latest financial year.
- At rival Credit Suisse the 1999 trading investments were SFr 123bn out of SFr 722bn. Credit Suisse has recently enlarged its presence in US investment banking by acquiring Donaldson Lufkin & Jenrette.

These are just a few examples taken at random from recent bank annual reports. But it would be hard to argue they are untypical. Investment banks run the biggest risks. But a disturbing recent trend has been the quest for size among investment banks, and also the degree to which some commercial banks have, since the effective demise of Glass–Steagall, increased their exposure to investment banking and proprietary trading.

Other than Nomura, the only example of a large bank reducing its exposure to this area has been Citigroup. HSBC, normally a byword for moderate trading and low exposure to proprietary trading, is periodically rumoured to be considering a merger with the likes of Merrill Lynch, a move that would undoubtedly increase the risks to which shareholders are exposed.

It is not so much the size of these numbers relative to the capital base of the banks concerned that is the disturbing element in all this, but the volatility of the numbers. One would have to question whether traditional bankers perhaps fully understand the risks their traders run, so volatile have been the returns.

The finance director of a large British company, which should perhaps remain nameless, once said to me, 'If we are using or trading a derivative product or security, the nature of which I cannot clearly explain to a non-executive director in a couple of minutes, and have him or her clearly understand what I am describing, then we shouldn't be trading it.'

Financial sophisticates may scoff at this. And bankers, of course, like to think of themselves as more financially sophisticated than most, and to some extent they are. But in large measure the same principle should be followed. One need only take a look at some of the other disasters that have befallen supposedly sophisticated institutions in recent years to drive the point home. Bankers are not immune to making mistakes. This is especially so when it comes to trading complex financial products.

It is almost a golden rule that, at some time, a bank employee will in any given period produce some spectacular losses. This will happen trading instruments that range from the mundane to the obscure. A good trader can, after all, lose money trading even the most humble bond or option. Barings' Nick Leeson bankrupted a 400-year-old bank using an instrument as simple as an option on a stock market index, making mistakes that would shame an amateur investor. That is not really the point. The point about operating a bank like a hedge fund is not the returns that are or are not generated, but the fact that their mistakes potentially can affect us all.

*   *   *

To understand how banks got into the mess they did with LTCM in particular, and how in general their involvement with hedge funds can be a destabilising influence on world markets, one needs to understand the symbiotic relationships that exist between banks and hedge funds.

As with most aspects of financial markets, the relationship has gone from strength to strength because of hunger for business on the part of the banks, because of the wealth of trading ideas that can flow from executing trades for hedge funds and their subsequent emulation by the banks, and because hedge funds have a need for low-cost execution and finance to carry out their trading.

If the relationship is looked at from the standpoint of the hedge fund managers, the role of the investment bank is essentially to facilitate the funds' trading activities, by providing a single point of contact through which the bank can gain all the services it needs. These range far and wide. There is straightforward deal execution in a range of world markets and across different types of instrument, whether equities, bonds, currencies, commodities, derivatives or other more exotic gambling chips.

Then there is the settlement of trades, the provision of basic back office functions, portfolio analysis, performance measurement, risk assessment, financing, either through loans or through other devices such as swaps, securities lending or repos, even down to the provision of office space, entertaining, and buying groceries for the office refrigerator.

The service that links banks and hedge funds is known as prime brokerage and it is booming even now. In fact, it continued to boom even in the immediate aftermath of the debacle of autumn 1998. One reason why it continues to boom is vested interest. Quite simply, it generates huge amounts of business for Wall Street firms and their banking parent companies. Margins are slim but the volume is huge.

Prime brokers are so discreet that few people, even well-informed investors, know the names of the individuals who head the firms and in good years are responsible for huge chunks of profit and massive return on capital. Executives like Richard Portogallo of Morgan Stanley, or Richard Harriton of Bear Stearns, are key individuals, but hardly household names outside the confines of Wall Street.

In the wake of the LTCM collapse, an article in *Forbes*, the US business magazine, described prime brokers in the following terms: 'The prime brokers are the madams; the hedge funds are the girls. Guess who makes the money and stays in the business longer?' Prime brokers make money out of hedge funds partly from commission and partly from lending them money or arranging stock loans or repo agreements for short positions. This was the type of leverage that sank LTCM and which threatened to sink the other blue-chip names that dealt with them and lent to them.

Interest is either paid out by hedge funds on their loans, or earned by the banks on the margin balances that the funds keep to support their activities. Prime brokers typically take a huge spread over their own cost of funds when lending to their hedge fund clients, often as much as 150 basis points (1.5%). They are at risk, of course, if a client defaults, but equally the prime broker knows as much if not more than the client itself about the risks it is running, and much of the financing is short-term routine stuff, liquidated and repaid quickly.

Stock loans, where banks can act as intermediaries between the hedge fund borrowers and the institutions who lend stock to generate additional portfolio income, are also a fee-earning activity for prime brokers.

One other big plus for the hedge fund manager in dealing with a prime broker is that while orders can be given to a variety of other brokers to execute, the prime broker masterminds the settlement and financing of the trades, handling settlement problems and arranging for stock borrowing to cover short sales. Other services offered by a prime broker are the ability of the hedge fund manager to participate in syndicated placements and also, not least, to have access to the research and analytical resources of the broker.

So valuable is stock loan activity for banks that there have been instances – though most banks vehemently deny it takes place – of banks offering to handle the custody activity of big investors free of charge in return for the ability to access their portfolios for stock lending activities.

There are obvious dangers in this practice all round. One is that, for example, the institutions dealing with a particular bank lending a particular stock on a conventional securities loan, have no knowledge of the purpose to which the stock loan is being put. The lender of the stock simply has to accept that in making the loan, fully collateralised of course, they are dealing with the bank as their main counterparty and ostensibly running no risk that they will fail to get their stock back.

While this is true, the stock could be used to support the trading activity of a hedge fund which is selling the stock short heavily, is borrowing the stock from several counterparties and is hoping to de-press the price and so make a profit. If this damages the confidence of investors in the shares concerned, there may be permanent harm to an institution's portfolio from lending the stock, however blue-chip the bank on the receiving end. Most likely it will be temporary or an outside chance. The bank could simply be lending the stock to another institution in order to solve a settlement glitch.

The point is that the lender of the stock has no knowledge of the purpose for which the loaned-out stock is being used, and no control over it for the life of the loan. As we noted in an earlier chapter, this practice reaches its apotheosis in the so-called repo market, when government bonds and other collateral are lent and re-lent in a spiral that produces ever greater levels of leverage. It is one reason why some large institutions, including at least one major US mutual fund group, will not countenance lending stocks in their portfolios, for fear of damaging their performance. They run the risk of being called financial fuddy-duddies, but it's a risk they're prepared to run.

Who are Wall Street's biggest prime brokers, and is the prime brokerage idea being exported? The answer is that if you think of a leading investment or money centre bank, the chances are it will have a prime brokerage operation, although the best known are those such as Bear Stearns, which fits into neither category. According to *Forbes*, Bear has 850 hedge fund clients. Other heavy hitters include Morgan Stanley, ING Baring Furman Seltz, Merrill Lynch and, of course, Goldman Sachs.

Hedge fund doyen Michael Steinhardt, interviewed in a US business magazine a couple of years ago, says he dealt with Goldman Sachs' prime brokerage operation for more than twenty years and calculates that he had traded as many as a million shares a year through them and generated at the peak of his activity some $60m in commission. And this is just one hedge fund out of many, albeit one of the larger and more active funds in its day. According to the latest Goldman Sachs annual report, investment services (the vast bulk of which are represented by prime brokerage services for hedge funds) contributed some $2.5bn to the firm's gross income of $12.6bn last year.

Rather like the bordello keeper and her tenants, Wall Street prime brokers essentially add their credibility and credit rating to the hedge funds that are their clients, providing them with the anonymity through which to seek stock loans and a range of other services. One of these is probably putting together hedge funds and potential investors. Merrill Lynch, for instance, played a large part in assembling an investor base for LTCM, while brokers have not been shy at the sort of lavish corporate entertaining – often involving golf courses – that puts hedge funds in touch with would-be investors, thereby stimulating demand for their own services.

Some prime brokers go even further. Montgomery Securities, part of Bank of America, is one example. It even kitted out a floor in its office building as accommodation for hedge fund clients, bringing a new meaning to the concept of the financial bordello, and extended its services to Friday lunchtime pizza deliveries.

There are also other ways in which prime brokers benefit from this symbiotic relationship. There are documented instances of hedge funds steering investment banking business in the direction of the parent companies of their prime brokers, often involving M&A activity in companies in which they hold a large stake. It's vaguely conspiratorial. But, one suspects, it goes on all the time. A more concrete example has recently cropped up in the courts. In a suit brought in October 2000 by Cromer Finance, Bear Stearns was accused of tipping off two large hedge fund clients (one of which was Moore Capital) about the impending collapse of the Manhattan Investment Fund – now a hedge fund cause célèbre. Manhattan imploded spectacularly as a result of alleged fraudulent trading by its manager, Michael Berger.

Prime broking looks likely to increase in importance in Europe, perhaps through the brokers spreading their wings and opening offices. European hedge funds are on the increase, and as they grow they will want the speed of response of a local player. Several big US players are considering establishing a presence. Morgan Stanley is currently understood to have the lion's share of the business.

Should a bank that's keeping your money really be involved to the extent it is in securities trading? It is perhaps ironic that the merger of Citibank and Travellers to form Citigroup was essentially predicated on the de facto repeal of the Glass–Steagall Act, the legislation enacted in the 1930s to prevent the mingling of banking and securities businesses. Since the merger, Citigroup has moved to reduce its dependence on securities trading. But others have seen the move as a green light to press ahead with mergers between investment banking and commercial banking, of which (at the time of writing) the latest example is the marriage of J.P. Morgan and Chase.

Glass–Steagall has long been seen as something of a dead letter. But it had unintended consequences. One was to ossify the structure of the US banking system, leading to too many banks for the system to be either efficient or economic. The de facto removal of the law should eventually produce a more efficient banking structure in America with fewer small regional banks. But unless this process is carefully handled, it may well increase the risks to the public.

Banks need little encouragement to lend or trade rashly, or to embark on injudicious mergers, as the experience of the post-war era has demonstrated. Some banks are better at trading than others, but even the biggest make mistakes, as the examples related to the LTCM debacle attest. If the likes of UBS and Nomura can lose heavily, then the rest of the banking fraternity are probably not far behind, but simply attracting less publicity.

The real problem that banks face in their dealing with hedge funds is that the best traders tend to migrate to hedge funds rather than stay in a restrictive corporate culture. The vogue for creating in-house hedge funds with hedge fund style bonus structures – also happening at European fund management groups too – is a question that may tax regulators who want to see risk within the banking system reduced rather than exaggerated. The fact that some hedge fund strategies are claimed to be low-risk arbitrage does not stop them blowing holes in even the biggest balance sheet.

The other part of the problem, aside from querying whether proprietary securities trading should really ever be part of a retail bank's activity, follows from the services that banks provide for hedge funds and other traders, most specifically the securities financing services of stock lending and repo trading which, again as LTCM showed, can have destabilising effects on the financial system if proper credit control systems are not followed. To those that argue that the lesson of LTCM has been well and truly learnt, one could counter that most banking debacles have been quickly followed by others, sometimes even more extreme.

The answer possibly lies either in creating pure retail banks whose assets and liabilities are ring-fenced from those of securities traders, and commercial and investment banks, whose activities solely consist of business lending, proprietary trading, repo, stock lending, prime brokerage and all the rest of the panoply of techniques that are employed to turn a profit.

Bank customers are forsaking the high-street banking model for online banks in sizeable numbers. Previously it has been assumed that the reason for this was the inefficient service and short opening hours of traditional banks, certainly in Europe. It could just be that traditional banks have also faced some loss of confidence in their unshakeable probity as a result of the fun and games in proprietary trading.

In the United States, however, things are slightly different. Household borrowings there are high relative to non-stock-market-related assets, whether or not via credit card or personal loan debt. The risk of a bank default is less worrying when it is you that owes the bank money rather than the other way round. Hence customers may feel little concern that Glass–Steagall is now defunct.

Regulating banks by ring-fencing securities trading from those parts of the bank that deal with the public may be viewed as a backwards step in this era of global capital markets and instant communications, but it has plenty of historical parallels. The response to the savings and loan crisis in the United States was to create the Resolution Trust, to act as a temporary holding zone for the assets of the shakiest institutions. In Japan and in developing countries (and even in some advanced European markets), it has long been a principle that problems in the banking industry are best dealt with by bundling all the assets into a single central institution, a so-called bad bank. Bad banks operate with public support (i.e. they use taxpayers' money) to work through any problems under the supervision of regulators. They thus preserve the remainder of the banking system with public confidence intact. That confidence may be sorely tested soon. A recent *Economist* article suggested that even conventional lending had severely over-stretched US banks and that 'the problems will probably be containable as long as stock markets do not crash and the economy does not go into recession,' both of which now look more and more likely.

Proprietary trading and stock lending procedures do not necessarily make for a 'bad bank'. But once credit control policies and risk management ease back somewhat (as they inevitably will), they could produce a systemic crisis in banking even greater than that experienced as a result of LTCM. If so, it may well originate at the interface between hedge funds, proprietary bank traders, and excessive leverage and concentration within the banking system. Even though some banking groups have all but abandoned proprietary trading, many have not.

Greater transparency may help to avoid the more outlandish risks. Are bank customers indifferent to the risks being run by these institutions to which they have entrusted their savings? The answer is probably not, although some financial regulators are sceptical about public awareness. More likely is that they are simply not fully informed about them. Making banks more open about the way they trade with customers' capital and the returns they make from it, and the variability of those returns, might give some pause for thought. It should certainly put pressure on some banks to pursue more controlled trading.

To do these things would achieve a major objective. It would take the risk seeking – bread and butter of the capital markets – and put it out in the open and a safer distance away from the savings of ordinary people, people only dimly aware of what a hedge fund does. Besides that, it would reveal how their bank might be operating as a hedge fund in disguise, lending excessively to one customer, the liabilities a potential time bomb buried deep in the balance sheet.

The next four chapters look at how the less desirable effects of the courtesans of capitalism are being contained: by risk management, by disclosure, by the participation of institutional investors in the market, and by regulation.

9

Finance's four-letter word

You can only pass it around, you cannot get rid of it
Tanya Styblo-Beder, Caxton Corporation

Separating institutions like banks from taking risks may be a vain hope. That is, to some degree at least, their reason for existing. It seems we can't expect banks to offer low-cost services without them taking calculated risks with the money we deposit with them. Most depositors are aware that banks lend money, but how many know that some also use it for high-stakes punting in the stock, bond and currency markets?

Depositors and investors want to feel that the risks taken with their money are being properly controlled and managed. At times there is an uneasy feeling that this isn't happening. It has long been painfully obvious that one reason for many past banking debacles has been a basic failure in prudent risk control procedures. This has sometimes been true at the banks that have been involved with hedge funds on a number of levels: as imitators of their trading strategies, as suppliers of leverage through loans and especially via repo transactions, and as trading counterparties.

It is possible to dismiss some of the shortcomings as human nature. Some are also doubtless the result of foolishness and greed in equal measure. Bankers may have turned a blind eye to one of the most basic rules of the market – that high returns do not come without high risks attached. In some cases the reason for ignoring obvious risks has been a desire not to be seen as out of step with their peer group by failing to chase the latest fashion in the market. In some cases it has been faulty modelling, or an overreliance on financial models to suggest a course of action when common sense might be a better guide.

In other cases the issue of moral hazard has reared its head. Traders have bonuses at stake, as have the senior managers who oversee them: the result is a desire to bend the rules of risk control to try and squeeze out some extra profit. One need look no further than the LTCM debacle for examples. This episode did not reveal the industry in a very good light: not the fund's own managers, nor its counterparties, nor the regulators. But precisely what were the failings and how can they be avoided in the future?

*   *   *

In the end, all of the problems for the financial markets resulting from the LTCM debacle had one main cause; the GAO report (Chapter 8) described it as a 'halo effect' surrounding the firm and anything it did. John Meriwether was admired for his record as a trader at Salomon Brothers. His team included Nobel prizewinners. So how could their strategies fail? In the end, this failure to look any deeper meant that the banks who were lending to the fund, and those who were trading with it, based their judgements more on the past reputation and credentials of those involved than on the more objective standards of traditional credit analysis.

The halo effect was compounded by the fact that, because LTCM employed so much leverage and traded in such massive size, its business was extremely profitable for the banks with which it dealt. There was intense competition to get on LTCM's list of favoured counterparties. There was no incentive for the recipients of this business to ask the questions they might have asked a less prominent or smaller fund about its creditworthiness. The GAO report also mentions other factors as contributing to the risks being run. One important risk was that the generally benign economic environment which had persisted for several years prior to the crisis also contributed to greater laxness in determining credit standing.

But not everyone succumbed to the Meriwether halo. Although a large number of investment banks, including what might be termed the great and good of Wall Street – Merrill Lynch, Morgan Stanley, Goldman Sachs, and so on – were prepared to relax their standards in order to deal with the firm, others were not; they were willing to suffer the derision of their peers. Several Wall Street firms refused to deal with the fund because of its reluctance to provide sufficient information about its trades.

One fundamental risk management point also highlights the limitations of conventional analytical models over solid commonsense controls. Models used by financial institutions to assess the risks inherent in LTCM assumed that because the fund's trades were diversified across several markets, the overall portfolio risk was reduced. This was, or so people assumed, straight from textbook financial theory.

There was a flaw in this piece of thinking. Although the broad markets themselves in which they had traded may have been only loosely correlated, the fact was that in each market LTCM had done essentially similar trades in similar instruments. Because of the linkages between global bond markets, they all went bad at the same time. It was a flawed assumption that the markets themselves would not react together in time of shock. Research shows that in such circumstances, selling affects all markets indiscriminately.

Risk management models used by the institutions that dealt with the fund also underestimated the liquidity risk posed by a failure, or potential failure, of an institution as influential as LTCM with which many market participants were fascinated. The glamour of LTCM was what was being watched, not the frumpy, boring risk management model in the back office. In testimony to the House Committee on Banking and Financial Services, the Federal Reserve's associate director, Patrick Parkinson, comments on the adulation that LTCM appeared to inspire:

> In our market-based economy, the discipline provided by creditors and counterparties is the primary mechanism that regulates leverage. If a firm seeks to achieve greater leverage, its creditors and counterparties will ordinarily respond by increasing the cost or reducing the availability of credit to the firm. . . .
>
> However, in the case of LTCM, market discipline seems largely to have broken down. LTCM received very generous credit terms, even though it

took an exceptional degree of risk. The inadequate risk management practices by LTCM's counterparties were also evident, albeit to a lesser degree, in their dealings with other highly leveraged firms.

In other words, the models that might have urged prudence were tossed out of the window in the rush to do business with the fund.

*   *   *

This raises the question as to whether or not regulators could or should have applied greater scrutiny of risk management procedures at any time during the whole episode. Parkinson's testimony continues:

> If market discipline is to be effective, counterparties must obtain sufficient information to make reliable assessments of its risk profile, both at the inception of the credit and relationship and throughout its duration. Furthermore they must have in place mechanisms that place limits on credit risk exposures that become more stringent as the firm's riskiness increases and its creditworthiness declines.

It is one thing saying this and another making sure it happens. The GAO report stresses, for example, that regulators had for years expressed general concern about the potential risks posed by hedge funds and the dangers to the system posed by declining credit standards, but appeared to believe that hedge funds' creditors and counterparties were taking appropriate measures to constrain these funds' leverage.

On the face of it, and with the benefit of hindsight, this now seems a pretty foolish position to have taken. Stringent examinations after the event uncovered the fact that the motley band of hedge fund creditors and counterparties weren't being as prudent or hard-nosed as they should have been. And in the case of the regulators, monitoring at a distance, the normal method of regulatory oversight had quite clearly failed to identify potential problems.

It is strange that regulators should have taken quite so much on trust from institutions (the commercial banks, investment banks and broker-dealers) whose decisions over the years have hardly been the byword for moderate and controlled risk taking. The banking community's tendency to jump on one fashionable bandwagon after another was ignored. More embarrassingly perhaps, the GAO highlights that the Federal Reserve investigated bank relationships with hedge funds in late 1997 and early 1998, surveying several large banks about their practices and procedures for dealing with these institutions.

It is tempting to conclude that the GAO asked the wrong people or the wrong questions, or it should not have believed the answers it got quite so readily. It did warn in June 1998 that banks should not allow competitive pressures to compromise standards, but it appears to have been singularly unaware of the extent to which credit standards had already declined.

Only after the crisis was over did it become clear what had happened. Investigation by the regulatory community after the event chanced upon a catalogue of errors. In the case of the mainstream banks it was found that inadequate due diligence had been performed, chiefly because of the belief that exposures were largely covered by collateral.

This was despite the fact this collateral itself could be subject to a diminution in value if the market went awry. It was also despite the fact that many hedge funds typically refused to provide data on their positions and investment strategies. When faced with this the banks declined to apply any measures either as sanctions or to reduce their risk. Last but not least, it was clear that inadequate credit risk stress testing had been performed. At investment banks and broker-dealers the situation was similar, with absent and unrequested information on aggregate portfolios, leverage, risk concentration, performance, or trading strategy, and no sanctions applied for this lack of disclosure.

It is perhaps significant that subsequent proposals for improving the system have focused on improving the flow of information between hedge funds and their creditors and counterparties. Few seem to blame or seek to correct the structural factors that gave rise to the manifest errors of judgement. Among the things ignored are conflicts of interest and potential for moral hazard to influence the outcome, the over-reliance on imperfect statistical models as a substitute for common sense, the bandwagon effect to which bankers are repeatedly prone, and other equally obvious targets for criticism.

*   *   *

Attempts at modelling risk often seem to bear passing resemblance to the search for the Holy Grail. Investors have often, perhaps naively and however irrationally, believed that it might be possible for the complex pattern of risks run by any trading strategy to be boiled down to a single number or group of numbers.

It is clear from the experience of LTCM and other hedge fund blow-ups that this is patently not the case. Indeed the confidence that this false precision brings is itself sometimes a factor in producing the very outcome that models like this seek to avoid. It can be likened to driving a luxury car. If you are cosseted and think you are safe from harm, you may not need to see the need to take extra precautions. But just because the car is an expensive one does not make it any less likely to crash if driven badly. And the fact that you have a speedometer does not stop you driving too fast or remove the need for the car having good brakes and tyres.

The best known of the models of risk adopted by the banking and securities industry takes the form of value at risk (VAR). First developed by researchers at J.P. Morgan, it grew out of the CEO's desire to be given a single and simple representation of the risks the bank was running in its trading. He wanted it available on his desk at 4.15 every afternoon in a form that could be calculated quickly, communicated easily and understood by non-technical senior managers. This has entered into the folklore of risk management. It is, rightly or wrongly, a process which Morgan itself has done little to discourage. The bank even alludes to the afternoon deadline in its software product Fourfifteen.

What a CEO asks for, he generally gets, irrespective of the wisdom or otherwise of the request, or the validity of the assumptions underlying it. To its major credit, J.P. Morgan has developed this idea into a wide-ranging methodology that it has made available to market practitioners in various forms. But the very idea of VAR raises a number of questions. Rather than make it easy for 'non-technical managers' to understand the intricacies of risk management by spoon-feeding them a spuriously accurate 'magic number', one could perhaps suggest that a more appropriate course of action might have been to educate these managers in greater depth about the true nature of portfolio risk and how to calculate it, and the danger signs to watch for. Reducing the issue to a single number arguably trivialises the whole nature and complexity of risk and the many forms it takes.

Barry Schachter, who operates a web site devoted to risk management, offers three definitions of value at risk, two are conventional statistical jargon but the third is rather more waspish: 'A number invented by purveyors of panaceas for pecuniary peril intended to mislead senior management and regulators into false confidence that market risk is adequately understood and controlled.' Having said all that, Schachter does have some sympathy with the purveyors of VAR, noting that 'it takes some courage to venture into unfamiliar terrain, and missteps are inevitable.' He notes too that the concept is still evolving and experimentation is to be encouraged.

Though VAR is intended to be a simple concept, defining it is far from easy. Taking one's cue from the modern portfolio theory of Markovitz and Sharpe, the basic idea is that risk can be assigned a value, the proxy for which is the standard deviation or volatility of a portfolio. It follows from this that, provided one can accurately measure standard deviation, then it is possible to create a framework of rules around it that will lead to optimal risk management decisions. Here is one possible rule: If volatility increases above x over a set period, then do y.

The problem is that applying criteria like this to day-to-day risk management decisions is difficult. What matters in the real world are profits and losses measured in cash terms, especially when compared to total capital. But the statistical model does not think in cash terms; instead it looks at the divergence of returns from an expected average by using the concept of standard deviations.

It is often the case that these divergences from the average are more pronounced when losses are incurred in trading portfolios, partly because of the widespread use of options and similar instruments to attempt to enhance return. In short, positive returns may be frequent, but any losses will be more extreme. They contrast with the theoretical assumptions underlying VAR, namely that returns occur symmetrically, or in statistical jargon, that they are normally distributed.

The VAR approach measures the spread of returns and attempts to estimate the loss associated with a particular event that has a small probability. Management can then be told that there is a 1% chance of losing a specific monetary amount over a period, an approach that is intuitively easy to understand. There are various ways of arriving at a VAR number, based either around simulating the impact on the portfolio of historical market changes or looking at how movements in particular stocks correlate with other portfolio constituents.

The major problem with the approach is that it is one-dimensional. It only measures market risk – what might happen to the portfolio if the market changes by a given percentage, other things being equal. So there are limits to the extent that it can be used to simulate how a portfolio will behave in the light of a specific 'event', such as a market crash.

A UK-based hedge fund manager observes, 'I think there is a risk in VAR methods, and a danger that a thematic approach can lead to a correlated pattern in both long and short side investments. We constantly review our risk procedures and now look much more closely at our portfolios' liquidity structure. There is a risk that VAR does not correctly identify correlations, nor discontinuities in volatility and liquidity.'

In other words, other things are almost never equal, especially in extreme market conditions. A market crash will in itself have an impact on liquidity risk, credit risk and a range of other variables. As one investment banker puts it, 'The only things that go up in a crash are correlations.' Stress testing can attempt to simulate this, but it is striking that each market crash has its own particular causes and characteristics, and therefore looking at how a specific portfolio behaved in 1987 or in 1998 may not be relevant to how it would behave in any future crash.

To give an example, one market crash might have at its root a loss of faith in the valuations applied to a sector (let's say the telecommunications sector) that had come to make up a significant proportion of major indices. Assume that an excessive amount of leverage had been taken on board by personal investors who had also been a big factor behind driving up prices in the previous period, and an initial fall in price will affect the market increasingly severely as margin calls fail to be met, with a crash as the result.

This chain of events is quite different, though just as damaging, to the impact that LTCM's near failure had on the markets. How, for example, a bond portfolio might react in the circumstances of a telecoms-induced crash will not be predicted by stress testing that only looks at how it reacts to the LTCM events.

VAR also suffers from another drawback, which is its dependence on assumed levels of volatility within markets. According to an *Economist* article in June 1999, these models are 'profoundly affected by rises and falls in volatility. Less volatile markets means a lower VAR, implying that for the same apparent risk, banks can pile up more assets. But if markets become more volatile, VAR goes up by a proportional amount . . . [with a bank then] faced with two choices: put in extra capital or reduce its positions, whatever and wherever they may be.'

Nor does VAR accurately explain the differences in liquidity risk between different parts of a portfolio, or the differences in the creditworthiness of various counterparties with which trades are conducted. Both of these factors can themselves be influenced by market events, indeed they are almost always influenced in this way. To take account of this latter point about credit risk, J.P. Morgan has developed a parallel CreditMetrics methodology alongside its RiskMetrics approach.

Schachter argues in fact that a VAR number is far from capable of being viewed in isolation by a non-technical manager. It is better for it to be used by a specialist risk manager as only one measurement among several used to assess risk. If so, it means that we have progressed some way away from the original concept. And that's not all. To these various types of risk – market risk (measured by VAR), volatility risk, liquidity risk and credit risk – one can add another element – model risk.

The slavish reliance on computer models is one of the banes of the modern financial system. The huge growth in computing power has brought many benefits. But it has not, on the whole, been matched by a heightened awareness, at least among those using them, that the results obtained from complex computer models need treating with a degree of scepticism if they run counter to normal common sense.

This is a separate point from the risk that computer models can sometimes be inaccurately constructed or, more often, are susceptible to corruption by their users. So-called model risk is assuming greater importance among hedge fund counterparties and bank proprietary traders, and the managers that supervise them. If one bears in mind that a hedge fund or investment proprietary trading desk may frequently have thousands of trades outstanding at any one time, modelling the individual and collective risk inherent in these trades is a task that can only be accomplished using computers.

Ironically enough, large macro traders, though making ostensibly riskier directional trades, are more likely to have fewer trades in fewer instruments to monitor than supposedly market-neutral arbitrage-style funds which have hundreds of complex offsetting trades in a complex web of instruments open at any moment.

Model risk, whether unwitting or deliberate, has been behind some recent big disasters in financial markets, dating back perhaps to Joe Jett's complex system of stripping and reconstituting US Treasury bonds in 1994. In 1997 the then NatWest Markets organisation was found to have a £50m hole in its options trading book which appeared to have arisen because of inaccuracies in the way the option pricing model used by the firm had been programmed, and the data that had been used. More recently an $83m loss in the derivatives area by Bank of Tokyo–Mitsubishi in 1997 was put down to model error, as was a $412m loss recorded by UBS in derivatives, even before it became involved with LTCM. The loss at UBS is thought by many to have precipitated the bank's merger with its long-standing rival SBC.

Models versus the market: survival of the fittest, a recent report published by Meridien Research and Capital Market Risk Advisors (CMRA), identifies four types of model risk:

- The risk that the model itself has been designed wrongly or is inappropriate for the application (this is pure model risk).
- The risk that the model is being applied improperly.
- The risk that the wrong inputs are being used in the model.
- The risk that the model is outdated or inconsistent.

Model risk is extremely hard to pin down, not least because the instruments the models are measuring are themselves highly complex. Meridien believes there are no ready-made solutions to the problem posed by model risk. It believes the problem can only be addressed through a series of linked systems and processes that are combined with procedures within the organisation. One point made by the report is that, despite the increasing evidence of a problem in this area, there has been little attempt by software designers to find a solution to the question of model risk.

The report highlights the work done by practitioners within banks to address these problems, citing Paribas as one of the few institutions to have set up an independent model risk management unit within the organisation to check on models used by traders. Ironically Bank of Tokyo–Mitsubishi, perhaps by virtue of its experience in 1997, is one of the few Japanese banks to have paid close attention to this issue in recent years.

* * *

There is no doubt that LTCM's collapse affected how financial institutions viewed hedge funds and the potential risks posed by their trading. Many observers remain to be convinced, however, that there will be any long-term improvement in the way these risks are viewed and managed. Unbridled competition within the investment banking arena and the prevalence of 'it can't happen to me' syndrome suggest there will always be someone prepared to take a risk.

Indeed the fact that John Meriwether was so easily able to raise several hundred million dollars to set up a new fund whose trading methods were unlikely to be much different from the old one, this might be construed as prima facie evidence that a return to the old freewheeling methods was well under way. However, there is objective evidence that, in some respects, banks and others who deal with hedge funds may be taking a more rigorous view of their exposure. A survey by CMRA undertaken about a year after the Russian crisis and the LTCM collapse indicated that improvements were beginning to happen.

In the immediate aftermath of the crisis, the firm had surveyed a range of counterparties to get a base level of data on the topic. Among the key things it found were a desire for an increase in frequency and quality of communication, and improved general reporting between hedge funds and their investors and other counterparties; greater use of mechanisms to reduce the concentration of exposures that the funds or their counterparties had built up; reduced leverage at hedge funds; and better stress testing by banks of the vulnerability of their exposures to particular strategies and related proprietary trading positions.

Another survey completed in late 1999 measured the extent to which these various features had changed since the original. One key feature was that within institutions that dealt with hedge funds, integration of market risk management and credit risk management functions was deemed essential. In August 1998 fewer than 10% of institutions adopted this policy; after the crisis, the figure had risen to 64%.

Risk also exists as a result of different types of documentation in the rules that provide for the unwinding of positions. Greater focus on this so-called documentation basis risk was apparent in the year following the crisis. More significant perhaps was the awareness institutions displayed and the risk adjustments they made to allow for large illiquid positions in securities. Adjustments for factors like this were made by 25% of the survey's respondents prior to the crisis but, not surprisingly, by 58% of them afterwards.

Stress testing of VAR assumptions was performed by around 50% of respondents to the CMRA sample prior to the August 1998 crisis, but by 80% of them afterwards. Explicit sharing with clients of the methods by which haircuts (the margin deposit built into collateralised loans such as repos) were calculated – what might be termed a 'get your house in order' type of conversation – was adopted by 42% of institutions before the crisis but more than 75% afterwards.

These results are particularly interesting because what the crisis showed up was that haircuts were practically non-existent for institutions like LTCM and that collateral in some instances was pledged several times over, making a nonsense of the whole concept. In theory a more explicit disclosure of the methods being used in this area makes it less likely that similar abuses will happen in future.

It is debatable whether stress testing has become more sophisticated. Compared with before the crisis, rather more firms now test both for shifts and twists in volatility curves; but when it comes to testing the degree of correlation between different categories of assets within portfolios, CMRA believes there's a lot more to be done.

Banks and other institutions appear to take the rather fatalistic view that for any type of asset, correlations would move immediately to +1 or −1 in any crisis – all assets would fall in value indiscriminately regardless of quality – making stress testing a waste of time. It was, however, an area where banks and other institutions involved in proprietary trading and dealing with hedge funds were planning greater testing in 2000. Finally, most institutions agree that greater internal coordination between their repo desks and derivatives desks helps to manage risks better. Some 58% had close coordination (or said they did) prior to the crisis, but it was 83% afterwards.

There are other areas where banks are planning to beef up management. Chief among them is adjusting for large positions. This perhaps implies greater supervision of proprietary traders and closer scrutiny of the exposures built up than was formerly the case. Banks have to some degree been put on notice that regulators believe they have an unsystematic and inconsistent treatment of risk. One concern is they have responded to past relaxations in capital adequacy requirements by treating them simply as an opportunity to take more risk for a given degree of capital, just because it was allowed but irrespective of whether it was warranted.

The charge, made by Alan Greenspan at a conference in late 1999, suggests that the ability to play fast and loose with capital requirements has undermined the efficacy of this method as a tool for regulating banks. Greenspan did note, however, that no two banks were alike in their risk profile, or in their risk management controls. More ominously, he observed that mergers within banking had also created the potential for unusually large systemic risks within the US and world economies. Since then there have been further mergers, the latest of which involves an investment bank (J.P. Morgan) and a commercial bank (Chase).

Dr Greenspan's solution to this is disclosure and reliance on effective market disciplines, as a way of creating further incentives for market participants to make improvements in risk management practices and technologies. In other words, disclosure will not just shame recalcitrant banks into making improvements in their procedures, but it will also highlight where their shortcomings are and therefore leave them at a competitive disadvantage to their peers, all of whom will have an insight into each other's policies in this area.

To some degree this echoes the recommendations of the Basel Committee and IOSCO, the international stock exchange body. Banks and securities firms should, the recommendations say, provide financial statement users with a clear picture of their derivatives and trading activities by disclosing 'meaningful' summary information, both quantitative and qualitative. They should also disclose information on their major risks associated with their trading activities and their performance in managing these risks.

More controversially, the recommendations also suggest that banks should disclose information produced by their internal risk measurement and management systems on their exposure and their performance in managing these exposures. Linking public disclosure to internal risk management procedures, the bodies suggest, will ensure that institutions keep pace with the latest advances in risk management technology.

In the real world, most seasoned market observers would be sceptical that such recommendations will ever be implemented in full. Banks, particularly investment banks, are sensitive about their trading methods, the risks they run, and their internal procedures for managing them. Airing too much dirty linen in public may, they argue, give their competitors an unfair advantage. In any case, as one fund manager observes, it is open to debate whether credit control and disclosure related to it would identify the interaction between funds, or reveal systemic risk before it happened.

Disclosure is not something that banks have ever been particularly good at, and there is no reason to suppose they will start now as a result of the exhortations from well-meaning international bodies, however authoritative.

* * *

Hedge funds have responded to the calls for their stricter regulation by issuing a series of proposals of their own. These proposals are contained in *Sound practices for hedge fund managers*, a report published in February 2000 and to which several of the more prominent participants have put their name. They include Bruce Kovner's Caxton Corporation, Louis Bacon's Moore Capital, Kingdon Capital, Soros Fund Management and Tudor Investment Corporation. These are big names but there were some obvious absences.

Not surprisingly perhaps, the funds do not advocate strict regulatory oversight, but seek to draw attention to the uniqueness of LTCM in employing leverage to enhance the relatively modest returns from its arbitrage strategies. As most of the signatories to the report are macro traders orientated towards large directional trades, it is perhaps not surprising that they should adopt this view, and claim (rather more dubiously perhaps) that they pursue these activities without resorting to 'excessive' levels of leverage.

This claim is, to say the least, contentious. Soros's much publicised bet against the pound in 1992, to take a single example, involved the use of leverage. In general, the point about macro funds is that although the levels of leverage have generally been less, the risks run have been no less great because for the most part they have been unhedged.

The report also makes clear the degree to which the interests of hedge fund managers and their investors are aligned by virtue of the fact that managers are frequently heavily invested in their own funds. Understandably it does not draw attention to the fact that on occasion these arrangements, when combined with the incentive payments that managers receive, can act as an inducement to take excessive levels of risk.

Be that as it may, it is impossible to disagree too violently with the recommendations proposed in the report. These include such key points as the fact that risk allocation and risk management should be managed together, in sharp contrast to the approach that a bank may adopt. This seems rather a function of the high degrees of risk that hedge funds assume, and the fact they are small, highly motivated organisations.

More conventionally perhaps, hedge fund managers are exhorted to remember that there is an interplay between different types of risk and that they should be clear on the ways in which liquidity might be impaired during times of stress in the market, in particular the risk that forced liquidations of positions due to inadequate liquidity may cause a spiral from which it is difficult to escape.

Leverage should, says the report, also be assessed on the basis of the risks being run, rather than accounting-based measures, and also that the ease with which leverage can be quickly reduced in response to market conditions should be noted. The report's appendix has a discussion of leverage with a Byzantine level of detail and complexity that seems odd coming from institutions that possess such seeming disinterest in the topic.

Other recommendations relate to the standardisation of documentation, and to the good sense of developing sound relationships with counterparties and regulators. Nonetheless, the extent to which the signatories of the report, and the hedge fund industry in general, are prepared to work with the authorities to reduce systemic risk is subject to the significant proviso that the confidentiality of proprietary information is preserved.

In a way this is really the crunch. LTCM was so reluctant to reveal its trading methods and positions that the market was in complete ignorance of the scale of its positions and the degree to which they were leveraged. The fund could have argued that it was not prepared to compromise the confidentiality of its proprietary information at any point up to the time it was forced to call for help because of its deteriorating financial position.

One does not perhaps expect hedge funds to advocate full disclosure of all their trading secrets, any more than one expects turkeys to vote for Christmas, but the self-serving nature of inserting a clause like this in these recommendations should be recognised for what it is. Even so, not all hedge fund managers agree. Michael Levitt at Harch Capital says, 'Secrecy is nonsense. It doesn't help a manager at all. What is proprietary are not the positions, but what the managers thinks about the positions.'

Despite this admirably dissenting voice, one must probably conclude that the hedge fund industry is congenitally incapable of reforming itself in any meaningful way. The tenor of the report seeks to apportion blame elsewhere, while the recommendations are flawed because of the proviso relating to keeping proprietary information secret no matter what.

Even according to the lawyers who helped draw up the report, the recommendations represent the best that can be expected. Significantly perhaps, of the five firms that sponsored the report, firms which collectively manage more than $15bn, not one has undertaken to adopt them all. Some practices have been adopted by some firms, but not all of them by every fund. One can draw one's own conclusions from that.

I conclude that it remains incumbent on banks, and other hedge fund counterparties, to keep a beady eye on those with whom they deal as much as they keep an eye on their own proprietary trading activities. To do this, banks arguably need to get a lot better at understanding the principles of risk management. But they also need to insist on greater disclosure from those with whom they deal, if the mistakes that contributed to the near meltdown in late 1998 are not to be repeated.

The problem is that the most favoured trading partners, the most successful hedge fund managers, know perfectly well they are highly desirable clients and are able to get away with minimal levels of disclosure for that very reason. At the very least, it argues for the adoption of compulsory minimum standards of reporting in order to ensure that innocent customers of the wider banking community – that's you and me – do not get caught up in the crossfire.

As the hedge fund industry becomes more institutionalised, it may have to accede to requests of this nature anyway, at least from larger investors. It might make sense for them to accept the idea with a show of willingness and a degree of good grace. Such sentiments, on past performance, do not come easily to hedge fund managers, many of whom are driven by a potentially self-destructive 'Masters of the Universe' ethos that contains little room for doubt and certainly no room for humility.

10

Dance of the seven veils

Sunlight is the best disinfectant
Justice Louis Brandeis

While there is a degree of allure in keeping one's more attractive attributes covered up, the courtesans of capitalism might find their prospects improved by revealing rather more than they are normally willing to do at the moment. Why? If hedge funds are to prove that the charges against them are exaggerated, they will only do so by giving more information about themselves to the world at large. If they don't, for whatever reason, it will be assumed they have something to hide.

* * *

In short, one of the supposed panaceas for the ills allegedly perpetrated by hedge funds is to force them to say more about what they are doing: what they are invested in, the leverage they use and their general investment strategies. Disclosure can be made to investors and to regulators, or even to the world at large.

Greater transparency would have prevented the shenanigans that accompanied the demise of LTCM because, with more information available, large financial institutions and their managers may have been less ready to invest in it or lend to it. Similarly, some of the problems inflicted by hedge funds on emerging markets might be moderated if there were greater knowledge, even after the event, about the positions taken by the funds.

While hedge fund managers are at liberty to ignore public opinion up to a point, knowledge that there would be disclosure of the position taken by a fund might give pause for thought before launching an attack on a weak currency and a poor country. Certainly governments and their agencies believe (or believed at the time) that greater disclosure would help curb the excesses of hedge fund behaviour. In April 1999 the US president's working group on financial markets recommended that the larger hedge funds be required to file quarterly statements. The chair of the Banking Subcommittee in the House of Representatives then moved to implement legislation giving effect to this recommendation so that reports would have to be filed by funds and fund groups with more than $3bn in capital, aggregate assets of $20bn or net assets of more than $1bn. The push for leglislation was approved in committee.

Not everyone agrees that this is the panacea it is claimed to be. Speaking at House hearings on the topic, George Crapple, chairman of the Managed Funds Association, a trade body, said that the disclosure of snapshot data by a few large hedge funds would not in any way address the credit risk management deficiencies associated with LTCM. Crapple's argument is that there are plenty of large potentially highly leveraged institutions that would not have to report under the proposed guidelines. In a memorable phrase, Mr Crapple was reported as saying that HR2924 (the House legislative proposal) 'would illuminate a few pixels and leave the rest of the TV screen blank.'

The Financial Stability Forum, an international body, has nonetheless added its voice to the calls for greater disclosure at a meeting in spring 2000. Britain's chief stock market regulator, Howard Davies, called for disclosure of total fund size and leverage for funds that have capital of more than $1bn. Australia's treasury has added its weight to international calls for greater disclosure, a particularly pointed move because of the way in which the Australian dollar was involved in the backwash of the 1998 crisis in Asian emerging markets.

In fact, in the United States the president's working group went further than most and suggested that not only should more frequent and meaningful information be made available about hedge funds, but also that public companies, and especially financial institutions such as banks, should also disclose more information about their exposure to highly geared investment vehicles such as hedge funds. There is obvious concern that banks may still not be applying sufficient diligence to the monitoring of hedge fund exposures. Forcing them to disclose what that exposure is might be a good way of keeping risk management up to scratch. The UK's Howard Davies said recently that he believes the lessons of LTCM have been too quickly forgotten.

Yet appealing though greater disclosure may sound, there are some reservations about these moves. The first thing to address is the issue of who should disclose what. Making hedge funds disclose information without requiring the same of bank proprietary trading desks is clearly inequitable. These institutions are pursuing the same strategies. Moreover, they are using equally high leverage and exposures. To exempt them is clearly only viewing part of the danger on the radar screen.

Second, there is the issue of whether or not disclosure means public disclosure and, if so, to whom it would be disseminated. Regulators may feel they need prior warning of the disclosures to be made, in order to take countermeasures necessary to neutralise any disclosures that might be likely to spook the market. Regulation FD, on public company disclosure of sensitive information, is already having a distinctly 'spooky' effect.

Third, though some levels of transparency are necessary so that would-be investors can properly assess the risks inherent in a fund, it is hardly reasonable to expect a fund to reveal too much of its proprietary trading methods in advance, assuming it has such methods.

Similarly, a leaking out of precise portfolio information can be picked up by other market participants, including perhaps companies or institutions with which the hedge fund has a relationship, against the hedge fund manager to the detriment of investors. Companies whose shares are being 'shorted' may not take too kindly to requests for information from the hedge fund manager if that information is disclosed.

There is also a philosophical point. Investing in hedge funds is always strictly on the basis of *caveat emptor* 'let the buyer beware'. To some degree, investing in any form of alternative investment involves lack of liquidity. The lack of liquidity – true also of venture capital investments – is part of the reason for the higher returns such investments purport to offer. But imposing greater disclosure without enabling higher levels of liquidity is simply a recipe for investor frustration and may do no one any good.

Arguably this is where the web comes in. The rest of this chapter explores several aspects of how hedge fund information is available on the web, ranging from general sources of information through to sources specifically dedicated to the topic. Then there is the new breed of hedge fund exchanges that aim to foster greater liquidity. Finally, there is the extent to which hedge funds themselves are present on the web, the quality of the information they could disclose and the amount they actually reveal.

There are striking difference in the way hedge funds approach the web, not all of them the obvious differences one might expect. If hedge funds are to attract more investment from institutions and have a more stable role within the international financial system, then this issue of web-based information disclosure is one that has to be addressed with a greater degree of focus than most funds have so far exhibited.

Certainly the web makes the means of information dissemination open to all: if hedge funds are not to continue to be perceived as international pariahs because of the actions of a few mavericks, then it is up to the industry to make a more concerted effort to argue the merits of its investment approach. More disclosure is the first step. At present it amounts to the sort of tantalising process not seen since courtesans performed the dance of the seven veils.

*   *   *

The first veil is information on generic performance. One thing the would-be hedge fund investor is not short of is information about the performance of different hedge fund styles. The web is helping enormously to make this information relatively freely available.

Hedge Fund Research (**www.hfr.com**) is run by Joe Nicholas. Nicholas is author of *Investing in Hedge Funds* and a well-known speaker on the hedge fund conference circuit. HFR's site allows users to access monthly performance data from 1996 onwards. The information is downloadable free of charge in PDF format for indices compiled on a variety of hedge fund styles. The site has definitions of the styles and explanations of how the indices are compiled. In addition, the site has news and a broadcast email list for any developments at the site. Subscribing to the full range of statistics costs some $200 per year. Registration for the inner reaches of the site requires the would-be user to be either a professional adviser or an accredited investor.

MARHedge (**www.marhedge.com**) is a publisher of regular newsletters and performance data on both hedge funds and managed accounts, typically run by US commodity trading advisers. Its site is not designed for maximum clarity but it does have some very useful information on hedge fund performance by style, in terms of month-by-month performance going back over several years, but also data on the median and upper and lower quartile performance of the various hedge fund styles.

Style definitions differ slightly from those adopted by Nicholas and don't include some of the more esoteric ones such as risk arbitrage and convertible arbitrage. Market-neutral styles are not analysed, at least in the publicly available data, into the constituent styles such as fixed-income arbitrage, equity hedge, and so on. The site also has news, editorial from the organisation's own staff, and links to the sites of a range of sponsors. MARHedge also periodically produces rankings of the top-performing funds in each category, ranked on an absolute return basis, by volatility and by Sharpe ratio (i.e. with returns adjusted for risk) showing performance rankings over one, three and five years.

Another site, albeit one that requires registration to gain access, is a site called Hedgefund.net (**www.hedgefund.net**), part of a group of sites related to the hedge fund and alternative asset investment scene run by Tuna Capital. Access to detailed fund information is restricted to qualified investors, but the site has a good databank of information.

It provides statistical analysis of the performance and performance rankings of individual fund styles, indices of performance of different strategies (in this instance a much greater variety of permutations of strategy than is available at other sites). Individual funds are ranked on the basis of individual monthly performance, performance over the year to date, Sharpe ratio, percentage of profitable months, and other variables.

A useful innovation is the ranking of performance of funds under the $10m mark, and the site also has an interesting table showing which fund pages within the site have been visited the most by would-be investors. The site's database is organised so that these rankings are produced in two parallel sites: one for US investors and one for off-shore (i.e. non-US) investors.

Another site is that of the Hedge Fund Consistency newsletter (**www.hedgefund-index.com**, not to be confused with the HedgeIndex URL). The site provides various statistical measures of hedge fund performance, although getting past the disclaimer page and registering to use the site is something of a feat.

VanHedge (**www.vanhedge.com**), a consultancy firm, also provides detailed generic performance data on hedge fund styles from an extensive database, as well as some narrative commentary on the trends in performance in the industry on a month-by-month basis.

The best recent initiative in this area, however, is undoubtedly HedgeIndex (**www.hedgeindex.com**), a joint venture between CSFB and Tremont, parent company of TASS, a well-known database of statistical information on hedge funds.

Launched in 1999 with the cooperation of a large number of hedge funds, including some of the largest and most prominent, this site, which is freely available, produces monthly index numbers of performance for all the classic hedge fund styles, along with related analytical tools and presentation of the data in a way that can be downloaded easily to spreadsheets for further analysis.

Construction of the index is weighted by asset, and funds must be greater than $10m in assets to qualify for inclusion. Moreover, funds must agree to provide regular performance data to be used in the index and must have audited financial statements. Funds are not removed from the index until they fail to meet the reporting requirements. The index is recalculated and rebalanced on a monthly basis and funds are reselected quarterly.

At the time of its launch, just short of 300 funds representing $100bn of assets were included in the index, subdivided into nine different styles, including all the classic styles mentioned in earlier chapters. The web site shows the returns for each style over periods which can be fully configured by the user and they go back to January 1994; more detailed analysis by fund style shows the mean return, worst percentage loss (sometimes called maximum drawdown) and the volatility. Volatility is the standard deviation of the monthly returns. These figures enable a variety of risk-adjusted comparisons to be made.

The index calculations are audited by a leading accountancy firm. The site also has a list of funds included in each sub-index. The obvious corollary of a product of this type is a tracker fund which replicates the movement in the individual hedge fund styles and which can be dealt in easily by the person in the street. At the launch it was stated that it was necessary for the index to become a credible product before such a move could be contemplated.

It might also help that some large funds which have thus far declined to participate are brought on board to make the index wholly representative. Nonetheless, as TASS's Nicola Meaden said at the time, 'There has been a big change in hedge fund managers' attitudes. Most have agreed to help.'

* * *

Hedge funds are not generally known for issuing press releases, although a select few do have web sites that contain information of this sort (see later). The second veil that needs shedding relates to news. Because they are newsworthy, business newspapers and magazines often run stories on hedge funds in general and individual hedge fund managers in particular.

The *Financial Times* (**www.ft.com**), *Forbes* (**www.forbes.com**) and *Fortune* (**www.fortune.com**) have freely searchable archives accessible to anyone and have often broken stories about hedge funds. The *Economist* (**www.economist.com**), *Business Week* (**www.businessweek.com**) and also the *Wall Street Journal* (www.wsj.com) have similar facilities, but they are only available to subscribers.

In general, however, those searching for news on hedge funds have to go to specialist sites and often have to register to gain access, although some sites allow partial access to non-investors. There is clearly no particular sanction that can be applied if you claim to be an accredited investor when in fact you aren't, and in some ways it's hard to see why some news-related sites insist on this requirement while others don't.

To recap, accredited investors should be able to demonstrate, or at least put their hand on their heart and say that they have either $1m in assets or $300 000 in annual income plus some degree of investing experience. Some sites will give access to bona fide researchers and consultants. From a news standpoint, general hedge fund industry news is available at a number of sites without entering a password-protected zone, while to search for news or reports on specific funds, a username and password are normally though not always required.

The MARHedge site has several news stories but Hedgeworld (www.hedgeworld.com) is probably the best site for tapping into general news about hedge funds. The content includes stories from the site's own journalistic staff and also from other relevant sources.

Hedgeworld is linked to the Tremont/TASS database on hedge funds, and as well as searching for news on funds, accredited users can also access a range of other resources, including a community section, a regularly updated top ten ranking of funds by assets, educational material on hedge funds and their investing styles, a short list of links to some related resources on hedge funds, including a very few individual hedge fund web sites, and so on. One of the main attractions for accredited users is subscriber access to detailed reports on individual funds from the TASS database. These reports show the following information on each fund:

- Summary performance statistics including returns, standard deviation, Sharpe ratio, its beta versus the S&P500, its alpha versus the

S&P500 and certain other statistics over a month, quarter to date, and over the last 12, 36 and 60 months.

- Basic information including style, whether or not the fund is open to investment, minimum investment, estimated assets, inception, contact details and a brief summary of its investment philosophy, software providers, custodians, administrators, industry bodies, and so on.

Tuna also has several seemingly dormant sites related to hedge funds, which may become more active in due course. There are few other worthwhile dedicated news sites related to hedge funds, although the newsletter Eurohedge (**www.eurohedge.co.uk**) has a limited selection of stories and reports available free of charge related to the European scene. At the time of writing, it offered a detailed report on the prime broker market in Europe.

Hedge Fund News (**www.hedgefundnews.com**) is another newsletter devoted to hedge funds but it has access to a modicum of news reports about hedge funds, and a particularly good list of interviews with hedge fund managers and industry figures, all available without registration. A database of hedge fund information is also available; users must register but the information appears to be free.

Hedge Fund Center (**www.hedgefundcenter.com**) has a reasonable series of feature articles on hedge funds, mainly written by the site's owners and their associates. The site also contains some news stories and a directory of hedge funds analysed by style, with a standard one-page summary of the fund's objectives, contact details, and so on. This is admirable in theory but, at the time of writing, the site only included a limited number of lesser-known funds.

Finally, Hedge Fund Resources (**www.hedgefundresources.com**) is a developing site with a small archive of articles about hedge fund investing and an assortment of related links and educational material.

*   *   *

There are a comparatively small number of industry associations devoted to the hedge fund industry, but their sites are fairly well put together, even if a little unimaginative, and they provide a reasonable degree of information about the industry. Another veil removed.

The site of the Alternative Investment Management Association (www.aima.org) has a good selection of educational material about hedge funds, a directory of members, and a library section, as well as a list of events relevant to hedge funds and other alternative investments. A newsletter at the site contains some articles which can be read without registration; others are password-protected and for members only. An interesting innovation is a generic multimedia presentation on the alternative investment industry, although this is not downloadable directly from the site; would-be users have to email the association for a copy.

Rather better value, for information on the industry, is the Hedge Fund Association site (www.thehfa.org). This site is constructed in a similar way to AIMA's but includes relevant press articles about hedge funds that date back to 1997 (all of them favourable of course) and press releases from the association itself, as well as links to member web sites categorised by function so that hedge fund managers can be identified from consultants, prime brokers and other service providers. Also interesting is a fairly active bulletin board, providing an insight into the workings of the industry, although a fair proportion of it appears to be devoted to those either seeking work at hedge funds or hedge fund managers seeking employees. Access to all the information on the site is available free of charge and without registration.

Last of all in this area is the Managed Funds Association. Somewhat more orientated towards independent futures trading rather than hedge funds, its web site is at www.mfainfo.org. The contents include a section on developments in the regulatory sphere in Washington, events, publications and documents (hard copy only), information about jobs at the association and some links. A bulletin board is available but seems hardly to be used.

As with the news sites and some other aspects of hedge funds on the web, explored later, there is considerable variation in the way the access is granted. Much of the information being displayed is of a similar type, yet some sites offer it freely with no need for the user to register or go through user verification, while others have heavy disclaimers and cumbersome registration procedures.

If it is to attract greater interest from the investing public and get itself a better press, the industry should try to arrive at some consistency about what is an acceptable level of access and what isn't. The average user could be forgiven for wondering why, if some sites allow unfettered access, others that are subject to the same regulatory constraints don't.

* * *

Consultants and other advisers fall into two categories: those advising would-be investors in hedge funds on the merits or otherwise of investing in particular funds and those firms that advise and act for hedge funds in their operations.

In the first category there are a range of firms with representation on the web. These vary from those advising individual investors seeking information on the way hedge funds work, and the merits of different hedge fund styles, to those acting on behalf of institutions who want to perform detailed checks on the background of hedge fund managers and the performance of their funds as part of the investment due diligence process.

In the first group, one of the best sites with information for individual investors is LJH (**www.ljh.com**). This is primarily a site for educating investors and has an excellent series of detailed white papers on the ins and outs of different hedge fund styles and how they work, all presented in a basic, no-frills, text-based format that is very user friendly.

Parker Global (**www.parkerglobal.com**) is a rather basic site aimed more at institutional investors; it also offers model portfolio construction, proprietary software tools, and a due diligence service.

Bookbinder Capital is a similar firm to LJH although its site is fairly basic (**www.bookbindercap.com**) and confined mainly to explanation of hedge fund terminology in rather less detail than LJH. There is, however, a good page of basic definitions.

KSP Capital (**www.kspcapital.com**) is another site orientated towards would-be professional investors in hedge funds, conducting due diligence on funds by means of extensive interviews and discussions with funds about their investment objectives, then attempting to match up funds with appropriate investors. The site has a good primer on hedge funds, and an excellent flow chart explaining how the consultancy process works.

Van Hedge (**www.vanhedge.com**) was mentioned earlier in the chapter in relation to its index measurement publications, many of which are available free of charge at its site, but the firm also offers a range of other professional advisory services.

Consultants or advisers to hedge fund groups may be classified as prime brokers, normally part of investment banking groups (their functions are discussed at some length in Chapter 8), advisers on risk management, and advisers on other aspects such as methods of securities financing like repo and stock lending.

Prime broker sites are something of a mixed bag. In many cases the details of prime broker services are buried deep in general investment banking sites, but the more imaginative have created stand-alone sites for their prime broking offshoots. Easily the two best sites are at **www.primebroker.com** and at **www.globalprimebroker.com**, respective offshoots from Bank of America Securities and Paine Webber (now part of UBS). In the case of **www.primebroker.com** there is a detailed exposition of the services on offer, a regularly updated newsletter about the services and detailed bios of the executives involved.

The Paine Webber site is probably the best of all the prime broker sites and is probably better considered as a general financial portal with some additional prime brokerage material, including the facility for clients to enter a password-protected area and upload and download datafiles relating to trades, valuation, and so on. One or two other prime broker sites are beginning to offer this facility.

Other sites dedicated specifically to prime brokerage, such as the ING Furman Seltz site at **http://prime.furmanseltz.com** and the Bear Stearns site at **www.bearstearns.com/about/** are fairly basic with textual descriptions of services offered and limited interactivity, although this may change over time as prime brokers and their customers become more familiar with using the web to communicate. Avalon Research (**www.avalonresearch.com**) is worthy of note as a prime broker specifically offering services to small and medium-sized hedge funds.

Outside of the prime broking area, a particularly good site is Capital Market Risk Advisors (**www.cmra.com**). This is a site particularly orientated towards helping hedge funds and others improve their risk management and offers a variety of services in this area, including auditing of trading systems for unintended risk factors (so-called model risk) and a range of other offerings.

* * *

Greater liquidity and transparency in the hedge fund arena is something of a Holy Grail. New initiatives do suggest, however, that at least some progress may be made towards improving this aspect of hedge fund investment. There have been two initiatives in particular, both utilising the web to deliver their services.

The Hedgeworld site (**www.hedgeworld.com**) has launched HedgeTrustExchange, in effect a bulletin board operated under the auspices of the Bermuda Stock Exchange (BSX). The site is designed to act as a crossing exchange for non-US-domiciled hedge funds to facilitate the matching of buyers and sellers.

The site allows users to place expressions of interest or firm buy and sell orders, with the aim of providing liquidity for investors in funds that are closed or that have restrictive redemption periods. All orders are anonymous unless either party wishes to indicate otherwise. Funds do not have to be listed on the BSX for trades to be done.

At the time of writing, there were a limited number of indications of interest available on the system, although more trades may have taken place behind the scenes. Information on the hedge funds themselves is available from the normal Hedgeworld access to the TASS database reports, which are updated monthly. More recently, Hedgeworld announced it was launching an online fund supermarket for hedge fund investors.

A parallel initiative, also utilising the BSX and with clearing through Euroclear and Clearstream, is PlusFunds.com (**www.plus-funds.com**). This works in a slightly different way. Hedge fund managers have to set up a new fund operated under the aegis of PlusFunds, if only so that standardised documentation can be used, but subscription and redemption, and secondary buying and selling are all catered for under the internet-based system. The funds thus created may mirror the existing portfolio of a hedge fund.

The big selling point for the system is that it is backed by Standard & Poor's real-time portfolio valuations along with risk profile data from Ernst & Young, so investors can have up-to-date information on the portfolio risk characteristics and net asset value (NAV), although not details of actual trades. Six global investment banks are reported to have agreed to be brokers on the system.

The site at the outset offered only around 43 funds, with only 35 funds having agreed to disclose their data, making its content look a little thin. However, more funds are set to participate, including some quite large ones, who are expected to create mirror images of their existing funds under the PlusFunds umbrella. If so, then by virtue of its independently verified up-to-date NAV numbers, the site could become something of a benchmark.

Ventures like this have got off to a slow start, but what the initiative shows is that web technology has the potential to improve liquidity or instruments that are notoriously illiquid in between redemption periods. It is generally in hedge fund managers' interests to encourage these moves, since it avoids the managers having to meet redemptions out of a fund's own cash reserves. The only drawback is the lack of any ability to vet the identity of the potential new investor in the fund.

A newer form of online interaction is designed to allow managers of hedge funds and other alternative investments sold via private placements the opportunity to circumvent the tedium of physical roadshows by providing an online medium for investors to see and hear presentations, and ask questions of hedge fund managers online, as well as providing investors with online access to due diligence material.

Using this system the manager could determine the level of access given to each would-be investor. It is said that hedge fund managers often spend as much as three to six months each year visiting investors and undergoing due diligence, and clearly any means by which this process can be streamlined will be of benefit to all concerned, provided it is not used by managers to introduce another layer of opacity into their dealings with investors. The service is currently being tested.

It allows managers to develop presentations in conjunction with the site operator that are then made available to selected investors, eliminating the need for an initial meeting between managers and investors. The site is paid by the hedge fund managers; it takes an initial fee and a small percentage of funds raised.

* * *

It is beyond any doubt that many hedge funds feel uncomfortable about the idea of web sites. So the sixth veil relates to hedge funds on the web. Part of the reason for hedge funds' nervousness about the web may be their relatively reclusive nature and part may be the advice from legal counsel that a web presence is tantamount to solicitation, and therefore not something to be contemplated at any price.

Another reason may simply be the fact that if a fund is closed, then there is little need for the hedge fund management firm to have a public presence at all. This assertion is probably unanswerable, except to point out that a hedge fund management firm may need to raise funds again in the future and, this being so, some form of public profile may be a good thing.

From the legal standpoint, hedge funds that do have web sites get around the objections in a variety of ways. Almost all have disclaimers that would-be viewers of material at the web site need to pass through before accessing any information. The next level up is that would-be visitors have to register for the site, verifying that they are accredited investors (usually by filling out a long form). Access is usually fairly speedily granted, sometimes immediately, and sometimes via a password and username being emailed later.

The most paranoid will usually only grant access to those who are accredited investors and personally known to the hedge fund managers. In this case the web presence is more like an intranet for existing investors and those who may soon become investors, rather than having any pretence of being a public site.

In the course of researching this book, I investigated hedge fund sites by combing likely directory entries at some of the generic sites and consultants and trade association sites mentioned earlier, and by conducting searches for hedge fund management group names on the most comprehensive internet search engine available. In all I found some 45 sites ranging across a variety of styles. A further 20–30 have web sites constructed to a standardised format and hosted by Hedgeworld.

The characteristics of the sites I documented were whether or not the funds themselves had a reasonable amount of information freely available about their activities without the requirement to register for a password; whether or not they had biographical details of the hedge fund managers and other personnel; and whether or not they had any particular sector focus or geographical focus.

Some 20 funds allowed access to information without registering, while a further six allowed access to some. The remainder of the sites required registration for a password. About 25 out of 45 sites had biographical details of fund managers available. In general, the list of sites offering biographies matched the list of sites offering either some information or a full range of information without requiring a registration procedure.

Looking at different fund styles to try and discern any pattern in the level of disclosure is conclusive. Those categorised as funds of funds or managers operating in a variety of different styles, 12 in all, tended to be the most open in offering some or all information without requiring passwords, although only 7 out of 12 had manager biographies available. Of 11 equity hedge funds (Zweig–DiMenna was the one site under construction at the time of writing), 6 required registration and only 6 had manager bios available.

Of four emerging market funds, all had manager bios and only one of the four required a password. Two of three fixed-income arbitrage funds offered password-free access and a decent range of information, including one that I reckoned was the best of all; it was the Ellington group of mortgage-backed securities funds (www.ellington.com).

In all only 13 funds out of 45 offered password-free access and complete information, including manager bios. Table 10.1 shows the funds in question. Links to all of the hedge fund sites I looked at are available (along with the other links mentioned in this chapter) on the hedge fund page of my web site at www.new-online-investor.co.uk. As a comparison exercise I looked in some detail at the Ellington site and also the password-protected site from Harch Capital Management (www.harchcapital.com). Harch Capital generously provided me with login details for the purposes of this research.

You enter Ellington's site by accepting the disclaimer and user agreement. Users then enter the site, which also has a closed section available only to Ellington investors and other registered individuals. Nonetheless, there is a considerable amount of information about the firm available at the 'about us' section of the site, with bios of all the main executives at the firm. In addition there is detailed information on the mortgage-backed securities market, its history and terminology, and about Ellington's role within it, the techniques it uses and the proprietary techniques it has at its disposal.

The design of the site is simple and uncluttered and the site provides a good degree of detail and context without overtly marketing the firm's funds. It seemed obvious to me that Ellington has taken a sensible view of the legal obligations on it and structured the site accordingly, and there seems no good reason why other firms could not follow its lead and disclose significantly more than they do at present without having to resort to cumbersome login and registration procedures.

At the Harch Capital site, there is a simple front page giving a brief summary and inviting users to complete a questionnaire to be allocated a username and password. In the body of the site, the firm

Table 10.1 Selected hedge fund web sites

Fund name	URL	Fund style	Info available?	Manager bios?
AKJ	www.akj.com	fund of funds	yes	yes
Austin Capital Management	www.austincap.com	fund of funds	some	yes
Aventine	www.aventineinvestments.com	equity hedge	yes	yes
Axiom Investment Managers	www.axiom-invest.com	emerging markets	yes	yes
Baron & Filtenbourg	www.bfcapital.com	various	yes	yes
Bayard Fund	www.bayard-partners.co.uk	equity hedge		no
Bowman	www.bowmancapital.com	equity hedge	password	yes
Canyon Partners	www.canyonpartners.com	event driven	yes	yes
Cardinal Fund Management	www.cardinalfund.com	various	yes	yes
Dominion Capital	www.domcap.com	managed futures	yes	yes
Dune Partners	www.dunepartners.com	equity hedge	some	yes
Eclipse Capital	www.eclipsecap.com	managed futures	yes	yes
Ellington	www.ellington.com	fixed income	yes	yes
Essex Investment Management	www.essexinvest.com	equity hedge	yes	yes
Estlander	www.estlander.com	various	yes	no
Evaluation Associates	www.eval-assoc.com	fund of funds	email	yes
Firebird	www.fbird.com	emerging markets	some	yes
FMG	www.fmgltd.com	various	yes	no
Folkes	www.folkes.co.uk	various	password	no
Gabelli	www.gabelli.com	event driven	password	no
Gordon House Optimal Fund	www.gham.co.uk	event driven	yes	no
Gottex	www.gottex.com		password	no
Harch Capital Management	www.harchcapital.com	event driven	password	no
Iris Financial Group (Ariston)	www.irisfg.com	emerging markets	password	yes
Magnum	www.magnum.com	fund of funds	yes	no
Maverick	www.maverickfund.com	equity hedge	password	no

Fund name	URL	Fund style	Info available?	Manager bios?
Momentum Asset Management	www.momentumuk.com	various	yes	no
Nelloadvisory	www.nelloadvisory.com	equity market neutral	yes	no
Niederhoffer	www.niederhoffer.com	managed futures	yes	yes
Owl Head (Hare Hedge)	www.owlhead.com	managed futures	yes	no
Park Place	www.parkplacecapital.com	various	some	yes
Pinnacle	www.piafunds.com	equity hedge	some	yes
Proprium	www.proprium.com	event driven	password	no
Regent Pacific	www.regentpac.com	emerging markets	some	yes
RR Capital Management	www.e-hedge.com	equity hedge	password	yes
Rumson Capital	www.rumsoncapital.com	managed futures	password	no
Sabre Fund	www.sabrefund.com	equity market neutral	some	yes
Scottish Value (Highlander)	www.scottish-value.co.uk	equity hedge	some	yes
Soros Fraternity Fund	www.fraternity-fund.com	global macro	password	no
TOR Fund	www.torfund.com		some	no
Towneley (Libre)	www.towneley.com	equity hedge	password	no
Trace Capital	www.tracecapital.com	equity hedge	password	no
Vision Funds	www.visionfunds.com	fixed income	yes	yes
Zweig–DiMenna	www.zweig-dimenna.com	equity hedge	soon	no

provides details of its funds (mainly in the fixed-income area with a total of about $400m under management at the time of writing).

The only significant difference between the two sites is that behind the password-protected area of its site, Harch is able to be a little more overt about displaying its monthly performance figures, and displaying its fund rankings, which have been very good. Users can also download a Microsoft PowerPoint presentation about the fund. Other than this, there are detailed bios of the fund's personnel, much as in some other publicly available sites.

More recently others have begun offering information on the web. Blackberry Capital Management, for example, is a new Toronto-based fund that is becoming something of a pioneer in the area of disclosure, with an approach likened to allowing investors to 'look over his shoulder'. Alexandra Investment Managers, a New York convertible arbitrage fund has begun listing statistics like its geographical allocation, up-to-date NAV and top ten holdings, plus other statistics related to its risk profile. The site is designed to answer many of the due diligence questions posed by professional investors. Initiatives like this point the way for others, although not all are so enlightened.

*   *   *

Hedge funds could disclose more than they do at their sites, but at least those funds and others I have mentioned have taken the trouble to construct sites and to present a public face. I searched for a couple of hundred funds in all, fewer than 10% of the total, but taking the larger and better-known fund groups with the larger size of assets under management. The hit rate on funds I searched for was around 1 in 6, with the remainder of funds included in my database culled from directories and other sources.

However, I believe the sample is large enough to be representative of the hedge fund industry as a whole, and that it shows the industry needs to be a little more proactive in displaying its wares if it is to get a better press and cultivate institutional investment interest. The current state of play in the hedge fund scene on the web is reminiscent of company web sites three or four years ago, when an enlightened few companies had sites and the remainder hid behind legal objections until the momentum for all companies to have sites became unstoppable.

Hedge funds will never make it to the mainstream investment arena unless this nettle is firmly grasped.

11

Attaining respectability

Not only did she refuse to meet Madame Swann, she conducted an out and out campaign to force her friends and acquaintances to do the same
                                    Marcel Proust, *Within a Budding Grove*

Courtesans craved acceptance by polite society. They usually attained (or attempted) it by marrying someone of good standing. Whether or not the acceptance into society is unqualified is another matter. Ladies with a more conventional background sometimes gave such newcomers the cold shoulder.

The same is true of hedge funds – the courtesans of capitalism. Despite the investment genre's raffish reputation, among the senior ranks of institutional investors there is an increasing acceptance that hedge fund investment, or the use of hedge fund techniques, can be legitimate. It is justified as a tool to enhance returns and reduce the dependence on more normal market exposure.

But the involvement in hedge funds, though increasing, is still rather tentative. Few institutions invest more than a small fraction of their portfolios in this area, and hedge funds have to compete for attention with other 'alternative investments', such as private equity and venture capital, commodity trading programmes and the like.

* * *

When the question of the involvement of big investors such as pension funds and insurance companies in hedge funds is raised, one name that usually crops up is the California Public Employees Retirement

Scheme (CalPERS). CalPERS announced in August 1999 that it was beginning to invest in hedge funds and was intending to inject some $12bn into the alternative investment sector over a period of years, a figure representing around a quarter of the actively managed portion of the $160bn fund. An initial $1bn allocation was recently approved. Though the CalPERS move lent a degree of credibility to the notion that institutional involvement in hedge funds was no longer beyond the pale, in fact the team at CalPERS were far from being the first professional investors to notice that hedge funds could form part of a 'normal' investment portfolio without the sky falling in.

But it may have seemed like that, especially in Europe. Fewer than five years ago, at an investment conference in October 1996, it emerged that around two-thirds of European institutional investors did not know the name of one hedge fund: this despite the role George Soros's Quantum Fund and others had played in the ejection of sterling and the lira from the ERM in September 1992. Most institutions now know the name of at least one hedge fund, but as an industry report recently noted, it would be a shame if one (LTCM) were to be the only name they knew. At the very least, and secretive though many hedge funds have been in the past, all investors need to understand how they work, if only because they coexist in the same investment environment.

US institutions have tended to be the most active investors in hedge funds and other alternative investments, though their exposure and their sophistication can often be exaggerated. The lack of discernment by some institutions investing in hedge funds was amply demonstrated by the LTCM debacle. Estimates put the total asset allocation to alternative investment by US pension schemes in the region of 2%, and as well as hedge funds this category also includes private equity and venture capital, and managed futures programmes.

That said, the 2% overall figure is being contributed by just 9% of this type of investor, suggesting that, of those who do invest, their individual exposure to alternative investments is much higher. Half as many again in percentage terms are said to be considering investing in hedge funds, so the proportion of funds committed from this source looks set to increase sharply. One reason for this may be that managers recognise the exceptional nature of the 1990s bull market and see hedge funds – in the classic Jones mould – as a way of maintaining respectable performance without surrendering gains in a subsequent bear market. At a conference on alternative investment in mid 1999 it was predicted, perhaps optimistically, that by the end of 2002 as much as $1000bn could flow into hedge fund investing from the US pensions industry alone.

University endowments in the US have been particularly promi- nent investors in hedge funds, perhaps because of the influence of modern portfolio theory in academia, and the personal financial inter- ests of trustees and professors. Not that the professors are necessarily the fund managers. Yale's outstanding performance in this area has been masterminded by David Svensen, a former Wall Street bond trader turned contrarian investor.

A specialist software house surveyed the field and found that between June 1995 and June 1998 (just prior to the LTCM debacle), the percen- tage number of college endowments investing in hedge funds had risen from 15% to about 23% and their average portfolio allocation to the category from 7.3% to 9.3%. Colleges had earned a comparable return on their hedge fund portfolios to those on their ordinary stock port- folios. Some studies have come up with a higher percentage for those investing, just short of 30%; a further 12% have said they might invest.

The interest of academic portfolios in hedge funds extends to the UK, where several Oxford and Cambridge colleges have been involved as investors. Generally, however, UK institutions have been slow to take to alternative investment. On most counts the UK and Germany have been least interested in hedge funds, while countries such as Switzerland and France have been most keen.

A recent survey conducted by Fulcrum Research on behalf of the financial public relations firm Ludgate Communications confirmed this. Based on a sample of 100 major institutional investors across Europe, it showed that some 17% of funds invested money in hedge funds and a further 39% were looking to do so in the foreseeable future, defined as the following two years. Institutions in France and Switzerland were keenest and those in Germany least likely to invest.

In the future, hedge fund investment looks set to increase most markedly in Scandinavia and the Netherlands.

The UK's lack of interest is not universal. There are exceptions. Aside from Oxbridge college endowments, some company pension funds have dipped a toe in the water (AstraZeneca and Cable & Wireless have been mentioned), while Nestlé and ABB in Switzerland are also said to have been active. Elsewhere, the Dutch have been relatively adventurous in the hedge fund and alternative investment arena generally, and look set (if the most recent survey is correct) to get more involved in due course. ABP, the public sector employees' pension fund, and other large funds are said to have allocated as much as 5% of their funds to a mix of private equity and hedge fund investments.

More recently, and in the wake of the CalPERS decision and the UK government's exhortation for pension funds to invest more in venture capital, the coal industry pension scheme (a £23bn fund) announced it would put up to 5% of the fund's assets in the alternative investment category. Several fund management groups in the UK – Schroder Investment Management, Merrill Lynch Mercury, Gartmore, Deutsche Asset Management and others – have either launched hedge funds or are considering doing so, partly to attract funds but also to retain staff who might otherwise defect.

Another big investor to spot the return-enhancing possibilities of hedge funds has been Warren Buffett. The homespun philosophy expounded by Buffett for consumption by his legions of private investor followers and the coterie of devotees among investment commentators, this is just one aspect of his character. The so-called Sage of Omaha is also a highly sophisticated investor by no means just wedded, as some commentators suggest, to value investing in the equity market. For evidence, witness his extremely profitable position in US Treasury zero-coupon bonds, a highly geared speculation on a downward movement in interest rates, a few years back, and his involvement as a would-be buyer of LTCM.

Buffett's involvement in hedge funds started earlier. In July 1998 he invested $270m in West End Capital, a bond arbitrage fund based in Bermuda. Strictly speaking, this fund isn't a hedge fund, since Berkshire

Hathaway (Buffett's company) is its only investor. Nor does it charge a performance fee in the conventional sense. But in most other respects its techniques are those of a conventional hedge fund. In March 2000 Buffett brought the fund more closely into his orbit, by promoting its chief fund manager to run the global financial products division of General Re, a Berkshire subsidiary. The day-to-day operations of the fund itself have been delegated to two specialist traders hired from a small Dublin-based bond arbitrage fund, Europlus Global Opportunities.

The strategy adopted by West End Capital, at least according to a *Wall Street Journal* article at the time, is essentially much the same as other fixed-income arbitrage funds. It uses leverage to enhance returns generated by playing differences in yield spreads. It invests a wide range of instruments primarily conducting arbitrage, but with about a fifth of the fund at any one time speculating in directional bets.

The fund returned a respectable 16% in 1999 but barely rates a mention amid the folksy rhetoric of Buffett's annual letter to shareholders in the Berkshire annual report. In fact, present or would-be investors in Berkshire would be hard put to deduce the company had any involvement in a quasi hedge fund at all; only deep in the notes to the accounts is there evidence of a sharply increased level of repo activity that betrays its presence. West End Capital may be small potatoes in the wider Buffett empire.

Buffett's investment methods are as much about a search for arbitrage profit as anything. His investment ideal of a long-term 'margin of safety' is in essence an arbitrage between the actual cost of an investment and its true underlying value. Buffett has long been as fascinated by complex financing structures with hidden value as with mainstream easy-to-understand brands, witness Berkshire's involvement in reinsurance and fractional aircraft ownership. So perhaps his involvement in hedge fund techniques such as fixed-income arbitrage is not so curious after all.

Not all investors have Buffett's astuteness. And hedge funds remain a minority taste. But hedge fund managers only need a minority of investors to part with their money to be able to raise sufficient funds. Many hedge funds of the type that institutions want to invest in are relatively small, and even a figure that represents a small investment for an institution can make a big difference to a fund.

Where the main sources of capital originate for alternative investments is fairly clear. For the category in general it is usually reckoned that private investors make up 60% of the total, banks (who may also be representing private individuals, especially if they are private banks) make up 10%, with the remaining 30% split between pension funds (around two-thirds) and corporate pension funds and insurance companies (one-sixth each). For hedge funds, individual investors remain vitally important. Participation here is often at one step removed, however, through funds administered by the so-called family offices of wealthy individuals and their families, or else via fund of funds products.

Private sources of capital, according to a report commissioned by RR Capital Management from KPMG, suggested 82% of hedge fund cash came from this source and, of the remaining 18%, some 8% from endowments, 5% from pension funds, 1% from insurance companies and the balance of 4% from various other sources.

There are big differences in the style of funds favoured by different types of investor. Individuals and family offices tend to opt more for aggressive growth, opportunistic and technology-orientated funds and they would doubtless also choose global macro funds if they were not generally closed to all but the largest investors. Corporate pension funds tend to opt for arbitrage, distressed securities and other event-driven styles, while mainstream pension schemes go for a mixture of arbitrage, macro and market-neutral strategies. Endowments often opt for distressed securities and convertible arbitrage.

There are several reasons why institutional investors are looking towards hedge fund investment. The trend also has implications for the hedge fund industry as a whole and its ability to function efficiently. Hedge funds have often worked best when they were little noticed and relatively small; the advent of large high-profile funds can sometimes be self-defeating, as revealed by Soros and Tiger. Equally there are very real issues for institutional investors to confront and reconcile when investing in hedge funds, not all of which are easy to resolve. These issues and the reason for institutional investors' involvement in the market are the subjects of the next two sections.

*   *   *

Cynics say that the main reason professional investors invest in hedge funds is so they can brag about it at cocktail parties to those less versed in the subject. Whether or not this is true, the main reasons lie elsewhere, in the fundamentals of the hedge fund concept. The most important point is that hedge funds, whatever their shortcomings from time to time, are dedicated to absolute return – they seek to produce a return that is consistently positive irrespective of market conditions.

Whereas most fund managers measure themselves on the basis of relative performance against a benchmark, the most common tool for assessing hedge fund managers, the Sharpe ratio, measures the rate of return in excess of the risk-free rate and compares this with the risk undertaken as measured by the volatility of the returns. It is a pure measure of return against risk.

It is of course self-evident that not all hedge funds achieve this all the time and some, though they may make spectacular returns from time to time, only do so at the expense of exceptional levels of volatility. If through investing in hedge funds by whatever means, a fund manager can generate (after paying hedge fund management and performance fees) a consistent return significantly greater than the risk-free rate with low levels of volatility, he or she should be considered to be doing a good job.

The absolute return characteristic of hedge funds has a particular attraction for pension schemes who face real liabilities now and in the future that have to be met by investment returns. Actual liabilities have to be met from positive returns. Even a consistent period of relative outperformance during a prolonged bear market would not help to pay the benefits on which pensioners depend. This is particularly important if, as some observers believe, the conventional share market may be entering a period of greater volatility and lower returns, after the spectacularly good performance posted in the 1980s and 1990s.

Another key facet of hedge fund investing as a concept is that institutions are not stuck with investing in a single fund. Indeed, in theory, investing in a mixture of funds should reduce risk still further. What is important is that institutional investors can invest in funds which operate in a defined way and which have specific risk and return characteristics.

Most important of all is the fact that funds can be chosen which still produce positive absolute returns, but in a way that is disconnected from the behaviour of the market as a whole. In statistical terms this is described as a fund having a loose correlation with the market and is measured by the statistical variable r^2. In this instance the level of r^2 is the percentage by which the movement in a fund is 'explained' by the movement in the market. A fund which aimed to track a particular stock market index would, for example, have an r^2 at or close to 100%, whereas some hedge funds have r^2 figures as a low as 20%.

This is interesting when it is combined with the fact that most conventional 'active' fund managers fail to beat the performance of the market. In other words, simply buying the index would be better than trying to pick an active fund manager on the basis of his or her past performance. Over a ten-year period, it is estimated in the UK unit trust industry, for example, that some 82% of managers fail to beat the index. If this is the case, why pay the fees of active managers when low-cost index trackers are available?

The more thoughtful of institutional fund managers, trustees and pension plan sponsors therefore come up with the idea that it is far better simply to index most of one's performance and to allocate a relatively modest percentage of capital to funds which are managed in a non-traditional way. This is especially the case if they have displayed positive returns that have been relatively uncorrelated with the market as a whole; in other words, the so-called alternative investment categories of private equity and hedge funds.

In most circumstances, at least theoretically, this should produce a better return per unit of risk for the fund, to the benefit of all concerned. As an investment policy, it would come into its own especially in times when the performance of the market as a whole is less than sparkling. Then, if things went according to form, the positive returns exhibited by the hedge fund component of the portfolio would bolster returns.

This is far from being an academic issue. The UK's Accounting Standards Board is proposing changes to pension fund accounting that will have the effect of making the returns made by pension funds more transparent rather than simply being the result of what a fund's actuaries believe it may be appropriate to show. The result may be that funds deliberately seek out investments, such as hedge funds, that can dampen the effect of market volatility.

In simple terms the combining of passive indexed investing with non-correlated returns from hedge funds and other alternative investments is the reason for the decision taken by CalPERS to invest in the hedge fund arena. What it does require, however, is intensive research on the part of the investing fund to make sure that managers are selected and monitored thoroughly. Considerable diligence is required because the managers that may be the best selection may not be the ones in the limelight, but rather those that modestly go about their business and produce consistent returns from a defined style over a lengthy period.

Investing in hedge funds may make sense logically for pension schemes and insurance companies, but there are some practical issues to confront along the way.

*   *   *

A big part of the issue for investors is simply the lurid publicity that some hedge funds attract. In the earlier sections of this book we have considered how some hedge fund operators inevitably attract publicity, not always of the most favourable variety. The fact that the hedge fund industry has attracted strong-willed mavericks does not necessarily endear it to pension fund trustees as a home for their funds' money. In cases like this, administrators face a 'career risk' if they opt for the wrong hedge fund. It is easier, and safer, to choose something more conventional.

However, it should also be clear that some hedge fund styles, particularly those that are essentially market neutral while avoiding high levels of leverage – the classic hedge fund in the mould set by Alfred Winslow Jones – can be construed as a highly suitable investment for institutional investors. Indeed a paper at a UK actuaries conference held in 1999 suggested that hedge funds merited investigation for those funds which based their investment strategy around a 'passive core' approach with 'satellite' investments designed to enhance returns, and it went so far as to suggest that as much as 10% of a fund could be invested in this way.

Chief among the objections to hedge fund investing are the fee structures most funds impose. Even allowing for the fact that a portion of fees is sometimes rebated to institutional investors, many investors have an in-built objection to performance fees, which are so generous and so tilted one way. In other words, investors who invest in hedge funds have to be content that they will give a fifth of any gains to the hedge fund manager, while bearing 100% of any losses, notwithstanding the fact that in some instances a portion of the manager's net worth is invested in the fund and that in the event of a decline, the funds often have to recoup any previous losses before performance fees resume.

At the core of the objection to this is the idea we alluded to in an earlier chapter, that there could be a temptation for a manager to indulge in excessive risk taking, especially if performance early in a fee-earning cycle starts to deteriorate, perhaps doubling up the risk to retrieve a negative position. At the same time, high fees bring a lack of tolerance of poor or inconsistent performance.

In the past the fee issue and some other less desirable aspects of the hedge fund industry have probably resulted as much as anything from a shortage of capacity in the hedge fund management industry. In other words, hedge funds were so sought-after by investors that managers regarded themselves as the elite of the industry and behaved with a greater degree of arrogance towards investors than may have been warranted.

Some observers now believe that if it becomes obvious that hedge fund investing by institutions is taking off, supply will increase and institutional investors may be able to demand that performance fees are reduced to more normal levels or that a formula will be devised where, if returns turn negative, a portion of fees previously paid will be refunded.

It is certainly true that if investing in hedge funds is to become a more accepted pastime for mainstream professional investment managers, then greater disclosure and transparency will be required. This is not just because institutions themselves require more information than hedge funds have traditionally been used to giving to satisfy their trustees, but also because institutions want the assurance that the actions of a hedge fund they might invest in will not damage their portfolio performance elsewhere in previously unforeseen ways.

Other issues related to transparency include the ability of investors to access real-time details of the returns made by funds, and even portfolio constituents via a password-protected web site (Chapter 10). But there are other items on the wish list as well. One is that a third party vets the data disclosed by a fund. Logically this could be the fund's prime broker or custodian. And very importantly indeed, the fund's investments should have been priced independently of the fund's managers, particularly over-the-counter investments such as derivatives, swaps and the like, but also any investments that are thinly traded.

However logical, it is a moot point whether or not the prime broker is the best originator of this information. Some might say that the broker's position as a key administrator of the fund is a problem. Being paid commissions by the hedge fund manager, a broker's independence may be compromised to some degree. Prime brokers compete ferociously for hedge fund business, and might not want to offend their current and potential future clients by getting involved in controversies over disclosure and performance measurement. Custodians may be viewed as potentially having fewer axes to grind.

Linked to the disparate nature of hedge funds is the issue of liquidity. Most professional investors are used to being able to liquidate investments quickly if the need arises. This option is rarely available for hedge funds, with their infrequent 'liquidity days' when redemptions are allowed. And institutional investment is not likely to be encouraged either when hedge funds, as occasionally happens, suddenly 'blow up' with little warning. The sharp correction in technology stocks in March/April 2000, for example, resulted in one fund losing 80% of its value in a matter of a week or so. Other disasters have since followed, some the result of fraud as their managers tried to bolster collapsing performance figures.

It is a moot point whether the fledgling development of web-based hedge fund exchanges (Chapter 10) will be sufficient to allay fears over lack of liquidity. With greater institutional exposure to the hedge fund sector there may come more of a secondary market in hedge fund participation. But as a would-be investor in a fund, would you wish to buy a participation when the seller perhaps had better information about the progress of the fund? The answer is probably no.

In other words, the creation of liquidity goes hand in hand with more disclosure, and extending that disclosure to non-investors. As if this were not enough, there are other drawbacks. One of them is the fact that hedge funds are not homogeneous. That is, their track records and the quality of their management vary considerably, both overall and within the different styles. The ability to have a hedge fund component in a portfolio that does the job it was intended to do depends crucially on the manager or group of funds selected, since the difference between the median return and the upper and lower quartiles can be not just significant but substantially different. Pick the wrong horse, and performance suffers.

A recent industry survey showed, for example, that US college endowments' selections of hedge funds over an extended period produced a return two full percentage points better than the norm, around a tenth better than the average it was compared with. What this really means is that there is a job for independent consultants to do, with the emphasis on independent. Very similar to the other main alternative investment category of private equity, independent consultants help institutions select the best managers with which to allocate money. Care needs to be taken to make sure these gatekeepers are not themselves exhibiting any bias when it comes to selecting funds, either inadvertently or otherwise.

Measuring the performance of hedge funds with the rigour that institutions normally expect to measure things is something of a conundrum as well. It is not just that in many cases the track record of hedge funds is short. But hedge funds also 'blow up' with alarming regularity and disappear off the radar screen. This means that the remaining performance figures of the group can be tainted with what is quaintly called survivorship bias. In other words, the performance figures quoted for the group might reflect only the figures of the funds still in existence and automatically exclude those whose performance has been dire to the point of extinction.

There is also debate as to how one should treat the performance figures of those funds closed to investment, since it is the past performance of the funds that are open and taking in new money at present that is the only really relevant figure for new potential investors. It is also probably fair to say that delegating part of the investment process to a hedge fund manager is far from being a soft option for an institutional investor. Alternative investments need to be closely monitored and, by the nature of the way they work, hedge funds require close monitoring and can also produce large amounts of documentation, both numerical and narrative, each month.

There are some common quasi-legal issues that hedge fund investors have to resolve. These range from straightforward prohibitions. For example, the state of New York prohibits by law its pension plan from investing in hedge funds, itself an interesting commentary on the laws of the state that is home to some of the biggest securities markets in the world. Some institutions are reluctant to invest, or prohibited from investing in entities that use high levels of leverage, and this may discourage investment in bond arbitrage funds, for example.

Event-driven strategies such as distressed debt or risk arbitrage create public relations problems for some funds and may be excluded by trustees on moral grounds. A similar bias is probably also evident against the purer short-seller funds. In other words, short selling is okay if it is part of a relatively low-geared long/short equity fund, for example, but not otherwise.

Another common legal stricture limits the degree to which some institutional investors, particularly insurers, can invest in limited partnerships. The rules currently suggest that no more than 5% of a fund can be invested in limited partnerships. Given that some real-estate investments are structured in this way and that some institutions have also invested in oil and gas partnerships, this may be a serious objection in some cases.

A more general issue is whether or not hedge fund investing sits comfortably, so far as US institutional investors are concerned, within the so-called ERISA guideline. ERISA (the Employee Retirement Income Security Act, passed in 1974) rules suggest that investors should behave with prudence and this, in some institutions' minds, may suggest caution towards hedge funds and indeed other alternative investments.

That said, ERISA may more often be used as an excuse for not investing in this way, to avoid taking a potentially controversial decision. On the face of it, there can be little wrong with the prudence of making an investment that would produce a comparable return to the stock market benchmark, with lower risk, and which would also be uncorrelated with that benchmark. Indeed, according to industry sources, there have been recent court rulings which clarify how the modern portfolio theory (MPT) of Sharpe and Markowitz can play a role in fund decisions.

Perhaps the most important issue for institutional investors is the phenomenon known as style drift and how to avoid it; in other words, the manager will start off producing returns from, say, a conventional long/short equity strategy but gradually branch out into other areas (say convertible arbitrage) or take more directional bets than might normally be expected, or introduce more leverage into the equation.

Mark Yusko, chief investment officer for the University of North Carolina at Chapel Hill, relates style drift to performance-based fees. Speaking at a conference in early 2000 he is reported by *Hedgeworld*

News to have said, 'When styles drift, it's an investor's worst nightmare. . . . When managers morph, it's not because they're managing my risk, it's because they're managing their own business risk. They drift because they're afraid of losing new money. Global macros may shift and reinvent themselves daily, but we hire a pure style manager to produce "alpha" in that style. If you have an edge, stick to it.'

* * *

Though in percentage terms the numbers may be small, it seems almost certain that a combination of factors will lead to a significant inflow of cash into hedge funds and other alternative investments. These factors range from the difficulty of conventional investment techniques matching recent historic returns from the great 1990s bull market; the growth of passive indexed investing; greater receptiveness to new investment ideas; and the loosening of ERISA guidelines to permit investments that can be justified on MPT grounds.

Many observers, however, see this inflow happening at best at a measured pace and with occasional pauses. There remain powerful obstacles to large-scale institutional investment in hedge funds, as described in the previous section. One is almost conceptual or philosophical in nature. Can hedge funds really succeed in becoming a mass-market pursuit, when to do so puts their managers at a disadvantage? Hedge funds are able to pursue the strategies they do because they are a relatively small and often secretive part of the investment scene, exploiting disparities and using techniques most fund managers are either unversed in or arguably not competent or willing to handle.

The very nature of this skill suggests that attempting to replicate it on the much larger scale required if institutional investment in hedge funds increases would potentially be self-defeating. The true investment talent to operate in this way is a scarce commodity, and the larger a fund run by a talented manager becomes, the less able it is to operate in the correct way. Some observers believe that the hedge fund industry is exhibiting the signs of a product life cycle beloved of management theory. It may be argued that mutual funds (known in Europe as unit trusts or open-ended investment companies) have already gone through this cycle of tentative trial, growth, proliferation and consolidation, the last part of the process seeing the emergence of fewer larger groups each offering an array of fund products.

In this instance the classic first stage of tentative use of new product is succeeded by a second stage of high revenue growth, many competitors, low barriers to entry and high profitability. Arguably hedge funds are in that stage now. The third stage, where mutual funds are now, is marked by maturity, universal use of the product by the mass market, slowing growth, greater price competition and consolidation. The KPMG report produced in conjunction with RR Capital Management and referred to earlier expands on this theme. It suggests that hedge funds today are in the same stage of development as mutual funds in the early 1980s and could see a sharp influx of capital in the next ten years before growth slackens.

But the corollary is that, as with mutual funds, the only logical way for the industry to develop is into multifund 'families' where the lower fees and adherence to specific styles that institutional investors expect can be countenanced because marketing and administration expenses are spread over several funds, not just one. Currently, though, there are few large funds. More than half of the 3000 plus funds in existence have assets of less than $20m. This is, if nothing else, testimony to the fact that the performance fees of a small fund can be such that a lone manager can make a good living. Even a fund of $10m making a 10% return would generate a combined management and performance fee (on the 1% and 20% basis) of $300 000 per year. Not large by Wall Street standards perhaps, but big enough to have a comfortable lifestyle in Middle America.

While one can argue logically that issues such as the more elderly managers cashing in their chips might be a reason for mergers between funds, the opposite is suggested by the eccentricities that made them successful managers in the first place. One can perhaps cite the example of Julian Robertson. He would rather close his fund down, distribute the proceeds to investors, and perhaps start again than pass control on to others. Even if the leading light of a hedge fund group is prepared to sell out, his or her main assets (i.e. talented younger fund managers and administrators) may resent the idea of the business being sold and leave immediately or in the future, making the purchase a risky one for the would-be acquirer.

The bottom line is that hedge fund managers do what they do because they are independent-minded individuals who do not want the constraints and bureaucracy of operating under a corporate umbrella. Even if downward pressure on fees is likely, many managers may make a quality of life decision that they would rather work independently for less income than become part of a larger organisation. Existing fee structures are such that it might be difficult for would-be acquirers to pay an economic price, at least on conventional valuation criteria, that would compensate managers for the loss of independence and the fee income that went with it. Hedge fund managers are only likely to agree to such a move if they foresee trickier times ahead.

In short, one suspects that hedge fund managers can live with demands to abstain from style drift and to provide more information (especially via the web). They can live with some of the other demands that institutional investors may place on them. And they may even live with some downward pressure on fees. What they would find harder to stomach is any change in the industry that resulted in a loss of independence. With such a loss would come a requirement to adhere to the bureaucratic stricture of a large organisation, perhaps similar to the one they left to start the fund in the first place.

The greater likelihood is that it will be regulatory pressure that causes individual hedge fund managers and small hedge fund management organisations to consider selling out. Having outsourced the administrative details required of them, in order to devote their full attentions to generating alpha, if compliance cannot be outsourced, then merger or a graceful exit from the business may be the alternative.

Our guess is therefore that institutional investors, while they might prefer dealing with larger management groups, might have to reconcile themselves to the extra administrative burden that investing in larger numbers of smaller funds brings with it, and for some time yet. If they accept that hedge fund techniques are a valuable counterpoint to their other investing activities, it will be a price they are prepared to pay to get the best talent on offer.

12

Taming Archimedes

Give me a place to stand, and I will move the earth
Archimedes, On the Lever

There are many contradictions about the hedge fund industry. Hedge funds began as a way of reducing risk to investors by eliminating the impact of the market on performance. Yet some have gone bust in spectacular style. Their originator was as modest as some of his successors have been flamboyant. Though their name suggests hedging, and hence caution, many of the best-known funds are essentially directional speculators.

By producing what may sometimes seem mediocre performance whose sole virtue is its lack of correlation with market benchmarks, hedge fund managers earn huge incentive fees. The fees are an incentive to perform well, which attracts new investors, yet the larger hedge funds get, the more difficult it is for them to do their job. Conventional fund managers and banks, seeking to mimic their success by creating internal hedge funds, may end up creating only envy and dissatisfaction among other employees and generating risks their customers do not want.

Some hedge funds castigate governments and corporations alike for a lack of transparency, yet they themselves rely on secrecy. They can threaten the stability of the financial system, yet they also provide it with liquidity. Equally some hedge fund managers, especially those with libertarian leanings, rail against 'crony capitalism'. They use this as moral justification for attacking the underpinnings of developing economies, yet display some signs of it themselves when their own livelihoods are under threat. While famously described as 'highway-men of the global economy' and seemingly functioning in a moral vacuum, some (though not all) hedge fund managers are generous to a fault with their private wealth, often espousing causes seemingly at odds with their competitive natures.

It is of course tempting to suggest that the hedge fund industry will ultimately collapse under the weight of its own contradictions, perhaps bringing the capitalist system down with it. The LTCM crisis seemed to suggest that, left to its own devices, this would be precisely the result. But an analysis like this doesn't really hold water. True hedge funds bring benefits, but those who seek excessive leverage (or the institutions with which they deal) need taming. Their lenders and counterparties need rules to adhere to. Observance of simple rules and greater disclosure can allow 99% of hedge fund managers to pursue their businesses, and gener-ate wealth for their investors and themselves unchecked. It can also allow, through the participation of institutional investors, the genuine benefits of hedge fund style investing to permeate through to the mass market via individuals' pension funds and collective investments.

Advocating any form of regulation is heresy to some hedge fund managers and their apologists, yet many others in the industry are alive to the risks they can pose and want something to be done. There are dangers still present in the system.

*   *   *

The beauty of the traditional hedge fund model is that it rewards pure talent. It is perfectly possible for a hedge fund manager to operate from a home office with a minimum level of technology and make a modest living managing ten million dollars or less if his or her tastes are not especially extravagant. If the fund performs, the rewards flow; if not, investors withdraw their funds and look elsewhere for a better man-ager. This suggests that the operation of what Jim Slater calls the 'Zulu principle' can work well in the hedge fund arena. A manager can specialise in a sector or in a particular style of trading, or both, and if successful, attract funds precisely because the style is so tightly defined.

Consistency in style and lack of market impact is precisely what institutional investors may seek in future if they are to allocate a greater portion of their funds to the alternative investment category and to hedge funds in particular. With some exceptions they will look with horror at the activities of large high-profile macro funds, and avoid managers who exhibit style drift when the markets are less favourable to their particular mode of investing. In some instances, signs that funds are making abnormal returns may be treated as prima facie evidence of an unwelcome drift in style.

With the greater transparency now becoming available through the existence of a number of hedge fund performance measurement web sites, and the readily available benchmarks of the performance of different style categories, it is now easier than it was to find those smaller managers who are the superior performers in a particular style and with a particular speciality.

In terms of numbers, most hedge funds are more or less true to the template originally established by Alfred Winslow Jones. Jones, it should be remembered, produced his stunning results through simple long/short stock picking, without much in the way of computerised analysis. This is the good side of the hedge fund industry: small, disciplined, specialist, truly hedged, modestly leveraged and unobtrusive; generating good returns but unlikely ever to pose a threat to the financial system.

In the other corner we have a less attractive member of the species; it can be unhedged, leveraged up to the eyeballs, egotistical, unscrupulous and potentially damaging. At least three of the seven deadly sins – pride, envy and avarice – are present in bank proprietary trading desks.

It is a caricature in both senses, but the small independent hedge fund manager is pitting their wits against the market at the same time as running their own business. Among big financial institutions, the picture is a less attractive one: 'prop desk' traders who are less talented than the independent funds, but who are maximising their own bonuses rather than serving their investors, who use market power for trading advantage and who, in my experience at least, at times trade as principals against the interests of their employers' other clients.

Though banks are regulated to a degree, there remains the grotesque notion that swaggering traders may indirectly be using customers' savings for grand-scale market speculation. Yet senior managers at most banks are too bound up in the process, both financially and politically, to reform the system. Blowing the whistle risks jeopardising bonuses and being branded a party pooper. Regulators seem too bemused to act.

You may have deduced I have a low opinion of proprietary traders, and bankers. It centres on several basic points. One is their size and the leverage they use, which dwarfs even the largest independent hedge fund group. Another is the fact that their sources of funds – at least for retail banks that indulge in this sort of thing – have no power of veto over the risks being run. For me this comes dangerously close to undermining the trust that is necessary between bank and depositor, if the financial system is to function properly. When banks take deposits from the public I would like to see them prohibited from indulging in proprietary trading. Savers can choose how to invest their savings – their banks should not be doing it for them.

The catalogue of misjudgements made by the banking industry at large – from sovereign lending in the 1960s through to technology investing in late 1999 – suggests that their acumen is not to be trusted. Some investment banks, even those with a reputation for aggressive trading, have stepped back from proprietary trading. Salomon, for example, now part of Citigroup, has essentially outsourced much of its in-house proprietary trading. Others may follow suit. Recent results show that even those regarded as the best proponents of proprietary trading – Goldman Sachs is a good example – can be just as much at the mercy of the markets as any tyro investor.

*   *   *

The counterpoint to the mass of 'true' long/short hedge fund managers are the big global macro funds. It seems they are in retreat. Julian Robertson's decision seemingly to retire from the fray and reorganise his fund management group follows a much earlier decision by Michael Steinhardt. And the scaling back undergone by George Soros, which has seen the objectives of his funds dramatically changed, investors withdrawing capital, and the departure of fund managers like Stanley Druckenmiller and Nick Roditi, might lead one to the conclusion that the macro style of trading has had its day.

Though tempting, this conclusion is not correct. Macro trading is a legitimate form of fund management, although it is a moot point whether it is really a hedge fund genre. In point of fact, the only common ground it shares with the true hedge fund (as defined by Jones) is the fee structure and the fact that leverage is used, since the investments of the macro funds are, more often than not, leveraged directional bets with little or no effective hedging.

Why have two of the biggest players effectively thrown in the towel? The answers are less obvious than might be supposed. In Tiger's case, Robertson's decision was announced prior to the downturn in technology stocks in March 2000. Essentially a value investor, Robertson professed himself unable to explain the rationale for price movements and valuation levels in the market at that time. In Soros's case the reasoning was characteristically opaque and masked by George Soros's philanthropic intentions. Seemingly concerned about his mortality, his ostensible desire is to leave behind something enduring.

Yet it was an accumulation of poor performances that left the funds unable to continue as before. The simple fact is that the performance of several Soros funds was rescued in 1999 by a late last-quarter conversion to technology stocks that, according to some competitors who specialised in the technology area, it knew little about. Investing in some size, the funds were unable to exit sufficiently quickly when the turnaround came and hence found their performance severely affected.

Underlying these statements is the true cause. It relates to a couple of features of hedge funds that are rarely talked about. In a speech in London shortly after the Soros announcement, Moore Capital's Louis Bacon talked revealingly of the problem that large hedge funds faced in effectively becoming 'the game' rather than being 'a player'.

So large and notorious that their moves are well telegraphed to the market, large funds find governments out to stop them, their competitors trading against them or else imitating their strategies, frustrating their moves at every turn. Investment banks, wary of risk, have tended to allow them less liquidity than before. Soros, while admitting that he has lost his investing touch, also noted that his fund group 'outgrew the optimum size'.

While Soros makes the best of it with a retreat into a more conservative style of investing which will ensure a flow of cash for his philanthropic activities, another reason for the strategic withdrawal also goes unremarked. This is the inability to attract and retain staff that stems from the oddities of hedge fund fee structures, notably the 'high water mark' provisions that mean underperforming funds have to recoup a period of dull performance before incentive fee payments will be resumed. This means no cash to pay fund manager bonuses. Hence in the money- and status-hungry world of Wall Street hedge funds, staff members leave. Envy and greed come to the fore, and traders and managers jump ship to rival funds, where bonuses are more assured.

That macro funds are not dead is for two reasons. First, it is possibly fair to say that the technology debacle which proved the final straw for the Soros group is hardly what macro investing is about anyway. The patchiness in Soros's performance in recent years reflects not the difficulty of macro investing, but the fact that several of the Soros group's bets went wrong. In Tiger's case it is fair to say that, though categorised as a macro fund, Robertson's forte was more as a value investor in individual stocks than as a spotter of broad geopolitical trends of the Soros style.

Several prominent macro funds remain very much in business, notably Leon Cooperman's Omega and Louis Bacon's Moore Capital. These funds have shunned publicity for their activity to the point of reclusiveness, so much so that few outside of the financial community have any idea just who they are and what they do.

That said, the future of macro investing could be somewhat different to the currency raiding and interest rate trend spotting of the past. Gabriel Burstein, in his book *Macro Trading and Investment*

Strategies (John Wiley, 1999), argues that the replacement for the classic macro trading will be a formula that plays macro trends, but in a hedged way, by spotting anomalies in the valuation of different sectors within the same market, and the same sectors between different markets. In other words, long/short macro trading replaces directional macro trading as the rationale for funds like this.

The switch is arguably necessary because low global inflation in the advanced world and convergence of bond yields and greater currency stability have resulted in fewer and fewer opportunities for classical macro trading to take place without undue risk being introduced into the equation.

Interestingly the book is dedicated to 'the brave pioneers of macro hedge fund investment: George Soros, Stanley Druckenmiller, Nick Roditi, Jerry Manolovici, Julian Robertson, Michael Steinhardt, Paul Tudor Jones, Leon Cooperman, Bruce Kovner, Louis Bacon, David Gerstenhaber, Victor Neiderhoffer and to the many other macro soldiers who won or lost on the battlefield of macroeconomic views-based trading.' Call me picky, but it is overdrawing things a tad to characterise those who created vast amounts of wealth for themselves as gallant soldiers in the service of an ideal. Those who lost were in a distinct minority.

* * *

It may sound sensational, but it is beyond belief that hedge funds do not end up unwittingly investing the proceeds of illicit activity, whether it is funds from Russian oligarchs or South American drug cartels. The popularity of Central American tax havens as locations for the hedge fund domicile, even if their managers operate from New York, is reason enough for this suspicion.

The geographical distance between them in fact lends credibility to the idea that the overwhelming majority of hedge fund managers do not know, or at least can plausibly deny, any knowledge of illicit cash being used to invest in their funds. If funds come from trusted third parties, who in turn get them from another reliable intermediary, which in turn is another link in the chain, it is hard to tell who is responsible. By the same token, just as legend has it that most bank-notes have traces of cocaine, so many other investment media are used for similar purposes and in similar ways. It is hardly fair to single out hedge funds for criticism in this respect.

Most hedge fund managers are undoubtedly honest. Just occasionally there is news of one that isn't. Some of these stories are mentioned in Chapter 4. Just occasionally too, though, there is a suggestion that hedge funds and organised crime may be linked. As an instance, a report by Molly Watson, New York correspondent of the *London Standard*, on the large-scale stock-pushing fraud involving small companies recently unearthed on Wall Street, cited a hedge fund manager as being among one of the 120 individuals arrested. A Reuters report at the time named William Stephens, of Husic Capital Management, as one of the defendants in the case, allegedly charged with agreeing to manage $300m in a union pension fund with the knowledge that a portion of this would be invested in corrupt deals.

Are there effective ways of combating the involvement of dirty money in hedge funds? One hedge fund manager suggests that the problem really resides in the moderate quality of staff employed by banks and auditors in tax havens, relative to those in major financial centres. This, it is said, makes it a comparatively easy matter for the unscrupulous and devious to funnel cash into investment vehicles domiciled there without attracting undue attention. Another British manager notes, 'I have been concerned that [some small offshore tax havens] have smaller labour pools with less experience than the big ones.'

More training for staff might help, as might a move of domicile, as might greater disclosure of the identity of investors to regulators. International action is tightening up the regime under which tax havens can operate, in an attempt to forestall the activities of those wishing to launder or invest illicit cash, but the application of these measures is regarded by many as at best haphazard. A senior investment banker observes, 'It does go on, without question. It is a big issue, and hedge fund managers are aware of the problem.'

Nonetheless most regulators, including Britain's FSA, see hedge funds as no more likely than any other investment medium to be targeted by money launderers, perhaps because their illiquid nature is less conducive than some other media to act efficiently as a means of washing dirty cash. If anything, cash of this sort is perhaps more likely to find its way back into a hedge fund once it has been legitimised rather than before.

As one fund manager puts it, 'There are very strong custodial sanctions on anyone involved in money laundering and managers must make active enquiries about this. However, where funds are wired from banks, it is the bank's primary responsibility. No manager wants to risk losing money for a criminal!' Another US hedge fund manager says, 'I know that we only take money from people we know or who are known by other people we trust, but as long as human beings are greedy, it will always be a problem.'

*   *   *

Regulating hedge funds directly is probably neither necessary, nor desirable nor practical, especially given the offshore status they enjoy. What is necessary is to ensure their activities do not harm innocent individuals or the financial system at large.

I have argued elsewhere in this book that I think this means some control should be exercised over proprietary trading by banks that are also involved in taking deposits from customers, since in many cases those customers lend their funds in good faith and do not expect them to be used for high-stakes punting. The moral case for this is unanswerable. It misses the point to say that clearing banks in the developed world effectively operate with a government guarantee, even if it were wholly true. If so, this merely becomes a problem for government itself to resolve.

Some regulators take a more detached view, however, arguing that disclosure levels are such that those who are interested in these things are able to acquaint themselves fully with the risks being taken, whereas those who find the subject of little interest must take their chances. One regulator cited the fact that surveys of public opinion suggest that most depositors are fairly apathetic about the performance of their banks in most respects, but this does not necessarily prevent stricter regulation, and such a relaxed view is at odds with the high level of consumer protection (almost to the point of nannying) in other parts of the financial services business.

Is high-stakes punting by bank proprietary traders a vital part of the financial system? In the sense that it provides markets with liquidity it may be, but the evidence of the LTCM debacle suggests that, while it may provide liquidity most of the time, it contributes to acute dearth of liquidity at the very time it is most needed. Few would deny that the villain of the piece is leverage, whether by borrowing or by the more subtle forms as practised in the securities markets via bond repos, futures trading and other devices.

In the wake of the LTCM collapse, the Basel Committee set up a working group under the chairmanship of Jan Brockmeijer to study 'highly leveraged institutions' and to investigate the implications of the collapse for banking supervisors. It defined the problem of excessive granting of leverage as down to inadequate monitoring and due diligence, excessive reliance on collateral without regard to its liquidity in adverse conditions, very favourable collateral agreements dictated by market conditions rather than objective assessment of risk.

The recommendations of the committee were to call for tougher credit control and greater transparency, but also to create an additional capital requirement to cover riskier repo and derivatives transactions. The committee also noted the problem of defining exactly what a highly leveraged institution was and the probability that direct regulation would simply lead to greater use of offshore tax havens.

The problem of definition is the most urgent one to be addressed. Banks, especially investment banks, interact with the hedge fund market in several ways. They transact business for them either directly or as prime brokers; in many cases they lend to them through the medium of the repo and swaps markets, and most importantly their proprietary trading desks also compete with them as de facto hedge funds themselves.

Chinese walls or no, this means that many banks, as key institutions in the financial system, not just in the securities markets but in some instances also as bankers to corporations and individuals, are the focal point for what many would view as an undue amount of leverage and risk. Combine this with the fact that bank traders are bonus-driven and often less competent than their hedge fund counterparts (otherwise they would leave and set up on their own, as many have done), plus the fact that bank managements by and large do not have the best record when it comes to a prudent and objective assessment of where their depositors' and shareholders' best interests lie, and we have a situation in need of some remedy.

To be fair, some of the more thoughtful investment bankers acknowledge that the problem needs addressing. One suggested remedy is a clearing-house system that would enable repo and swaps desks to have more insight into the precise levels of leverage being adopted by the hedge funds and other counterparties with whom they deal. But are they arguing this in order to reduce the level of risk within the system? Possibly. Yet such knowledge might also give their proprietary trading desks an advantage in the market.

It is, in any case, depressing to record that banks appear to be taking little notice of the exhortation to be more cautious in their dealings with highly leveraged institutions. An article in the *Wall Street Journal* in January 2000, little more than 15 months after the debacle, noted that banks in the developed world already appeared to be relaxing their standards for dealing with hedge funds. The FSA's Howard Davies has also warned that the lessons of LTCM have begun to be forgotten.

The Basel Committee, quoted in the article, noted dryly at the time that there were indications that competitive and business pressures were starting to reassert themselves and to influence credit standards imposed by banks in their dealings with hedge funds. The committee did acknowledge that banks had been reviewing their strategies and had more clearly codified their approach to them, for a time cutting back their exposure and establishing clear management responsibility for the approval of large risks. But they also observed that this process had not gone far enough and that banks were still lax in their credit documentation and the information they sought from funds, while hedge funds themselves remained reluctant to share information with them.

Matthew Lynn, writing in the UK newspaper *Sunday Business* in early April, made an amusing comparison: 'In truth the risk to the stability of the world's financial system posed by the existence of these massive vehicles of risk has not gone away. We have just chosen, in the main, not to think about it – in the same way that wives sometimes choose not to think about whether their husbands are really always working that late at the office. The implications of thinking about it are just too scary.'

In March, after a meeting in Singapore, the bank supervisors stopped arguing for voluntary solutions to the problem and advocated that funds with more than $1bn in capital should be obliged to disclose more about their investments. US legislators have flirted with measures that suggest much tougher regulation of hedge funds. However, short of prohibiting hedge fund investment completely, something impossible to enforce, the reality is that clipping hedge funds' wings to make them less of a danger to the system has to be done through greater control and disclosure by the banks.

In early June 2000 there were signs of moves along these lines, at least in the United States. The Federal Reserve announced that it intended to put in place stiffer disclosure rules about banks' risk control measures, in the hope that such disclosure would in itself prevent banks from employing overly simple risk measurement and management techniques that could be picked up by competitors, or indeed from running excessive risks that might incur the wrath of stockholders. By December 2000 there were moves afoot to force banks into more detailed disclosure of their futures and options positions in financial statements.

Bank mergers, said the Fed, had created large complex banking organisations which 'mistakenly assume they are too big to fail'. It also makes it harder to assess whether or not they have adequate risk controls in place, hence the need for greater disclosure. The Fed's Laurence Mayer noted, 'Some large banks are, surprisingly, behind the curve in developing their own internal risk classifications.' And sometimes banks use data sets that are too small and models that are too simplistic.

Although Mayer did not say as much, it is tempting to conclude that the reason some banks have paid too little attention to this is the self-aggrandisement that accompanies large takeovers, and the influence possessed by traders over the management processes of the institutions, and hence the reluctance of some to impose stricter risk controls.

Where this debate will end is anyone's guess. But without moralising unduly, banks clearly have a duty to ensure the stability of the financial system. In the longer term, since the thriving of the financial system is their raison d'être, they themselves have an interest in ensuring that it does thrive. This does not, however, seem compatible with the norms of behaviour at some banks, where bonuses come first.

This is really the nub of the regulatory issue – banks have to be made to act in their own long-term best interests, and decisions must not be made on the basis of narrower short-term considerations imbued with a large helping of moral hazard. There are signs that banking regulators worldwide are taking this on board and attempting to make sure the recommendations made by global regulators in respect of large complex financial institutions are adhered to and the mechanisms exist for ensuring compliance.

* * *

For the courtesans of capitalism, the moral dilemma faced by the banks may well be the cause of some amusement. Hedge fund managers have never been short on ego, and no doubt feel that the conflicts of interest that were brought out into the open at leading banks as a result of the LTCM debacle are no more than the banks themselves deserve, for treating their own businesses with markedly less discipline than the hedge funds themselves apply.

Hedge funds will always trade up to the limits of what is allowed by the market, because it is very much in their financial interests – incentive fees make it so. If the market will allow them to leverage heavily in strategies they are confident about, they will take advantage of it, even if in objective terms that leverage may be unhealthily high. Michael Steinhardt's 'live by the sword, die by the sword' comment quoted in a previous chapter demonstrates the indifference with which hedge fund managers view the investment banking community.

It is a moot point whether greater institutional interest will produce changes in behaviour at hedge funds. Macro funds that have strong links to existing investors will continue to be in demand, not least because fund of funds products probably need to have a macro component to be representative. At the moment the perception is that macro funds have somehow become less dangerous because a couple of high-profile players have withdrawn from the scene and because there are fewer opportunities for sashaying around the international system in the fashion of times gone by.

This view is probably mistaken. Macro funds will return to raiding currencies and betting on variations in economic performance and interest rate levels when volatility returns. It is simply that the US stock market in the past year or so has offered greater opportunities for trading than international ones. Or so it seemed, except for the fact that those who tried to second-guess the technology market got it wrong.

The reason for being encouraged about the influence of greater institutional investment on the hedge fund marketplace is not that macro funds are somehow going to be tamed, but because institutional investment focus is likely to be on smaller specialist funds that can be mixed and mingled according to performance and style attributes, much as commodity trading advisers are currently used by some US pension funds. The real threat for the financial system at large comes not from the hedge fund community itself, but from those who often have much larger capital at their disposal and who seek to mimic hedge fund techniques, yet with less discipline and control.

Raffish though some of the exploits of the hedge fund community have been in the past, it is the risks run by the banking community as hedge funds in all but name, or as ill-disciplined lenders to hedge funds all too ready to take advantage of the facilities they offer, that pose the greater threat to financial stability. They require the urgent attention of regulators if LTCM-like crises are not to recur at some future date when central bankers are less able or less well prepared to cope with them. Constant vigilance and tougher regulation of the banking industry, these are the only ways to prepare properly and give ourselves a chance to avoid crises like this in the future.

Bibliography

Headline or title	Author	Publication	Date
Chapter 1			
Another Year in Hedge Funds	Greg Newton	Managed Account Reports	2.7.99
Background Note on the Hedge Fund Industry		Financial Stability Forum	1999
European Hedge Fund Report	Simon Kerr	Banking Technology	1999
Europe's Hedge Fund Visionaries	Sudip Roy	Global Investor	Sept 1999
Fear not all Hedge Funds	Peter Coy	Business Week	14.12.98
Hedge Funds Risk & Reward		FOW	Oct 1999
Hedge Funds Risk & Reward 2		FOW	Spring 2000
Hedge Funds. Trimmed, not axed		Economist	27.2.99
Hedge Funds: Protection Against An Aging Bull	Dion Friedland	www. magnumfund.com	1998
Hedge fund universe nearly $400bn	Pete Gallo	HedgeWorld	7.7.00
Survey of Fund Management		Economist	25.10.97
Taking the Mystery Out of Hedge Funds	Dion Friedland	www. magnumfund.com	1998
The Case For Hedge Funds	TASS Investment Research	Tremont Partners	1999
The Cutting Hedge	Ian Morley	Money Marketing	10.2.00
The Hedge Fund Dilemma	Robert L. Kearns	Babson Staff Letter	11.12.98
What Every Investor Should Know About Hedge Funds	James P. Owen		1998
Why Hedge Funds Will Defy the Odds	Laure Edwards	www. magnum.com	25.8.99
Chapter 2			
A Big Player Sidelines Himself	Gary Weiss	Business Week	23.10.95
America's Richest People's Right-hand Men		Forbes	10.11.99
Bacon, the game and tell-tale signs		HedgeWorld	5.6.00
Brown quits Tiger fund	Mike Foster	Financial News	16.1.00
Cooperman acquires 5.8% stake	Newstraderz	Motley Fool	17.9.98
Does college count?	Peter Brimelow	Forbes Global	6.4.98
Edgar lives on		Financial News	4.9.00

Headline or title	Author	Publication	Date
Education of a Speculator (book review)	Patrick Young	Applied Derivatives Trading	1999
Elephant hunting for profits	Victor Niederhoffer	Managed Money	Mar 1995
Euro and Tech blamed	Mike Foster, Niki Natarajan	Financial News	7.5.00
Fall of the Wizard	Gary Weiss	Business Week	1.4.96
Founders Keepers	Riva Atlas	Institutional Investor	28.9.99
Fund Management		Financial News	22.8.99
Fund manager 'earns £50 last year'	Richard Northedge	Telegraph	2.10.96
George Soros' Letter to Investors	George Soros	HedgeWorld	28.4.00
Hedge Fund Manager Sues CME	Nikki Tait	Financial Times	17.5.99
Hedge Fund Terms		Bookbinder Capital Management	1999
Hedge Funds		www.deanlebaron.com	22.2.99
Hedge funds (Do they have a future?)		Financial Times	
Hedge funds, leverage and lessons of LTCM		President's working group on finance	28.4.99
High-growth warning to hedge funds	Astrid Wendlandt, Joshua Chaffin	Financial Times	21.3.00
How a Cat Becomes a Dog	Holman W. Jenkins	WSJ Interactive	5.4.00
John Henry to consolidate	Pete Gallo	HedgeWorld	19.10.00
Kovner is hedge fund king	Mike Foster	London Fin News	8.1.01
Kozeny alleges official payoffs	Steve Levene	Wall Street Journal	11.9.00
Living with the bull	Peter Brimelow	Forbes Global	6.4.98
Mining Profits From Microdata	Peter Coy	Business Week	1.12.97
Moore Capital to return $3bn	Joshua Chaffin	Financial Times	2.1.01
Moore's chief equity strategist quits	Joshua Chaffin	Financial Times	18.5.00
Soros billions		Sunday Business	15.8.99
Pruned: hedge funds		Economist	12.8.95
Quantum Manager Druckenmiller Resigns	Ken Brown, Paul Beckett	Wall Street Journal	2.5.00
Radical plan to stem Tiger redemptions	Mike Foster	Financial News	13.12.99
Rationality flies out of the window	Larry Black	Sunday Business	2.4.00
Robert Soros takes a leading role	Gregory Zuckerman, Sara Calian	Wall Street Journal	16.7.00
Robertson close to winding up Tiger fund	Various	Financial Times	30.3.00
Robertson's Tiger winds up	Niki Natarajan	Financial News	9.4.00
Roditi on leave from managing Soros funds	George Trefgarne	Telegraph	28.10.98
Roditi's $1.5bn fund	Mike Foster	Financial News	18.10.99

Headline or title	Author	Publication	Date
'Safer' Soros abandons high-risk strategy	Carl Mortishead	London Times	16.6.00
Shopkorn joins ex-Soros man		Financial News	28.8.00
Some tigers are better extinct	Graham Searjeant	London Times	1.4.00
Sony slump warning	Carl Mortished, Lea Paterson	Financial Times	7.1.00
Soros crashes 10%	Duncan Hughes	Sunday Business	4.7.99
Soros ends era	William Lewis, Joshua Chaffin	Financial Times	30.4.00
Soros fund chief to take break amid shake-up		Financial Times	27.10.98
Soros hit for $2bn more	Iain Jenkins	Sunday Business	6.9.98
Soros liquidates up to $6bn of assets	Joshua Chaffin	Financial Times	16.5.00
Soros moves to shore up flagship Quantum fund	Adam Jones	London Times	9.8.99
Soros set to close fund to new investors		Financial Times	5.1.99
Soros to name ex-Bankers Trust treasurer of Soros Fund		Financial Times	10.8.99
Soros tops list of Wall Street's big earners	Charles Pretzlik	Telegraph	23.8.97
Soros to stand trial		Associated Press	23.12.00
Soros Urges ECB to Help Euro		Wall Street Journal	5.5.00
Soros wants external managers to take $1bn	Mike Foster	Financial News	19.6.00
Stan's man		Financial Times	11.8.99
Stock picker throws in the towel		Sunday Times	21.5.00
Stock Volatility Hits Market Value	Gregory Zuckerman	Wall Street Journal	8.4.00
Terms of Dissolution		HedgeWorld	30.3.00
The man who lost billions	Larry Black	Sunday Business	15.8.99
The Secret Financial Network Behind 'Wizard' George Soros	Various	www. freerepublic.com	2.12.98
The Stock Whiz You Never Heard Of	Debra Sparks	Business Week	19.7.99
The Taming of the Shrewd		Economist	6.5.00
This Sure Thing Isn't So Sure Anymore	Dean Foust	Business Week	29.1.96
Tiger chief gives mauling to Europeans	William Lewis	Financial Times	8.10.99
Tiger group wound down	William Lewis	Financial Times	31.3.00
Tiger hedge funds suffer $7bn setback	Mike Foster	Financial News	16.7.99
Tiger Management changes redemption liquidity	James T. Gillies	Hedgenews.com	10.8.99
Toothless Tiger Fund	Duncan Hughes	Sunday Business	26.12.99
Warning to offshore finance centres	John Willman, Michael Peel	Financial Times	26.5.00
Whatever voodoo he uses, it works	Greg Burns	Business Week	2.10.97
Why Currencies Are the World's Most Profitable Trading Market	Delong Foreign Exchange	www.forex-trc.com	31.8.99
Wizard of Wall Street	Garth Alexander	Financial Times	2.4.00

Headline or title	Author	Publication	Date
Chapter 3			
Dealing with Myths of Hedge Fund Investment	Thomas Schneeweis	www. magnum.com	Winter 98
Does your fund manager pass the alpha test?	Philip Coggan	Finacial Times	10.00
France seeks a crackdown on tax havens	Dan Atkinson	Guardian	12.5.00
Fund of hedge funds	Robert Maharajh	Sunday Business	21.5.00
Global Macro Hedge Funds	Anita Jain	Wall Street Journal	18.8.00
Global Macro Investing	Dion Friedland	www. magnumfund.com	1998
Hedge fund assets quadruple in six years	Joshua Chaffin	Financial Times	7.9.00
Hedge fund bets on conservative strategy	Ursula Miller	Cincinnati Enquirer	26.10.98
Hedge Fund Strategy Definitions		HFR Technologies	1999
Hedge Funds & Listed Options		CBOE	1999
Hedge Funds. Their role and influence in today's financial marketplace		Chapman, Spira & Carson	1.9.99
Hedge Funds: A Guide		Economist	3.10.99
Hedge Funds: An Introduction	Discovery Capital Management	AIMA	1.9.99
How a Hedge Fund Uses Derivatives in Corporate Action Arbitrage	Patrick J. Hess	University Capital Strategies Group	28.1.00
Introduction to Hedge Funds	Neil A. Chriss	www. math.nyu.edu	Dec 1998
Investor Confidence in Funds Soars	Jamie Larea	Hedgenews.com	1999
Lessons of Hedge Funds	Nick Wyld	Financial News	27.9.99
Market Neutral Long/Short Equity Trading	Dion Friedland	www. magnumfund.com	1998
Risk? It depends how you look at it	Edward Chancellor	Financial Times	12.12.98
So you want to get rich?	Robert Budden	Financial Times	17.5.00
TASS Asset Flows Report		TASS	Sept 2000
The respectable face of hedge funds is revealed	Simon Kuper	Financial Times	11.8.98
Chapter 4			
A Hedgie Bets on Baseball	David Whitford	Fortune	26.4.99
A New Breed of Philanthropist		Business Week	6.10.97
A tract for the times		Economist	1998
About the Foundation for National Progress		www. mojones.com	1999
About the Thomas B. Fordham Foundation		www. edexcellence.net	1999
ADDA 100 Club		www.add.org	1998
Ayn Rand philosophy for futures brokerage	William B. Crawford Jr	Rand Financial Services (Chicago)	15.2.93
Ballybunion Manager Pleads Guilty	Christopher Faille	HedgeWorld	12.7.00

Headline or title	Author	Publication	Date
Bermuda Triangle		Dow Jones Business News	31.1.00
Black, White and Grey	Adam Bryant	Newsweek	19.4.99
Bogus Hedge Funds	Carlo Cannell	Red Herring	Feb 1999
Bulldog's $200m Foxhound Fund	Alex Shogren	Hedgenews.com	7.4.00
Cayman's tax evasion 'is tip of the iceberg'		Sunday Business	8.8.99
Children's Scholarship Fund		PR Newswire	27.9.98
Clampdown on tax haven	Mark Atkinson	Guardian	28.10.99
Clothier joins Plantation old boys' reunion	Andrew Clark, Sundeep Tucker	Telegraph	12.3.98
Council on Foreign Relations: Mission Statement		www.foreignrelations.org	1999
Fund Manager Concocted Fraud	John R. Wilke	Dow Jones Business News	20.1.00
George Soros: Agenda for Drug Legalization, Death and Welfare	Rachel Ehrenfeld	www.tmr.no	1999
George Soros Supports Foundation to Aid Haiti		Philanthropy News Digest	25.5.99
George Soros: Open Society 'Crusader' in Retreat	David Callahan	Civnet	Spring 1999
Hedge fund admits using false figures	Joshua Chaffin, William Lewis	Financial Times	15.1.00
Hedge Fund CFO Charged with Fraud	James T. Gillies	Hedgenews.com	1999
Hedge Fund Chief Accused of Fraud	Joshua Chaffin	Financial Times	20.1.00
Hedge fund chief accused of fraud by the SEC	Joshua Chaffin	Financial Times	23.2.00
Hedge fund managers to increase fees	Joshua Chaffin	Financial Times	2.8.00
Hedge fund twist on an old game		HedgeWorld	18.8.99
Hedge Funds Face Coolness	Chip Cummins	Wall Street Journal	13.4.00
Hedge Funds: Law and Regulation	Helen Parry, Barbara Matthews	Bharat Book Bureau	3.4.00
How to beat the hedge-fund cheats		Investors Chronicle	10.9.00
Immobility in Washington	Chakravarthi Raghaven	www.twnside.org	Oct 1998
Interview: Rob Johnson		www.pbs.org	1999
Investors Sue Blue Water	Deborah L. Cohen	HedgeWorld	3.7.00
Island of content for the money men	Clare Gascoigne	Financial Times	17.10.99
Juilliard School Launches a Five-Year Campaign		www.juilliard.edu	28.4.99
Justice Dept, SEC announce that Caxton & Steinhardt will pay $76m		www.usdoj.gov	Dec 1994
Lehman Brothers sues Yagalla	Pete Gallo	HedgeWorld	20.10.00
Leon's Lament		www.pathfinder.com	1999
Lincoln Center Receives $25m Gift	Ralph Blumenthal	Philanthropy News Digest	16.9.98
Manhattan Hedge Fund Files for Chapter 11 Bankruptcy		Wall Street Journal	3.9.00

Headline or title	Author	Publication	Date
Market slip sends hedge funds to dog house	Joshua Chaffin	Financial Times	17.4.00
Mother Jones 400		www.mojones.com	Apr 1996
Natale admits hedge fund fraud	Mike Foster	Financial News	19.3.00
New Foundation to Help Mend Small Town Race Relations	Chris Burritt	Philanthropy News Digest	26.11.97
Niederhoffer Investments	Laura Jereski, Aaron Lucchetti	Wall Street Journal	30.10.97
Paradise Isle	Conal Walsh	Sunday Business	7.11.99
Paul Tudor Jones does it again	Katy Hogan	Hedgenews.com	6.4.00
Paul Tudor Jones II Supports Everglades Clean-up Campaign		Philanthropy News Digest	2.10.96
Princeton Global Fund closes itself	Clay Harris	Financial Times	17.9.99
Private Client Services		Rand Financial Services	1999
Quiet man with a loud impact	George Trefgarne	Telegraph	2.8.97
Results-Oriented Philanthropy Attracts Donor		www.cwire.com	17.12.97
Salomon's US bond arbitrage unit closed	Richard Walters	Financial Times	7.7.98
Searching for good return	Debra Nussbaum Cohen	Jewish News	1998
Smirlock accused	Pete Gallo	HedgeWorld	26.12.00
Soros Goes West	Paul Demko	Chronicle of Philanthropy	5.9.96
Soros opts for smaller returns	Niki Natarajan	London Fin News	30.10.00
Sotheby's to sell the single-owner collection		www.shareholder.com	1998
Team Leadership Board of Directors		www.worldteamsports.org	1999
Thanks to $15m in funding		Philanthropy News Digest	26.11.97
Top Soft Money Donors to RNC		www.ccsi.com	June 1996
Trout Sibling's Rift	Ann Davis	Wall Street Journal	4.3.00
Trustbusters	Susan Lee, Christine Foster	Forbes	6.2.97
What vouchers can and can't solve		Business Week	10.5.99
With Big Money and Brash Ideas	Judith Miller	New York Times	17.12.96

Chapter 5

A new approach to financial risk		Economist	17.10.98
An optimist on the sidelines	Robert Lenzner	Forbes	16.11.98
Archimedes on Wall Street	Robert Lenzner	Forbes	19.10.98
Backers of LTCM face data inquest	Tracy Corrigan	Financial Times	22.6.99
Blood on Wall Street	Naem Mohaimen	Daily Star Bangladesh	1999
Cash is king when markets crash		Sunday Business	11.10.98
Currency chaos spills over into bond markets	Alasdair Murray, Oliver August	London Times	10.10.98
Dash for Cash		Financial Times	10.10.98
Dream Team	Leah Nathans Spiro	Business Week	29.8.94

Headline or title	Author	Publication	Date
Failed US gurus return		Financial News	3.9.00
Failed Wizards of Wall Street	Peter Coy, Suzanne Woolley	Business Week	21.9.98
Fear of 'flight to cash' by investors	Ian Jenkins, Nils Pratley	Sunday Business	4.10.98
Financial stars who fell to earth	John Gapper	Financial Times	7.9.00
Fool on the Hill	Louis Corrigan	Motley Fool	1998
Hedge Fund Chief Expresses Remorse	Gregory Zuckerman	Wall Street Journal	21.8.00
Hedge fund fear factor		Personal Investment Magazine (Australia)	Dec 1998
Hedge fund guru	Gary Siverman, Joshua Chaffin	Financial Times	21.8.00
Hedge fund LTCM returns $800 million more to banks		Yahoo! Finance	28.9.99
Hedge Funds Galore	Richard Thompson	Financial News	9.1.00
Hedge funds repair Long-Term damage		Sunday Business	5.9.99
Hedge funds, leverage and the lessons of LTCM (pages 1–9)		President's working group on finance	28.4.99
Hedge-Fund Wizard or Wall Street Gambler?	Gretchen Morgensen	New York Times	2.10.98
How the Eggheads Cracked	Michael Lewis	www.cob.ohio-state.edu	24.1.99
How the eggheads fell to earth	Michael Lewis	Guardian	1.2.99
Investors dump bonds in worldwide flight to cash	Jeremy Grant	Financial Times	10.10.98
Lesson learned?		Economist	2.9.00
Long-term gamble	Roger Lowenstein	London Times	1.9.00
LTCM bonds sale sparks explosion in sterling issues	Edward Luce	Financial Times	22.10.98
LTCM chief acknowledges flawed tactics		HedgeWorld	21.8.00
LTCM chief in public display of remorse	Adam Jones	London Times	22.8.00
LTCM colleagues invest	Andrew Hill	Financial Times	15.12.99
LTCM founder puts finishing touches on new fund	Apu Sikri	Yahoo! Finance	5.11.99
LTCM pays final debt	William Lewis	Financial Times	17.12.99
LTCM returns banks $1bn		Guardian	7.7.99
LTCM returns investors' funds	Tracy Corrigan	Financial Times	7.7.99
LTCM to repay debts		CNNfn	18.6.99
LTCM: one bad apple		www.assetpub.com	Nov 98
LTCM's Italian Job	Nicholas Dunbar	Financial News	15.11.99
Meriwether fund seeks investors		London Times	10.11.99
Meriwether struggles to raise funds	Joshua Chaffin, Gary Silverman	Financial Times	21.8.00
Meriwether fund plummets by 44%	Oliver August	London Times	4.9.98
Meriwether struggles as hedge funds boom		Sunday Business	30.7.00

Headline or title	Author	Publication	Date
Picking up juicy yields from corporate bonds	Angus McCrone	Sunday Business	1.11.98
The long and short of it	Matthew Guarente	Sunday Business	10.9.00
The LTCM Episode (pages 10–21)		President's working group on finance	28.4.99
The lure of learning and leverage	Philip Coggan	Financial Times	17.12.99
The return of the hedge fund	William Lewis, Andrew Hill	Financial Times	24.9.99
Turmoil forces hedge fund to liquidate $1.5bn bonds	Oliver August	Times	14.10.98
Turmoil in Financial Markets		Economist	17.10.98
Two more LTCM partners to quit	Tracy Corrigan, William Lewis	Financial Times	20.6.99
When the sea dries up		Economist	25.9.99
Worldwide jitters spur stampede to super-safe havens	Edward Luce, Philip Coggan	Financial Times	6.10.98

Chapter 6

Headline or title	Author	Publication	Date
Acquisition of Companies		Chapman, Spira & Carson	1999
Apollo Cashes Out Big in KKR Buyout	David Carey, Josh Kosman	www.thedailydeal.com	1999
Apollo on Building Maintenance Pact	David Carey	www.thedailydeal.com	1999
Bay Harbour Partners		www.magnumfund.com	2000
Broader scope for vulture funds	Nigel Adam	Asset International Inc.	8.9.94
China approves mortgage-backed debt	James Kynge	Financial Times	25.4.00
Convertible Arbitrage Evolves		HedgeWorld	10.3.00
DE Shaw Sells Business to KBC		Wasswestein, Perella & Co.	8.10.99
Dealing in duds		Economist	9.5.98
Distressed assets sale	Gillian Tett	Financial Times	19.4.00
Distressed Securities Investing	Dion Friedland	www.magnumfund.com	1998
Ellington Funds File Suit Against UBS Warburg	Kristin M. Fox	HedgeWorld	19.6.00
Former Wall Street Barbarian	Joshua Chaffin	Financial Times	30.6.00
Fruit of the Loom takes Chapter 11	Christopher Bowe	Financial Times	30.12.99
Hedge Funds: Their Role and Influence in Today's Financial Marketplace		Chapman, Spira & Carson	1999
Hermes Lens to launch shareholder activist fund	Simon Targett	Financial Times	17.2.00
Hermes plans an expansion	Sara Callan	Wall Street Journal	7.7.00
Hermes sets up 'name and shame' fund	Simon Targett	Financial Times	7.7.00
How to Avert a US Economic Crisis		Time Inc.	1996

Headline or title	Author	Publication	Date
Icahn raises bet on Reliance	Christopher Oster	Wall Street Journal	28.12.00
Investors and companies must trust each other	Alastair Ross Goobey, Peter Butler	London Times	5.7.00
King of the corporate raiders	Christoper Bowe, Andrew Edgecliffe-Johnson	Financial Times	25.8.00
Klesch issue	Janet Lewis	Financial News	16.4.00
Leon Black: Wall Street's Dr No	Phillip L. Zweig	Business Week	29.7.96
Liquidity trap catches Shaw	Tracy Corrigan	Financial Times	19.10.98
Merger Arbitrage		Financial Times	1.12.99
Merrill buys DE Shaw unit	Tracy Corrigan	Financial Times	21.2.99
Michael Vranos		www.worth.com	6.98
Mortgage Backed Securities	Dion Friedland	www.magnumfund.com	1998
Mr Icahn and the new maximizers	James K. Glassman	Wall Street Journal	6.7.00
Philosophy of Investing in Bankrupt and Distressed Securities		www.amph.com	1997
Reducing Market Risk with Merger Arbitrage	Dion Friedland	www.magnumfund.com	1998
Reviewing Hedge Strategies	Iain Jenkins	International Fund Investment	
Suit highlights testy dealings	Lanthe Jeanne Dugan	Wall Street Journal	20.7.00
The $700 Million Mystery	Gary Weiss	Business Week	18.12.95
The Battle within the Battle	Yvette Kantrow	www.thedailydeal.com	1999
The Case for Convertibles	Dion Friedland	www.magnumfund.com	1998
The Reincarnation of Peter Cohen	John Rossant, Leah Spiro	Business Week	29.3.99
Turning distress into investment		Bank of Bermuda	1999
Vultures Grab Distressed Debt	David Carey	www.thedailydeal.com	1999
What's Special about Special Situations Fixed Income	Dion Friedland	www.magnumfund.com	1998
Where are the opportunities in down-sizing Europe	Gary Klesch	www.ljh.com	1997
Wilco to buy DE Shaw business		Financial News	30.5.99

Chapter 7

An open letter to the government of Thailand	Patrick Young	Applied Derivatives Trading	7.97
Asset Managers Shut or Restructure	Craig Karmin	Wall Street Journal	26.4.00
Bank warns of increase in hedge fund activity	George Graham	Financial Times	18.6.99
Bond traders urged to share burden	Steven Fidler	Financial Times	10.12.99
CDRC Chief Touts Success	Leslie Lopez	Wall Street Journal	14.4.00

Headline or title	Author	Publication	Date
Close the World Bank and the IMF	Kenneth R. Timmerman	Wall Street Journal	13.4.00
Debt defaults rise to £27bn	Arkady Ostrovsky	Financial Times	19.1.00
Did Bank of Japan have yen to save funds?		London Times	28.8.97
Diminishing returns		Economist	9.10.00
Early warning system starts		Financial Times	12.5.99
Effects of the Financial Crisis in Hong Kong		www.igcc.ucsd.edu	4.3.00
Hedge Funds and International Financial Markets	Takehiko Nakao	www.mot.go.jp	July 99
Hedge funds and their effect on the Pacific Rim Crisis		Chapman, Spira & Carson	9.5.99
Hedge funds: what do we really know?	Barry Eichengreen, Donald Mathieson	IMF	Sept 99
HK growth keeps pace with Asia	Rahul Jacob	Financial Times	9.3.00
HK official chides West's attitude to hedge funds	Peter Montagnon, Tony Tassell	Financial Times	1.5.99
Hong Kong. Fair Shares		Economist	31.10.98
How to avoid the debtor's prison	Martin Wolf	Financial Times	18.10.99
Issues on Hedge Funds		y2000.mas.gov.sg	4.3.00
Keynote Address	Mahathir Mohamed	Conference on Managing the Asian Financial Crisis	3.11.98
Korea bail-out plan	John Burton	Financial Times	18.5.00
Krugman supports hedge fund conspiracy theory	Wong Sulong	The Star	8.12.00
Kuala Lumpur avoids capital flight	Lanathan Birchall	Financial Times	2.9.99
Let the good times roll		Economist	15.4.00
Mahathir pulls out of Apec summit	Gwen Robinson, Jonathan Birchall	Financial Times	3.9.99
Mahathir urges Muslims to embrace technology	Sheila McNutty	Financial Times	27.6.00
Mahathir finds new demon	Sheila McNulty	Financial Times	23.4.00
Mahathir secures his position	Sheila McNulty	Financial Times	12.5.00
Malaysia goes from outcast to money magnet	Lachian Colquoun	Financial Times	9.7.00
Malaysia prepares expansionary budget	Jonathan Birchall	Financial Times	29.10.99
Malaysia wants role in G7 talks on hedge funds		Reuters	14.9.99
Malaysia's great survivor	Sheila McNulty	Financial Times	11.5.00
Malaysia's New Stock Market	Chen May Yee	Wall Street Journal	25.6.00
Quotes on currency speculation – international media and leading spokespeople		neac.gov.my	10.11.98
Ready, steady		Economist	21.8.99
Russian Fall-out		Financial Times	26.8.98
SC pushes for direct regulation of hedge funds		Business Times	3.6.99
Slowly lowering Thailand's mountain of debt	William Barnes	Financial Times	20.1.00

Headline or title	Author	Publication	Date
Some Believe Soros's Moves Caused Emerging Market Fall	Angela Pruitt, Carol Remond	Wall Street Journal	8.5.00
Soros turns attention back to Asia region	Gillian Tett et al.	Financial Times	31.3.00
The Asian Crisis and the Global Economy	Robert Wade	www.wright.edu	Nov 98
The Asian Financial Crisis	Jeffrey D. Sachs, Wing Thye Woo	rebuildasia.com	21.1.99
The future that might have been		Economist	16.12.00
Top Chinese currency official	James Kynge	Financial Times	14.5.00
US hedge fund batters baht in new raid		Reuters	1.9.99
World Bank warning on Asian recovery	Rahul Jacob	Financial Times	23.3.00

Chapter 8

Bank rules in disarray		Economist	27.11.99
Bankers emerging from cover after crisis	Joshua Chaffin	Financial Times	12.11.99
Bankers Trust takes derivatives hit	Richard Irving, Anuj Gangahar	Financial News	26.9.99
Banks in trouble		Economist	28.10.00
Banks set to make a stand on reputation risk	Richard Irving	Financial News	14.11.99
Banks, hedge funds and regulators			
Battle over Barings	Jon Ashworth	London Times	12.10.99
Biggest banks record sharp rise in profits	John Willman	Financial Times	4.7.00
Black Box or Black Hole?	Corey Bock	www.assetpub.com	3.9.91
Buoyant Goldman defies sceptics	Lisa Buckingham	Guardian	24.6.99
Chase fires senior trader	Gary Silverman, Adrian Michaels	Financial Times	2.11.99
Chase overstatement		London Times	2.11.99
Citigroup		Financial Times	18.10.99
Citigroup executive warns banks on lending	Joshua Chaffin	Financial Times	11.9.00
Citigroup's Quarterly Profit		Wall Street Journal	20.7.00
Commerzbank could face 45m bond loss	Richard Irving	Financial News	23.1.00
Derivatives under the spotlight after Chase sacking		Sunday Business	7.11.99
Deutsche team in London	Niki Natarajan	Financial News	3.7.00
Europe is where the action is		Internatinal Fund Investment	
European Hedge Fund Report (chapter 9)	Simon Kerr	Banking Technology	1999
Fed capital asset cover plan attacked	Gary Silverman	Financial Times	10.4.00
Fed prepares new capital guidelines	Jathon Sapsford	Wall Street Journal	15.3.00
Finance and Economics		Economist	29.7.00
FSA chair says lessons of LTCM	Pete Gallo	HedgeWorld	17.8.00
FSA investigates Goldman Sachs		Financial News	6.12.99
Goldman fails to impress the market	Ian Kerr	Financial News	10.10.99

Headline or title	Author	Publication	Date
Goldman figures beat expectations	William Lewis	Financial Times	22.9.99
Goldman in row		Guardian	18.5.00
Goldman Sachs beats forecasts	Gary Silverman	Financial Times	21.6.00
Goldman Sachs delivers 30% increase	Andrew Edgecliffe-Johnson	Financial Times	24.6.99
Goldman Sachs loses its glister	Matthew Lynn	Sunday Business	18.6.00
Goldman Sachs suffers loss	Arkady Ostrovsky, Clay Harris	Financial Times	19.8.99
Goldman slip may not be the last	Ian Kerr	Financial News	5.9.99
Goldman's 2nd-Quarter Profit		Wall Street Journal	21.6.00
Growth of prime brokerage	Brian Bollen	Financial News	29.8.99
High-tech fall hits Goldman	Caroline Merrell	Wall Street Journal	21.6.00
Hotimsky resurfaces	Richard Irving	Financial News	30.4.00
How the mighty can fall	John Adams, Jack Evans	Investors Chronicle	13.11.98
Japan's big three brokers	Nakao Nakamae	Financial Times	12.5.00
J.P. Morgan receives boost	Gary Silverman	Financial Times	14.7.00
Morgan Stanley Beats Forecasts	Gary Silverman	Financial Times	23.6.00
Morgan Stanley buys hedge fund consulting firm		Reuters	2.12.99
Morgan Stanley Forms Venture	Kopin Tan	Wall Street Journal	20.3.00
Morgan Stanley Posts 30% Advance	Lynn Cowan	Wall Street Journal	23.6.00
NatWest fined for options scandal	Jill Treanor	Guardian	20.5.00
Nobody wants to kill the golden goose	Matthew Schriffen, Caroline Waxler	Forbes	14.12.98
Prime Brokers		www.hedgefunds.org	28.10.99
Salomon proprietary trading shake-up	Caroline Merrill	Guardian	18.10.99
Salomon set to start hedge funds monitoring venture		Financial News	22.2.99
Salomon spin-off within sight	Richard Irving	Financial News	18.10.99
Silver glint appears	Mike Foster	Financial News	22.11.98
Staff Bonuses	Gary Silverman, Andrew Hill	Financial Times	5.12.00
Suit says Bear Stearns	Pete Gallo	HedgeWorld	5.10.00
The business of banking		Economist	30.10.99
The Prime Broker's Oyster	Emma Davey	FOW supplement	Oct 99
The trader's lament		Economist	16.10.99
The wisdom of Salomon (book review)		Economist	13.5.00
UBS left out	Larry Black	Sunday Business	19.12.99
US investment banks spot prime opportunity in Europe	Lynn Strongin Dodds	Financial News	16.5.99
Value would overshadow rest	Gary Silverman, Joshua Chaffin	Financial Times	15.9.00
Warburg answers its critics		Financial News	30.9.99

Headline or title	Author	Publication	Date
Chapter 9			
A Walk on the Wild Side	Penny Cagan	Online Inc.	Dec 99
Are hedge funds the 'black holes' of the financial markets?	Andreas Grunbichler, Heinz Zimmerman	NZZ Online	Oct 98
Basle bust-up		Economist	16.10.99
Dependence on Risk Models		Meridien Research	13.1.00
European Hedge Fund Report (chapter 8)	Simon Kerr	Banking Technology	1999
Finance & Economics		Economist	12.6.99
Five Hedge Funds Respond	Mitchell Pacelle	Wall Street Joural	9.2.00
Greenspan hits out at way banks treat risk	Nancy Dunne, George Graham	Financial Times	12.10.99
Guidelines awaited on risk management	Tracy Corrigan	Financial Times	21.6.99
Hedge funds control	Jill Treanor	Guardian	10.5.99
Hedge funds give advice on risk	Joshua Chaffin	Financial Times	9.2.00
Hedge funds, leverage and the lessons of LTCM (testimony)	Patrick M. Parkinson	Federal Reserve Board	6.5.99
J.P. Morgan to build online derivatives link	Gary Silverman	Financial Times	1.2.00
LTCM	Various	GAO Report	Oct 99
Commercial Banks' Relationships with Hedge Funds		The presidents' working party	28.4.99
Protection markets run dry	Richard Irving	Financial News	10.10.99
Recommendations for Public Disclosure	Basel Committee/ IOSCO		1995
Recommendations for Public Disclosure	Basel Committeee	www.bis.org	28.2.00
Russian/LTCM Crisis Survey		CMRA	1999
Sound Practices for Hedge Fund Managers	Various	Sound Practices for Hedge Fund Managers	Feb 2000
The Market: Survival of the Fittest		Meridien Research	1999
Value at Risk Resources	Barry Schachter	www.gloriamundi.org	1997
Chapter 10			
A hand of diamonds	John Katz	Sunday Business	31.10.99
Alexandra Turns to the Web	Kristin M. Fox	HedgeWorld	22.6.00
Baker proposal on hedge fund reporting		Hedgenews.com	16.9.99
Call fo better monitoring	George Graham	Financial Times	25.1.99
CSFB and Tremont to unveil hedge fund index		Financial News	15.11.99
CSFB Tremont venture	Stephen Foley	Financial News	15.8.99
CSFB/Tremont Hedge Fund Index Unveiled		CSFB Tremont	16.11.99

Headline or title	Author	Publication	Date
Direct Regulation of Hedge Funds Not Out of the Question		HedgeWorld	3.27.00
'Down Under'		HedgeWorld	13.3.00
Drive to tackle hedge fund risks	Richard Wolffe, Tracy Corrigan	Financial Times	2.3.99
Hedge fund managers to get new internet site	Phillipa Jones	Financial News	26.9.99
Hedge funds' real-time revolution starts in September	Pete Gallo	HedgeWorld	23.8.00
Hedge funds step out from shadows	Joshua Chaffin	Financial Times	8.12.99
Hedgetrust Exchange		HedgeWorld	18.10.99
House to hear bill on more hedge fund reporting	James T. Gillies	Hedgenews.com	1999
It's love at first electronic sight		HedgeWorld	31.3.00
Learn more overview		PlusFunds	1999
Leverage and prudent risk-management		Finacial Stability Review	June 99
Online group in hedge fund move	Joshua Chaffin	Financial Times	26.1.00
Online hedge fund service to launch		Financial News	13.12.99
PlusFunds looking to Europe	Juliette Pearse	Financial News	27.2.00
Precipitating Declines in Falling Markets		Chapman, Spira & Carson	1997
Report: Hedge Funds Need Watching	Marcy Gordon	Yahoo! Finance	19.11.99
Untangling the Transparency Web	Deborah L. Cohen	HedgeWorld	5.7.00
US may legislate on hedge fund disclosure	Andrew Hill, William Lewis	Financial Times	23.9.99
Website to offer hedge fund stock trades	Joshua Chaffin	Financial Times	22.12.99

Chapter 11

Alternative asset weightings to grow		Financial News	15.5.00
Appetite grows for neutral funds	Niki Natarajan	Financial News	7.5.00
ASB fuels drive towards alternative investments	Mike Foster	Financial News	14.11.99
Baring tests hedge funds		Financial News	13.12.99
Buffet hires bond arbitrage managers		HedgeWorld	2000
Calpers allocates $11 billion to hedge funds	James T. Gillies	Hedgenews.com	1999
Calpers approves $1bn	Susan L. Barreto	HedgeWorld	14.11.00
Calpers' hedge fund first		Financial News	30.8.99
Coal pension scheme	Simon Targett	Financial Times	21.9.99
Dark stars of the investment galaxy	Simon London	Financial Times	19.6.99
European Hedge Fund Report (chapter 4)	Simon Kerr	Banking Technology	1999
European Hedge Fund Report (chapter 8)	Simon Kerr	Banking Technology	1999
Finding a place for hedge funds	George Palmer	www. assetpub.com	1998
Funds of the future	Daniel Bogler	Financial Times	9.8.99
Hedge Funds Join the Herd	Joe Neidzielski	Wall Street Journal	6.3.00

Headline or title	Author	Publication	Date
Hedge Funds Demystified	Goldman Sachs	Pension & Endowment Forum	July 1998
Hedge funds fail to tap	Alex Skorecki	Financial Times	7.12.00
Hedge Funds Flourish in Europe	IFI (interview)	International Fund Investment	
Hedge funds growing up		Economist	20.11.99
Hedge funds head for mainstream market		Investors Chronicle	5.11.99
Hedge funds open their doors to small investors	Gregory Zuckerman	Wall Street Journal	2.8.00
Hedge funds set to bloom	Philip Coggan	Financial Times	26.6.99
Henderson launches new hedge fund	Nick Gilbert	Financial News	31.10.99
In-depth fund report: Europus Global Opportunities Plc		HedgeWorld	2000
Institutional Investing	Kim Hunter	FOW	Spring 2000
Investors wake up to hedge funds		HedgeWorld	31.7.00
Investors warming to hedge funds	Philip Coggan	Financial Times	1.3.00
Lipnick scours Europe	Michael Foster	Financial News	10.10.99
MAM to enter hedge fund arena	Simon Targett	Financial Times	8.5.00
Mercury makes hedge fund debut	Mike Foster	Financial News	8.5.00
MLM set for long/short equity fund		Business News	3.1.00
Not even a skunk could ruin this garden party	Kristin M. Fox	HedgeWorld	17.4.00
NY Teachers Thinking		Business News	14.5.00
Orient Express		Economist	13.5.00
Paribas loses Hadizdad	Michael Foster	Financial News	19.9.99
Pension fund in strategy shift	Tom Forenski	Financial Times	12.5.00
Pensions manager to invest in hedge funds	Andrew Edgecliffe-Johnson	Financial Times	1.9.99
Pockets of Popularity	Sarah Munson	International Fund Investment	
Report on Highly Leveraged Institutions	Financial Stability Forum		1999
Research shows increasing European institutional interest in hedge funds	Fulcrum Research	Ludgate Comms, Eurohedge	1.3.00
Schroders positive on hedge funds		Financial News	17.4.00
The Coming Evolution (III)		RRCM Corp.	Mar 1998
The Coming Evolution (V)		RRCM Corp.	Mar 1998
The Coming Evolution (IV)		RRCM Corp.	Mar 1998
The Eleventh Commandment	Jennifer Hopfinger	Hedge Fund Forum	8.5.00
Vive La Difference Continentale	Iain Jenkins	Internatinal Fund Investment	
Warren Buffet Thrives	Chip Cummins	Wall Street Journal	13.4.00

Chapter 12

120 charged with Mafia plot	Jill Treanor	Guardian	15.6.00
A New Breed of Small Funds	Gregory Zuckerman	Wall Street Journal	2.5.00
All things to all men	Lionel Barber, Gillian O'Connor	Financial Times	2.12.99

Headline or title	Author	Publication	Date
As hedge fund champs fade	Gregory Zuckerman	Wall Street Journal	8.6.00
Banking system a 'magnet' for money launderers	Charles Pretzlik	Financial Times	14.3.00
Banks in 11 Nations	Joe Rebello	Wall Street Journal	26.1.00
Banks plan trading network	Jill Treanor	Guardian	11.4.00
BIS survey shows arbitrage contraction	Richard Irving	Financial News	5.11.99
British Virgin Islands Comes Under Attack	Michael Allen	Wall Street Journal	
Brussels seeks derivatives reform	Deborah Hargreaves, Michael Peel	Financial Times	17.1.00
Calpers takes stake in manager	Elizabeth Wine	Financial Times	5.6.00
Conclusions and Recommendations (pages 29–43)		President's working group	28.4.99
Creeping growth of the hedge funds	Howard Davies	Financial Times	8.8.00
European chief quits Soros	William Lewis	Financial Times	9.6.00
Fed plans disclosure system for banks	Sathnam Sanghera	Financial Times	1.6.00
Financiers play with fire again	Matthew Lynn	Sunday Business	9.4.00
For the Mafia it's not just crime	Duncan Hughes	Sunday Business	18.6.00
French Report Says Monaco Fails		Wall Street Journal	22.6.00
FSA to tackle market abuse	Pete Gallo	HedgeWorld	29.8.00
Goldman Sachs profits rise	Gary Silverman	London Times	22.12.99
Greenspan questions derivatives reform plan	Nikki Tait	Financial Times	22.6.00
Greenspan wants derivatives freed up	Gerard Baker	Financial Times	11.2.00
Greenspan worries about the world's leverage	Stephen Fidler	Financial Times	21.5.99
Greenspan, Summers Oppose Proposal		HedgeWorld	21.6.00
Hedge funds move to invite scrutiny	Joe Niedzielski	Wall Street Journal	10.8.00
House Subcommittee Passes Hedge Fund Disclosure Bill	Staff	HedgeWorld	17.3.00
How to control hedge funds	Stephen Fay	Independent	18.10.99
Hundred arrested in stock fraud	Adam Jones	London Times	15.6.00
Husic Strategist Named	Kristin M. Fox	HedgeWorld	14.6.00
IMF applauds Thai comeback	Tom Wright	Wall Street Journal	10.5.00
Jersey Regulator issues warning	Pete Gallo	HedgeWorld	29.8.00
Laundering rules	Anthony Hilton	Evening Standard	23.6.00
Lawyers face tough rules	David Lister	London Times	3.7.00
Mafia spins stock market scam	Garth Alexander	Guardian	18.6.00
MFA chairman takes issue	Staff	HedgeWorld	12.4.00
'Near live' testing	Anuj Gangahar	Financial News	29.8.99
Optima Fund Management's Founder	Chip Cummins	Wall Street Journal	15.6.00
Pension funds see less risk in derivatives	Simon Targett	Financial Times	14.10.99

Headline or title	Author	Publication	Date
Plan to force options disclosure	Robert Bruce	London Times	14.12.00
Public Policy Issues (pages 23–28)		President's working group on finance	28.4.99
Russia and Israel head money laundering list	Charlotte Denny	Guardian	23.6.00
Russia, Others Cited	Kenneth Maxwell, Michael Allen	Wall Street Journal	23.6.00
Secret no more		Economist	15.4.00
Shifting winds are filling hedge fund sails	Jennifer Hopfinger	HedgeWorld	9.6.00
Soros makes a quantum leap	Juliana Ratner	Financial Times	16.6.00
Stability of the international financial systems		Financial Stability Review	June 99
Taskforce hits at money launderers	Guy de Jonquieres	Financial Times	23.6.00
The Mob at the Wall Street casino	Andrew Hill, John Labate	Financial Times	16.6.00
US banks slump	Adam Jones	London Times	27.5.00
US Officials Nab 120		Wall Street Journal	13.6.00
US securities fraud crackdown	John Laban	Financial Times	15.6.00
Van's chairman on proposed new hedge fund regulation	George P. Van	www.vanhedge.com	18.5.99
Wall Street rocked by Mafia link	Molly Watson	London Times	15.6.00
Why the hedge fund is back in favour	Philip Manduca	Sunday Business	7.5.00

Books

Against The Gods	Peter L. Bernstein	Wiley	1996
Apocalypse Roulette	Richard Thomson	Pan	1999
Debt and Delusion	Peter Warburton	Penguin	2000
Fiasco	Frank Partnoy	Profile Books	1997
Fundamentals of Hedge Fund Investing	William J. Crerend	McGraw-Hill	1998
Hedge Fund Giants	Beverley Chandler	FT Pitman	1998
Hedge Funds: an introduction to skill-based investment strategy	Richard Hills	Rushmere Wynn	1988
Hedge Funds: investment and portfolio strategies	Jess Lederman, Robert A. Klein	McGraw-Hill	1995
Inventing Money	Nicholas Dunbar	Wiley	2000
Investing in Hedge Funds	Joseph G. Nicholas	Bloomberg	1999
Liar's Poker	Michael Lewis	Hodder & Stoughton	1989
Macro Trading and Investment Strategies	Gabriel Burstein	John Wiley	1999
Manias, Panics and Crashes	Charles P. Kindleberger	Macmillan	1989
Market Wizards	Jack D. Schwager	Harper	1990
Money, Greed and Risk	Charles P. Morris	Wiley	1999
Rogue Trader	Nick Leeson	Warner	1996
Soros on Soros	George Soros	Wiley	1995
Soros: The Unauthorized Biography	Robert Slater	McGraw-Hill	1996

Headline or title	Author	Publication	Date
The Alchemy of Finance	George Soros	Wiley	1994
The Education of a Speculator	Victor Neiderhoffer	Wiley	1997
The Hedge Fund Edge	Mark Boucher	Wiley	1999
The Laundrymen	Jeffrey Robinson	Simon & Schuster	1994
The New Market Wizards	Jack D. Schwager	Wiley	1992

Index

3M, 120
Absolute return, attractions of to pension funds, 217
Accounting Standards Board, 219
Accredited investors, 50, 196
Adjusting for large positions to eliminate risk, 183
AIG, 106
AIMA, 198
Ainslie, Lee, 37
Alexandra Investment Management, 208
Alpha, 15, 53
Alternative investments, sources of capital for, 216
Amroc Investments, 129
Anonymity, importance for hedge funds, 47
Arbitrage, 54, 98
Arbitrage, Warren Buffet style of, 215
Askin Capital Management, 3
Askin, David, 3, 7, 119
Astaire, Edgar, 23
Australian treasury department, 190
Avalon Research, 201
Aziz, Nazri, 145

Bacon, Louis, 41, 67, 84, 233, 234
'Bad banks', 169
Ballybunion Capital Partners, 77
Bank customers, supposed indifference to proprietary trading, 170
Bank managements, reticence over involvement in proprietary trading, 156
Bank of America, 122
Bank of Thailand, 141, 142
Bank of Tokyo–Mitsubishi, 180
Bankers Trust, 4
Banking community, as hedge funds, 242
Banking community, competitive pressures on, 175
Banking community, ill-disciplined lending to hedge funds, 242
Banking community, tendency to jump on bandwagons, 175
Banks, bureaucratic corporate culture at, 159
Banks, compulsory minimum standards of reporting of hedge fund exposure, 188
Banks, desire to move in step with their peer group, 171
Banks, internal procedures for managing risk, 185
Banks, investments in internet start-ups, 155
Banks, involvement with hedge funds, role of credit control, 238
Banyan, 149
Barclays, 161
Barclays, involvement in LTCM, 160

Barings, 4, 75, 91, 157, 163
Basel Committee, 184, 238, 239
Bear Stearns, 120, 130, 166
Berkshire Hathaway, 214
Bermuda Stock Exchange, 201
Beta, 15, 53
Black, Fischer, 15
Black, Leon, 126, 128
Blackberry Capital Management, 208
Black–Scholes, 11
Bleichroder, A&S, 23
Bluewater Fund, 77
Boesky, Ivan, 7, 56, 113
Bookbinder Capital, 199
Brady bonds, 154
Brockmeijer, Jan, 238
Buffett, Warren, 105, 106, 214

CalPERS, 211, 219
Canary Wharf, 127
Capital adequacy requirements, misuse of by banks, 183
Capital controls, role in thwarting hedge funds, 150
'Career risk', for managers picking hedge funds, 219
Carlebach, Schlomo, 85
Caveat emptor, 191
Caxton Corporation, 36
Cayne, James, 107
CDC Gamma, 67
Cerberus International, 67
Chapman, Spira & Carson, 13
Chapter 11 bankruptcy, 59
Chemerow, David, 120
China, success of capital controls in, 139
Chinese renminbi, 145
Citigroup, 168
Citigroup, trading investments vs assets, 162
Clearstream, 202
CMRA, 181, 201

Collateral, diminution in value of, 175
Collateralised mortgage obligations, 116
Commerzbank, 161
Consultants, as gatekeepers in hedge fund selection, 222
Conventional risk models, limitations of, 173
Cooperman Foundation, 85
Cooperman, Leon, 41, 68, 234
Core–satellite investment approach, 220
Corrigan, Lou, 110
Corzine, Jon, 106
Crapple, George, 190
Credit limit disciplines, 92
Credit Lyonnais, acquisition of film studio, 154
Credit Suisse, 161
Credit Suisse, trading investments vs assets, 162
Creditors committee, importance in distressed securities trading, 58
'Crony capitalism', 139, 229
Cronyism of banks and hedge funds, 144
CSFB, 194
Custodian, role in monitoring hedge funds for investors, 221
Custody and portfolio administration, 157

Deutsche Bank, 4
Deutsche Bank, effect on trading exposure from takeover of Bankers Trust, 162
Deutsche Bank, takeover of Bankers Trust, 154
Development of multi-fund families, 226
DiMenna, Joe, 36
Distressed debt trading, 124
Distressed securities arbitrage, 57

Distressed securities funds, returns from, 66

Documentation basis risk, 182

Domino effect of Asian currency collapses, 139

Donaldson Lufkin, 120

Drawdown, 17

Drexel Burnham, 119, 127

Druckenmiller, Stanley, 26, 27, 233

Druckenmiller, Stanley, position in technology stocks, 28

Duquesne Capital Management, 27

Ellington Group, web site, 205

Ellington, lawsuit against UBS Warburg, 121

Ellington Mortgage Partners, 120

Emerging market hedge funds, 148

Emerging market hedge funds, returns from, 149

Emerging markets, lack of role in regulating hedge funds, 146

Entrepreneurship in banking, 153

Equity hedge style, returns from, 66

ERISA, 224, 225

ERM debacle, 5, 23

Euroclear, 202

Eurohedge, 197

European institutional investors, attitudes to hedge fund investment, 213–214

Europlus Global Opportunities, 215

Event-driven hedge funds, public relations problems for some investors, 223

Event-driven strategies, 54, 57, 123

Event-driven style, returns from, 131

Fairfield Sentry, 67

Fama, Eugene, 15

Federal Reserve, implementation of tougher disclosure rules for banks, 240

FHLMC, 116

Financial models, risk of over-reliance on, 172

Financial Stability Forum, 190

Financial system, real threat to, 242

Fixed-income arbitrage, returns from, 67

'Flight to quality', 173

Florida Marlins, 41

FNMA, 116

Friedland, Dion, 61, 121

Fruit of the Loom, 130

Fulcrum Research report, 213

Full disclosure, impossibility of by hedge funds, 187

Futures contracts, gearing inherent in, 101

Fuxiang, Li, suicide of, 140

GAO Report, 159, 174

Gartmore, 214

Gateway buyout, 155

Gecko, Gordon, 56

Generic hedge fund performance, web-based information on, 192

Glass–Steagall Act, 162, 168

Global macro funds, 150, 216, 231, 242

Global macro strategies, 61, 63

GNMA, 116

Goldman Sachs, 52, 106, 130, 173, 232

Goldman Sachs, gearing during LTCM, 159, 160

Goldman Sachs, involvement in prime brokerage, 166, 167

Grand Metropolitan, 130

Granite, 119, 120

Gray, James, 120

Greater transparency, desirability of, 189

Greenspan, Alan, 79, 141, 184

Gutfreund, John, 94

Haircut, 101, 183

Harch Capital Management, 80, 187
Harch Capital Management, web site, 205, 208
Harriton, Richard, 164
Hedge Fund Association, 198
Hedge Fund Center, 197
Hedge Fund Consistency, 194
Hedge fund industry, institutionalisation of, 18
Hedge fund intranets, 204
Hedge fund managers, independent-mindedness of, 227
Hedge fund managers, investment in own funds, 186
Hedge fund managers, investment in own funds, 71
Hedge Fund News, 197
Hedge Fund Research, 66, 192
Hedge Fund Resources, 197
Hedge fund, involvement in stock pushing fraud, 236
Hedge fund, origins of the term, 9
Hedge funds, ability of investors to spread risk between, 218
Hedge funds, action to destabilise currencies, 139
Hedge funds, and money laundering, 49, 235, 236, 237
Hedge funds, as a mass-market pursuit, 225
Hedge funds, asset allocation by US pension funds, 212
Hedge funds, classification of, 45
Hedge funds, contradictions of, 229
Hedge funds, hunting in packs, 135
Hedge funds, impact of technology debacle on, 234
Hedge funds, importance of consistency of style, 231
Hedge funds, in banks, 64
Hedge funds, lack of correlation with main market benchmarks, 218
Hedge funds, limited numbers of investors, 50

Hedge funds, need for rules for lender to, 230
Hedge funds, no public offerings in, 49
Hedge funds, product life cycle similar to mutual funds, 225
Hedge funds, role of private capital in, 216
Hedge funds, secrecy of, 12
Hedge funds, total amount under management, 12
Hedge funds, variation in returns between styles, 64
Hedge funds, web sites of, 203
Hedgefund.net, 193
HedgeIndex, 194
HedgeTrustExchange, 201
Hedgeworld, 196
Henry, John, 40, 68
Henry, John, purchase of Florida Marlins, 87
Hidden options, 116
Higgins, Michael, 77
High water mark provisions, 234
Highbridge capital, 67
HK crisis, government intervention in, 146
HK dollar, 136, 145
HMKA, 145
House Committee on Banking and Financial Services, 173
HSBC, 162
Hypothecation, 101

Icahn, Carl, 124
IMF, 137, 138, 139, 142, 143, 146
Incentive fees, 4, 32, 71, 229
Incentive fees, bias to excessive risk seeking of, 72
Indonesian rupiah, hedge fund role on collapse of, 142
Inflexion point, 24
Information cascade effect, 134
Information, improving flow as a way of reducing risk, 175

ING, 75
ING Baring Furman Seltz, 166
Institutions, concern over hedge fund liquidity, 221
Institutions, concerns over hedge fund opacity, 221
Institutions, limitations on investments in limited partnerships, 224
Institutions, problems with hedge fund fee structures, 220
Institutions, problems with lurid publicity given to hedge funds, 219
Internal coordination between bank trading desks, 183
Internal hedge funds, 159, 229
Inverse floaters, 118
Investor types, which hedge funds favoured, 216
IOs, 118
IOSCO, 184
'It can't happen to me' syndrome, 181

Japanese banking collapse, 155
Jett, Joe, 75, 113, 180
Jones, Alfred Winslow, 7, 16, 18, 36, 45, 46, 98, 220, 231
Jones model, how it worked, 18
Jones, Paul Tudor, 39, 68, 80
Jones, Paul Tudor, charitable activities, 84
J. P. Morgan–Chase merger, 168, 184
J. P. Morgan, development of VAR, 176
J. P. Morgan, trading investments vs assets, 162
Junk bond financing, 54
JWM, 109

Kaufmann, Henry, 153
Kazarian, Paul, 124

Kidder Peabody, 75, 113, 120
Kingate Global, 67
Kingdon Capital, 185
Klesch Capital Partners, 126
Klesch, Gary, 124
Komansky, David, 107
Korean crisis, 139
Kovner, Bruce, 35, 67, 185
Kovner, Bruce, charitable activities, 85–86
Kozeny, Viktor, 42
KPMG, 226
Krugman, Paul, 138, 147
KSP Capital, 200

LaBow, Ronald, 124
Lasry, Marc, 129
Latinvest, 149
Leeson, Nick, 7, 75, 91, 157, 163
Lehman Brothers, 159
Lending to California property market, 155
Leverage, 18, 186, 242
Leverage, access through futures and options, 100
Leverage, excessive levels of, 185
Leverage, importance to LTCM, 98
Leverage, mechanics in bond arbitrage, 99
Lewis, Michael, 94, 95
Lewitt, Michael, 80, 187
Liquidity days, 50
Liquidity options, 109
Liquidity risk, 108
Liquidity, 97
Liquidity, importance of, 47
Liquidity, problems with lack of in bond markets, 51
LJH, 199
Long/short strategies, 60
Loomis, Carol, 9, 10, 98
LTCM, 2, 3, 6, 11, 48, 52, 66, 89, 90, 95, 97, 98, 101, 102, 106, 107, 110, 153, 160, 173, 190, 212, 238

LTCM, bailout of, 74, 150
LTCM, collapse of, 122, 134, 141, 172
LTCM, futile attempts at secrecy, 104
LTCM, impact of policy of minimum disclosure, 105
LTCM, leverage of, 172
LTCM, mimicking of trades by banks, 6
LTCM, secrecy of, 187
LTCM's leverage, 103

Macro traders, 180
Magnum Funds, 61, 121
Malaysia, 5
Malaysian capital controls, 139, 140
Malaysian ringgitt, 142
Managed Funds Association, 195, 198
Margin calls, 91
Margin calls, in LTCM situation, 103
Margolis, Lou, 111
MARHedge, 193
Market impact, 46
Market intervention, role in thwarting hedge funds, 150
Market-neutral strategies, 52
Markets, illogicality of for short periods, 97
Markowitz, Harry, 15
Marron, Donald, 107
'Masters of the Universe', hedge fund managers as, 69
Maverick Capital, 37, 38
Meaden, Nicola, 195
Merger arbitrage funds, returns from, 66
Merger arbitrage, 54
Meridien Research, 181
Meriwether, John, 2, 3, 7, 51, 67, 90, 113
Merrill Lynch Mercury, 214

Merrill Lynch, 123, 130, 173
Merrill Lynch, gearing at time of LTCM crisis, 159, 160
Merrill Lynch, involvement in prime brokerage, 166
'Me too' trading, 104
Milken, Mike, 7, 127
Miller, Merton, 15
Minnesota Power & Light, 120
Model risk, 180
Modigliani, Franco, 15
Mohamed, Dr Mahathir, 5, 140, 143, 144, 146, 147
Moore Capital, 28, 41, 67, 70, 185, 233, 234
Moral hazard, 73, 74, 92, 108, 156, 157, 172, 175, 241
Morgan Stanley, 173
Morgan Stanley, position in prime brokerage, 166
Morgan Stanley, trading investments vs assets, 162
Mortgage-backed securities arbitrage, 115
Mortgage-backed securities, lack of transparent pricing in, 118
Mortgage-backed securities market, 114
Mortgage-backed securities trading, zero-sum game nature of, 118
Mutual funds, hedge funds not to be confused with, 48

NationsBank, 123
NatWest Markets, 161, 180
Nicholas, Nicholas J., 120
Niederhoffer, Victor, 3, 7, 79
Niederhoffer, Victor, art collection of, 87
Nomura Securities, 161, 168
Nomura Securities, trading investments vs assets, 162

Odey, Crispin, 68

Offshore domicile, 49
Offshore tax havens, 4
'Old George', 88
Olympia & York, 128
Omega Advisers, 41, 234
Open Society Foundation, 83
Options, use for leverage in risk
  arbitrage, 56
Orphan equity, 59
Over-the-counter (OTC)
  derivatives, 102

Parker Global, 199
Pearson, 126
Penn Central, 125
Pequot, 67
Permal, 149
Perry Partners, 67
Philippine peso, 142
Pines, Isadore, 120
PlusFunds.com, 202
Portogallo, Richard, 164
POs, 118
Price, Michael, 124
Prime broker, 221
Prime broker, as bordello keeper,
  167
Prime broker, role in pizza deliveries,
  167
Prime brokerage, 5, 164, 165
Prime brokerage, in Europe, 167
Prime brokers, web sites of, 200–201
Prohibitions on hedge fund
  investing by public bodies in
  certain US states, 223
Project Death in America, 82
Proprietary private equity funds, 155
Proprietary traders, 153, 180
Proprietary traders, greater
  supervision of, 183
Proprietary trading, 51, 64, 74, 75,
  136, 155, 156, 158, 168, 191, 231,
  237, 238, 239
Proprietary trading, and stock
  lending, 170

Proprietary trading, central banks'
  concern over, 76
Proprietary trading, potential for
  undermining confidence in banks,
  232
Proprietary trading, role in LTCM
  collapse, 104

Quadrex, 125
Quantitative techniques, 37
Quantum Fund, 24, 67, 81, 212
Quota Fund, 28, 67

Rand, Ayn, 79
Reflexivity, theory of, 24
Rehypothecation, 101
Reichmann brothers, 127
Relative value strategies, 52
Repo markets, workings of, 100,
  165, 166
Repos and swaps, possibility of a
  clearing system for, 239
Resolution Trust, 169
Retail banks, 169
Risk allocation and risk
  management, done together by
  hedge funds, 186
Risk arbitrage, 54, 55
Risk aversion, 17
Risk control, importance of, 40
Risk control procedures, failure of, 171
Risk, definition and measurement of,
  14
Risk, separation and identification of in
  mortgage-backed securities, 117
Risk-seeking funds, 47
RJR Nabisco, 155
Robertson, Julian, 12, 30, 67 133, 147,
  226, 232, 233, 234
Robertson, Julian, charitable activities,
  83–84
Robertson, Julian, hot temper of, 30
Robertson, libel case versus *Business
  Week*, 31, 48

Roditi, Nick, 27, 28, 67, 233
Rogers, Jim, 149
RR Capital Management, 226
Russian default, 102, 134
Russian default, impact on LTCM, 91

Sachs, Jeffrey, 138
Salomon Brothers, 93, 105, 172
Salomon Smith Barney, 160
Salomon Smith Barney, withdrawal
    from proprietary trading, 157
Savings and loan debacle, 155
Scholes, Myron, 11, 109
Schroder Investment Management,
    214
Secrecy, supposed importance of to
    hedge funds, 47
Securitisation, 115
Settlement problems, role of prime
    broker, 165
Sharpe ratio, 15, 17, 39, 217
Sharpe ratio, definition of, 16
Sharpe, William, 16
Shaw, David, 122
Shopkorn, Stanley, 28
Short selling, 8
Singer & Friedlander, 23
Size, problems of in hedge funds, 41
Soros Fund Management, 133, 147,
    150, 185
Soros, George, 5, 6, 10, 12, 23, 62, 67,
    78, 134, 233, 234
Soros, George, espousal of liberal
    causes, 82
Soros, George, flexibility of approach,
    24
Soros, George, forays in UK gilt
    market, 25
Soros, George, intuitive understanding
    of leverage, 24
Soros, George, testimony before
    Congress, 26
Sortino ratio, 17
Standard & Poor's, 202

Standard deviation, 14
Steinhardt Management/Caxton
    Corporation, DoJ case, 87
Steinhardt, management style of, 34
Steinhardt, Michael, 10, 32, 67, 80, 90,
    166, 233
Steinhardt, Michael, charitable
    activities, 85
Stock lending, 165
Stock lending, lack of knowledge of
    lender of use to which loan is being
    put, 166
Stock market bubble, 110
Stress testing of VAR, 182
Strips, 117
Style drift, 224
Survivorship bias, 223
Svensen, David, 213
System trading, 62
Systemic crisis, as a result of proprietary
    trading, 170
Systemic risks, 184

Tactical trading funds, 61,
TASS, 12, 194, 196, 201
Thai baht, 136
Thai baht, forward sales of, 141
Thatcher, Margaret, 12, 32
Tiger Management, 30, 67, 133, 138,
    150
Tiger Management, problems of size, 31
Tiger Management, role in baht
    speculation, 142
'Toxic waste', 115, 119
Transparency, disadvantages of, 191
Transparency, need for to prevent
    excessive risk in bank trading, 170
Trout, Monroe, 38, 67, 79
Trout, Timothy, 80
Tudor Investment Corporation,
    185
Tuna Capital, 193

UBS, 4, 167, 168

UBS, involvement in LTCM, 154
UBS, merger with SBC, 180
UBS, trading investments vs assets, 162
UK company pension funds, investment in hedge funds, 214
US Treasury, evidence on LTCM, 105
US universities, investment in hedge funds, 213
US universities, returns from hedge fund portfolios, 222

Vairocana Fund, 78
Van Hedge, 194, 200
VAR, 176
VAR, limitations of 176–179
Volatility, 195
Volatility curve, testing for shifts in, 183
Vranos, Michael, 113, 120

Vulture capitalists, 123

Wade, Robert, 141
Web-based hedge fund exchanges, 222
Weill, David, 78
Welch, 'Neutron Jack', 114
West End Capital, 214
Westgate International, 67
World wide web, role in greater transparency, 192
Wriston, Walter, 153
Wyly family office, 38

Yam, Joseph, 146
Young, Patrick, 143

Zell, Sam, 124
Zulu principle, 230
Zweig, Martin, 36, 67
Zweig–DiMenna, web site, 204